IN SU[illegible]S CIRCUMSTANCES

INTRODUCTION BY

Edward Woodward

BOXTREE

First published in Great Britain in 1993
by Boxtree Limited

10 9 8 7 6 5 4 3 2 1

Typeset by DP Photosetting, Aylesbury, Bucks
Printed and bound by Cox & Wyman

Boxtree Limited
Broadwall House
21 Broadwall
London SE1 9PL

A CIP catalogue entry for this book is available from the British Library

ISBN 1 85283 413 7

Disclaimer
No photographs used in this book portray actual members of the public. All photographs were taken from the Granada series and posed by the actors.

Contents

Acknowledgements

This book has been written by the *In Suspicious Circumstances* research team. We should like to thank the many people who helped us with these eleven cases, some of whom we cannot name without betraying a confidence. Our particular thanks go to those who generously recalled painful memories of family tragedy for our benefit. We are indebted to: Molly Anghinetti, Hazel and Ken Batchelor, Jack Birtley, Frank Burslem, Ronnie Charlton, Ann Colwell, Gladys Dry, Mary Duff, Daniel Farson, Brian Ford, Gertrude Freeman, His Honour Bernard B. Gillis QC, Nigel Green, Helen Grindrod QC, Joan, John and Pem Hattersley, Freda Heath, the Jewell family, Moira Kirke, Phyllis Kenion, Dorothy Love, Lady Lucinda Marchant, Juliette Marshall, Paul Menzies, Chrissie Mills, Patrick Morley, Eileen and Bob Pollard, Keith Skinner, Dudley Stephens, Ed Vale, the staff of the Forensic Science Laboratory, Chorley, Andrew Brown of the Metropolitan Police Archive, Frances Grey of the Crown Prosecution Service Archive, Jeannette Harkin of the Lord Chancellor's Office Archive and Mrs S. Smith of the Home Office. We should also like to thank our scriptwriters: Glenn Chandler, Frank Cottrell Boyce, Chris Fallon, Brian Finch, Stephen Lowe, Julian Roach, Peter Whelan, Jane Woodrow and Barry Woodward.

Sue Durkan, Producer, *In Suspicious Circumstances*.

Introduction

Dear Reader,

When my grandfather, Albert Smith, was a young man, for leisure and pleasure there was no television service and no radio. There was theatre, which for the working man meant the music hall, and the early flickerings of the cinema. But above all, there were the newspapers.

If there was a juicy murder 'on the go' – and there usually was – there would be a word-for-word trial report and pages and pages of stories about the victim, the suspect and the respective families and households of both. Every day – day after day. The public interest was constant and never ending: who did what to whom and where, when, how and why?

I still vividly remember sitting in the gaslit parlour of my grandfather's cottage as my cousin John and I listened to the old man (he must have been all of 55 years old!) tell my grandmother the 'plot' of a recent Croydon murder and compare it with the 'storyline' of the Jack The Ripper Whitechapel murders of his youth.

From that moment in the late 1930s, my reading was almost exclusively of famous trials, murder and mayhem. My hero was the late great Sir Bernard Spilsbury, long-term Home Office pathologist and forensic pioneer. He was like a real-life version of the greatest fictional detective of all time – Sherlock Holmes. From 1910 to the 1950s this man kept the nation thoroughly intrigued and suitably horrified.

All you had to do then was buy a newspaper. Well, all

you have to do now is to watch the series and read this book. There are some real 'prizewinners' here, cases that will I know fascinate, intrigue and sometimes puzzle.

Good reading to you.

Edward Woodward OBE
Cornwall, October 1992

1: Mrs Bravo Regrets

Alice Cooper

Florence Bravo was a very beautiful young woman: before our drama even began her life was already marred by scandal and rumour. By the time she was thirty she had outlived one drunken and violent husband, and her affair with James Gully, a married doctor thirty years her senior, had shocked Victorian society. Then she met Charles Bravo – a handsome barrister from a respectable background. He was not as well heeled as she but they were attracted to one another. They fell deeply in love almost immediately and were married. He objected to her excesses. He claimed she drank too much and that she was extravagant. Did the grounds require that many gardeners and keeping four horses in the stable was surely unnecessary? Apart from these minor domestic troubles, which are to be expected in any marriage this seemed an ideal union.

But Florence had a companion, Jane, who lived with them and Charles was said to resent the amount of money she was paid. After Florence had suffered two miscarriages in quick succession, Jane often shared a room with her and as a result Charles could not always claim his 'conjugal rights'. With his hot-blooded masculinity spurned perhaps, he grew to dislike Jane and maybe she anxiously suspected that her days at the Priory were numbered. One night Charles fell ill. He started vomiting violently and within three days he was dead. The doctors declared it was antimony poisoning. Antimony was used to de-worm horses but it was not good for suicide – other drugs like chloroform or morphine were much less painful. So did someone murder Charles Bravo? And if so who? Two inquests didn't even find the hint of a culprit. But if the police found little to go on, the press certainly had plenty of material.

It was a story thick with sex, violence, adultery and financial intrigue. But most attractive of all the story showed the upper classes to be as wanton and uncontrolled as those they professed to look down upon. The police couldn't pin it on anyone, but with society beauties, spurned lovers, jealous husbands and loyal companions involved, the press had no end of suspects. The Charles Bravo Affair became a *cause celèbre* – everyone had an opinion on who killed him and why. But no one was ever sure of the truth.

The Victorian era was an extremely repressive, albeit hypocritical, period in our history. Florence, with her early marriage to the dashing guardsman Alexander Ricardo was once the very emblem of glamorous Victorian society. She was to become its victim – Victorian codes of behaviour favoured devoted, sober virgin brides who endured demanding husbands and ensuing unwanted pregnancies without complaint. When the inquiry began into the death of Florence's second husband she was in effect on trial – as much for crimes against the mores of the time as for Charles's murder. She got what she had coming to her because, in the eyes of contemporary society, sex outside marriage was almost as evil as murder itself.

Florence Campbell had married Alexander Ricardo in 1864 when she was only nineteen. Bride and groom both came from wealthy backgrounds and made an impressive pair. She was a blue-eyed auburn-haired beauty and he was a real live, tall, dark and handsome hero. But Alexander had a drink problem and although Florence must have known about it soon after the wedding, it did not become problematic until about three years later. The couple travelled a great deal and managed to cope with the situation, but Florence became more distressed by Alexander's bouts of boozing, occasional violence and his horrifying symptoms of delirium tremens whenever he tried to abstain.

Florence consulted a doctor first. Her mother had also suggested that the then fashionable water cure in Malvern might help her daughter's frazzled nerves and ease Alexander's addiction. On this advice, Florence left for Malvern, to be joined by her husband a few weeks later.

It was in Malvern in April 1870 that Florence renewed her acquaintance with Dr James Gully. He had been a family friend for years and she had met him for the first time when she was only twelve. By 1870 he was sixty-two and she was barely twenty-five. He was no dashing guardsman but after the drunken ravings of her husband he was dignified, attentive and kind. Gully had always been known for his charming, almost magnetic personality and he would listen endlessly to Florence's woes. He may have been the wiser older man but there was a youthfulness about him too that Florence could not help but fall victim to. It was not long before their friendship attracted gossip although it seems that, at this stage, they really were just good friends. Polite society was not horrified by the age difference between the two, as this was not uncommon, but rather by the fact that Gully was a married man. Admittedly his wife was an invalid, some ten years older than he, but that did not alter the fact that his wooing could only lead to disappointment and disapproval.

Florence and Alexander stayed at Malvern until June 1870 when yet another drunken spree took Alexander away, but they were back in August in company with Florence's mother to take the cures again. The cure consisted of various types of baths some of which were taken in mud, as well as the application of cold sheets to the body. They were very fashionable at the time and leading figures like Dickens and George Eliot visited the place. Gully was one of the first exponents of homeopathy and despite a degree of cynicism from orthodox medical minds he was well known and respected in society.

But the Malvern cure was not enough for Alexander – he could not shake off the demon drink. He was still guzzling the stuff and his behaviour was becoming more and more erratic. Florence and Alexander had rented a house in Malvern but in November she went to stay in Dr Gully's house to get away from Alexander's temper and moods. She now seemed to be greatly reliant upon Gully's friendship and protection. Soon after this she returned to her parents' house whilst Alexander stayed in London. In March 1871 she filed for a separation and Dr Gully and Florence's solicitor, a Mr Brooks, acted as trustees. She had been married only seven years. In the same month Alexander went to Cologne and set up home with an old flame.

By April he was dead, apparently from the booze. The glamorous partnership was over, and Florence was a rich widow. Her husband's £40,000 fortune came to her. Fate may have been unkind but it was certainly more than generous. The errant husband was brought home and buried at the Brompton Cemetery.

Florence was staying with Mr Brooks when she heard of the death of Alexander. Within a month of the funeral Dr Gully found lodgings near the Brooks' house in Tooting and began to pay Florence regular visits. The doctor was in love and no one approved. Her parents were worried about her reputation. In polite society a widow like Florence was not supposed to be visited so keenly by an elderly married suitor. Mr and Mrs Brooks found the doctor's frequent presence hard to stomach too and there were arguments. On one occasion Gully threatened to bring a slander action against Mrs Brooks. So Florence became alienated from society, from her family and from her friends and all because of her strange affair with the sixty-three-year-old doctor. The doctor too caused concern to his circle. Surely a man of his position and age was making a fool of himself in running after Florence. Although his Malvern practice did not suffer, the two became the subject of keen gossip.

In June 1871 Florence went again to Malvern with her hostess's two daughters. She stayed until September and defiantly spent much of her time with Dr Gully despite all that was being whispered about her behind her back. One can only speculate as to what the two saw in each other: although he was elderly, he was comforting, reliable and a man of the world; and as we all know, any man in his sixties can become fixated by a beautiful woman half his age.

Florence had become friendly with the Brooks' governess, Mrs Jane Cox, a widow, who taught their youngest daughters. The two women got on well and when Florence finally left the Brooks in January 1872 she was sorry to bid farewell to Jane.

In January 1872 Florence finally set herself up in a rather grand house in Leigham Court Road, Streatham. She called the house Stokefield and promptly hired a butler, a cook, two maids and a gardener. But before she finally moved into the house she went on yet another spree with Dr Gully, this time to Italy. They were accompanied only by her maid and his butler and they were gone for six weeks. When they returned Gully moved to Streatham too. He severed all ties with Malvern, moved into a house across the road from Florence and visited her constantly. Yet again tongues wagged and Florence cannot have felt the most welcomed of newcomers to the neighbourhood. The two claimed that their friendship was still above board at this stage but against the romantic backdrop of the Italian spring who can say what had passed between them.

In May 1872, when Dr Gully would have been a constant visitor to Stokefield for five months, Florence hired Jane Cox, the Brooks' governess as a live-in companion. Jane arrived in August and was paid the very princely sum of £80 per annum, an enormous wage at the time. But she was worth the money – with a reputable gentlewoman in the house the visits of Dr Gully could not be frowned on quite so easily. She was sufficiently friendly with Florence to know when to be in evidence and when to leave her employer to her own ignominious devices. She gave the situation an air of respectability without cramping Florence's style and it was vaguely rumoured that Jane had a soft spot for Doctor Gully herself. So it seemed that for the three friends life was domestic bliss. The doctor popped in for meals at his leisure, Jane lent a sympathetic or advisory ear when needed and peace reigned at the house in Streatham.

It was only the estrangement of her parents that truly upset Florence at this time. They still disapproved of her liaison with Dr Gully and claimed that there could be no reconciliation between Florence and her family until she had ended the affair. Florence could not bring herself to do this and so chose Gully above her family.

By this time Gully and Florence were lovers.

Whatever the status of their liaison they certainly wished to be alone a great deal and at Christmas-time in 1872 they were finally able to stay in the house unchaperoned for the first time since May. Jane took her sons off to Brighton for the festive season and Florence and the doctor were alone at last. It was now over a year and a half since Florence had been Gully's constant 'friend'. She was young enough to crave love and devotion and if Gully was not quite the romantic hero she had once had in mind, his charm and attentiveness certainly held Florence's interest.

In August 1873, perhaps again in an effort to be unchaperoned, the couple went to Germany. Alone, save for Florence's maid Humphreys, the lovers made their way to a picturesque Bavarian spa town. Kissingen was a romantic place where there were tree-lined streets, wooded valleys and a castle looking down on the town from the nearby mountainside. Gully, with this beautiful woman on his arm, must have thought he had landed in heaven; surely nothing could disturb their peace. Only the rather unpleasant water and mud bath cures that Gully insisted Florence make use of marred their bliss. Poor fools – their happy existence was about to be shattered by pregnancy and by a rival for Florence's love.

They returned in September and in November Florrie realised that she was suffering from a miscarriage. The pain and sickness were unbearable and it was then that Florence decided to withdraw her sexual favours for good. Jane Cox denied all knowledge of the true nature of Florence's illness as did Gully, who claimed it was a 'kind of tumour' that he had removed successfully. A rumour circulated that the illness was actually an illegal abortion that Gully had been forced to perform upon Florence.

After the illness it seemed that life at Leigham Court Road continued as before. But all passion had now cooled and Florence and Gully really were now just good friends. Florence did not want to risk another pregnancy but she still enjoyed Gully's almost constant company and had no plans to stop seeing him. Gully protested about the new nature of their friendship but he made no attempt to force the issue.

After convalescing Florence made more grand plans to change her life. A bigger and more impressive house was sought and in March 1874 she moved into the Priory, Bedford Hill Road, Balham, with Mrs Cox yet again in tow. With ten acres of land, two lodges and an impressive staff, this was life in the grand style. And poor old love-lorn Dr Gully came too, devoted as ever, moving into another new house, again just down the road from the Priory. He was given a key to one of the garden gates and once more came and went as he pleased, dining often with Jane and Florence. There was something vaguely comical about Gully's trips through the vegetable garden to the house – but he knew only too well that this was as near as he would get to marriage. They went on trips and excursions and although it was a rather circumscribed existence it seemed to suit them.

Or did it? Was Florence yearning for a new grand passion and perhaps even the respectability that she had lost since the death of Alexander? And what kept Gully as attentive as a lapdog? His obsessional devotion seemed to know no bounds however humiliating the situation might become.

In May 1874 Florence was introduced to Mr and Mrs Bravo, a couple who were close friends to Jane Cox and who had known Jane's dead husband. Six months later Florence finally met their handsome and charming son over tea at the Bravo's stylish home, Palace Green. The event passed quietly enough amongst the clinking tea cups. After all, havoc and chaos don't always announce their arrival – sometimes they just slip in, unnoticed, biding their time.

Meanwhile the inseparable threesome of Dr Gully, Florence and Jane continued to live in peace at the Priory. There were visits to the West Country in early 1875 and another to Italy in March. Florence and Gully were getting along very well again but, according to Mrs Cox, they were not lovers. She slept beside Florence during their travels and we are to believe that Gully had a room of his own. But can we be convinced of their restrained behaviour all that way from home in the beautiful countryside and the warm spring sunshine?

Their peace was finally to be shattered on their return home. Mrs Cox and Florence took a trip to Brighton in September of 1875 and whilst driving along the Prom. they spotted the dashing figure of Charles Bravo. Florence was about to experience a rapid and radical change to her life.

Charles Delauney Turner Bravo was nearly thirty when Florence met up with him that autumn. He was a handsome and affable young man: tall, clean cut, with fashionable mutton-chop whiskers. He was also intelligent, ambitious and determined. Although his law practice did not earn him a great deal of money, he had a considerable private income from his family. His father was dead but his stepfather, a successful and affluent merchant, looked upon Charles as his own flesh and blood.

A whirlwind romance took place down by the seaside. The two saw each other as often as they could and even managed to meet alone on a few occasions. If they made a match of it Florence would be free of the reputation she had gained by accompanying a married suitor about the country and the Continent. But what *was* she to do about Gully? Was she strong enough to cut herself off from him completely? She had been wondering all summer if she was ever to extricate herself from that strange partnership. The companionship of an old man and a matronly widow were comforting but was this *all* there was to life? The disapproval of her family and friends came as extra punishment for this dull existence. She was twenty-eight by then and she wanted the excitement of someone new in her life. She was beautiful and she knew that a marriage to Charles Bravo might regain for her all that she had lost.

But when Dr Gully arrived unexpectedly in Brighton, back from Italy only a day or two before, Florence could not bring herself to tell him that she wanted to end their friendship. Riding along the front with a blissfully ignorant Gully by her side, they saw Charles walking by. He raised his hat and Gully innocently asked who the man was. Florence told him but could not bear to tell the doctor the true nature of her new friendship. Florence could only bring herself to break with James in a letter. Gully was shocked by events but said he only wanted her to be happy. He accepted the new situation like a gentleman and never acted as the enraged and rejected lover, but simply walked away. One cannot help but feel sympathy for him. An old man really, who had sacrificed his reputation for the love of a beautiful young woman. In all the events that followed it seemed that perhaps Gully was the most honourable character of all. The two returned all the gifts they had given one another, even Florence's locket containing a picture of the doctor was handed back. Perhaps most poignant of all, Gully's own key to the garden gate was restored once more to the Priory: it symbolised so well the nature of his furtive, almost pathetic, little trips to visit Florence. Now, all traces of their life together were gone.

Charles took the opportunity shortly after Dr Gully's departure to confess his own somewhat immoral past. He confessed to having 'kept an establishment in Maidenhead for the last four years' and with this news Florence realised that he would be in a poor position to disapprove of her own history. Mrs Cox had advised Florence to confess all to Charles, perhaps in an effort to scupper the relationship. Jane knew that her services would be surplus to requirements if there was a husband at the Priory and she did after all have her own very particular fond feelings for Dr Gully. But Florence respected Jane's advice nonetheless and eventually told Charles the full account of her love affair with Gully. Her version of events suggested that she and the doctor had only been lovers on one occasion and Charles was prepared to accept this apparently minor indiscretion. He told her, 'I am quite satisfied to make you my wife, but of course you must never see Dr Gully again.' The only person who had not been told of Florrie's shady past was Charles' mother who needed little encouragement in disliking anyone who came between her and her son.

With that Charles and Florence were engaged. It was the end of October 1875. Now, with her old suitor out of the way and a new and presentable fiancé in tow, Florence could win back the approval of her family. Bravo was to gain Florence's considerable fortune in marriage and it seemed that he was actually in love with her. And Florence, suddenly had everything that had been denied her. Her social position was improved and the problem of Gully had been dealt with, but it seemed unlikely that she was passionately in love. After all they had become engaged after a courtship of approximately two weeks and Florence seemed to be far more concerned with the change in her lifestyle than with true love.

One last hitch lay in front of the couple. The law then decreed that all property passed into the ownership of the husband once a woman married unless a legal settlement dictated otherwise. Florence's lawyer drew up a settlement of the money she had inherited from Alexander and the lease of the Priory, but when he attempted to include all of Florence's personal effects and furniture Charles became incensed. He had no objection to her settling the money on herself but he could not abide living in a house where 'the very furniture he sat upon did not belong to him'. She was to leave them out of the settlement or there would be no marriage. This may seem a rather dramatic overreaction but at that time it was not that unusual. Women were accustomed to being the property of their husbands and even Florence who had been independent for so long seemed unsurprised by events. However she was vexed that Charles was quite so furious about it and sought advice from the only person she truly trusted. Yet again gullible Gully behaved impeccably and advised Florence to go along with Charles' request. He even wished her luck. 'I hope it will turn out well and that you'll be very happy, my dear.' There was no recurrence of their earlier passions and they parted politely – he to a life of solitude and she to a long and happy marriage, or so she thought. But this little incident showed us something else – Charles had a keen eye on Florence's finances. He wanted things his way and never more so than in the area of money.

With the church bells ringing above their heads the happy couple were married on 7 December 1875 and they made an impressively handsome pair. But Mrs Bravo could not bring herself to witness the departure of her adored son. One other person was absent from the jolly occasion and that was George Griffith who had been in service with Florence since her stay in Malvern. However he had recently been discovered driving Florence in her carriage in an 'irresponsible' manner up New Bond Street and had subsequently been dismissed on Charles' insistence. On the day of the wedding Griffith was spotted in the Bedford Hotel, Balham, and when the subject of the marriage came up was heard to remark, 'Poor fellow, I shouldn't like to be in his shoes. He won't be alive four months!' Quite how he came to this startling conclusion we can never be sure but you can rest safe in the knowledge that we shall return to the subject of Mr Griffith.

Charles enjoyed the comforts of the Priory. Apart from the occasional nagging worry he had about the financial outlay of running the place, he and Florence and indeed Jane all got along swimmingly, or so it appeared. His mother encouraged him to question the amount spent on gardeners or keeping ponies, but he risked the formidable wrath of Florence when he brought the subject up. During those early days things went well for the two of them and life at the Priory seemed happy. In one letter to Florrie he suggested that by getting rid of two cobs (favourite horses of Flo's) and Mrs Cox they could save £400 a year, but this seems never to have been mentioned again.

In April Florence had her second miscarriage since she had married Charles – contraception was fairly basic in those days and Florence must have been beginning to wonder if the continuing ardour of her husband would leave her permanently weakened or worse through miscarriage or childbirth. Jane had nursed Florence during those periods and had taken Charles' place beside Florence in bed in order to do so. Florence was in no hurry to see Charles return to the marital boudoir, in fact she positively discouraged it. Charles now slept in his dressing-room alone. With perhaps more miscarriages or the terrifying prospect of childbirth to look forward to, it is not hard to understand Florence's point of view. But was this reluctance to sleep with Charles more than just fear of pregnancy? Had she fallen out of love with him as quickly as she had fallen in?

The 18th of April was the first day since Florence's illness that she had felt like venturing out. Charlie too had gone on a shopping spree with Florence, then left her to her own devices while he lunched with his friend MacCalmont at St James's Hall, Piccadilly. Florence had managed to buy Charles some tobacco and was lying on the sofa when he got home just after 4.30 p.m. He admired the present and then, not stopping for a smoke, leapt into his riding breeches and bounded to the stables. Before long he was astride Cremorne, one of the much maligned cobs, and was belting out of the yard.

But Charles was to regret his post-lunch energy when the horse duly bolted with him, causing him to have to ride an extra five miles. He returned home bruised, aching and somewhat sorry for himself. What with having had a toothache the previous day he was beginning to feel that his body was under siege.

Mrs Cox had been to Worthing on that fateful Tuesday to arrange the rental of a house for Florence to convalesce in. She arrived late and rushed into the house apologising for keeping them waiting for their supper of whiting, roast lamb, anchovy eggs on toast and a liberal supply of wine. Charles seemed depressed by his experiences in the saddle and Florence was tired after all the unaccustomed activity since her illness. He drank at least four glasses of burgundy and the ladies downed a bottle of sherry each. The atmosphere was a bit gloomy. At about nine Florence, who had promised Charles she would retire early, went upstairs with Jane to help her to prepare for bed. But at the foot of the stairs Florence asked Mrs Cox to get her a glass of water with a little Marsala in it and made her way alone up to the bedroom. A few minutes later Florence and Mrs Cox were alone in the bedroom, the requested drink having been fetched. Twenty-five minutes later Mary Ann appeared with hot water.

Again Florence asked for more wine and when Mary was bringing it upstairs she passed Charles in the corridor looking like thunder and quite ill too. He followed Mary Ann into Florence's dressing room where in front of both the servant and Mrs Cox he said to his wife, 'You've sent downstairs for more wine. You've drunk nearly a bottle today!' But he said it in French so that Mary Ann at least would not be able to understand. This was quite a common thing to do in those days, known as *pas devant* (not in front of). Mary Ann hastily retreated and hid in the main bedroom until she heard the master pass the door. Then she left the bedroom meeting Florence and Mrs Cox, who now shared the bed there, as they were coming in. Mary Ann tidied the dressing room and then returned to the bedroom to check that nothing more was needed of her by the mistress of the house. Mrs Cox told her everything was done and that all Mary had to do was check on the whereabouts of Skye, the pet dog. Mary Ann bade her goodnights and was on the upstairs landing calling softly to the dog when Charles burst out of his room wearing only his nightshirt. He looked very ill, pale and gasping, 'Florence! Hot water!' he yelled and again louder and more panic-stricken he yelled the same thing, 'Florence! Hot water!'

The events of that night and more particularly the order in which they happened are vital to our case. You should be paying attention to when and how quickly Mrs Cox called the doctors that appeared that night and exactly what she said to them when they arrived. During the next few days things were to look decidedly uncomfortable for the loyal companion – had her extreme devotion caused her to act above and far beyond the call of duty?

Mary Ann stood and stared at Charles as he rushed back into his room. But no one else stirred, no one, not even the two women sleeping just across the landing seemed to have heard. Mary Ann ran into Florence's room. Florence appeared to be fast asleep in bed and indeed, after all the sherry that she had drunk that evening, this was hardly surprising. But Mrs Cox sat fully dressed on the edge of the bed perfectly able to run on to the landing should any emergency occur – either she really had not heard it or she had simply refused to move.

And then suddenly all hell broke loose.

Mary Ann ran into Florence's room but she still lay asleep apparently oblivious to the din. The sherry was still acting as an excellent sleeping draught or was Florence giving the performance of her life?

Mrs Cox followed Mary Ann into the master's bedroom – he stood at the window and was vomiting out of the open casement. Mrs Cox acted quickly, sending Mary Ann for hot water and mustard to act as an emetic and instructing the coachman Parton to ride out for Dr Harrison in Streatham. Between them Mary Ann and Jane poured mustard down the now almost unconscious Charles, put his feet in a mustard bath and rubbed them, and got camphor and coffee, in a desperate attempt to keep him awake. And still Florence lay oblivious through it all. Finally Mary Ann tried to wake her and with Mary Ann she arrived to see Charles slumped on the floor of his room. She was convincingly concerned telling Parton to go again for Dr Moore who lived much closer than Harrison. Dr Moore was grave – Charles' heart had nearly stopped beating – he doubted that the patient would recover – his pupils were dilated and he could not swallow the brandy they tried to force down him.

With this fatal news Florence began to sob and Mrs Cox became mistress of the hour: calm, supportive, and a shoulder for Florence. When the other doctor, Dr Harrison, arrived at eleven, Jane told him what had happened – Charles had taken chloroform, she said, for his toothache. But she had never mentioned this before to Dr Moore – why on earth not? There was a bottle of chloroform on the mantelpiece – but in those days that was not unusual especially for a man who'd been suffering from toothache. Both doctors were very pessimistic – all they could do was force brandy and water into the patient and this eventually stimulated his heartbeat. The two doctors looked around for the chloroform that Jane had mentioned and saw the empty bottle but they could not smell chloroform in the room or on his breath. They also found laudanum and ammonia camphor compound in the room but none of these would have had such a violent effect on the patient.

Florence was distraught and threw herself down beside her husband clutching and clinging to him. 'My dear Charlie, what is the matter? Do speak to me Charlie, dearest.' Eventually she was pulled away from him for fear she would squeeze what little life he had left out of him. While Florence became more and more uncontrollable, Mrs Cox's resilience grew all the greater.

Yet another doctor was sent for – Royes Bell – he had nursed Florence once already. He was Charles' cousin and a good friend too. Florence was sent to rest until he arrived while the rock-steady Jane, Moore and Harrison kept vigil.

At 2.30 a.m. Royes Bell arrived, with yet another doctor, Dr Johnson from Kings College Hospital. It was then that Charles began to vomit and pass blood and Johnson suggested that Charles had been poisoned. By now Charles could utter a tiny whisper and when asked what he had taken would only say, 'I rubbed my gums with laudanum and may have taken some.' But Johnson was firm: 'Laudanum won't explain your symptoms, Mr Bravo.' And even in his great pain and distress Charles was adamant, 'Well, I've taken nothing more.' If there was even a hint of suicide it was not going to be confessed by Charles Bravo.

Now an extraordinary development took place that implicated both Jane and Charles too. She took Royes Bell to one side and told him that Charles had said to her, 'I've taken some of that poison but don't tell Florence.' He was never clear exactly when Charles had supposedly told her this. Royes Bell was understandably furious. 'It's no good sending for a doctor if you don't tell him what's the matter!' When Johnson was informed of Charles' supposed confession he was astounded.

'But didn't you ask him what he had taken or when he'd taken it or why?' But Mrs Cox said that that was all he had told her and that she hadn't pressed him further. If he really had said such a thing surely Jane would have acted upon it. By saying nothing she had contributed to Charles' worsening condition. And if she was making it up? What on earth was she making it up for – to try to suggest suicide instead of something worse? At least if folk thought it was suicide, they wouldn't go hunting for a murderer. All three went to ask the fading Charles again about the poison but he seemed puzzled and repeated the story of the laudanum for his neuralgia. And he insisted, 'If it wasn't laudanum, I don't know what it was.'

But why had Mrs Cox not mentioned the poison story to Harrison or Moore earlier? 'I quite thought that I had told Mr Harrison,' she demurred. And with that, Moore, Harrison and Johnson departed leaving Royes Bell in charge. It was 5.00 a.m. on Wednesday.

High Victorian melodrama now took over. If we did not know it was true, we would think it came straight from the pages of a novel – if only. Charles gasping for breath but able to smile asked Royes Bell to read some prayers. He told Mary Ann that his next trip would be to the churchyard and not Worthing and he told his wife, 'When you bury me, Florence, make no fuss over me.' Florence had tears streaming beautifully down her face. 'Oh don't say so, Charlie. But I won't if it's your wish.' Next a will was made up giving everything to Florence and he told her, 'You must marry again, but not a word of the past.' He loved Florence enough to want her to make a new life free from scandal and shame. The short but cataclysmic drama was building to its hysterical and inevitable finale. Royes Bell, when alone with his friend and patient, asked if Charles had anything on his mind. But Charles as if not even realising that his cousin was suggesting some kind of confessional said only, 'No – I've not led a religious life.'

At 3.00 p.m. on Wednesday the other three doctors arrived as well as Charles' parents and a servant called Amelia who had known Charles since he was a boy. Mrs Bravo could see that Florence was inconsolable and was more affectionate towards her daughter-in-law than usual. But she insisted on nursing Charles herself with the help of Amelia. Florence with no protest but some resentment found herself giving over not only her wifely duties at the bedside but also her room. Charles asked his mother always to be kind to Florence. 'She's been the best of wives to me.' Florence then went up to share a room with Mrs Cox.

It was Amelia who received yet another nugget of information from Florence that would again cast the net of suspicion in Florence's direction. 'What a dreadful thing. The only thing by which I can account for it is that Mr Charles took lunch at St James's with a friend and had something cooked in a coppery pan which has disagreed with him,' were Florence's words to Amelia. What was all this of coppery pans? She had mentioned this strange thought to Mary Ann and Jane but not to the doctors. Was Florence clutching at straws or was she in fact trying to confuse any suspicion that might arise about her.

The doctors questioned Charles again but could get no sense out of him, 'If I knew what I was suffering from, why the devil should I send for you?'

On Thursday morning Charles was so weak that Florence sent a telegram to her mother saying, 'No hope for my darling. He cannot live long. Florence.' The tests done on Charles' vomit found no sign of arsenic as Johnson had hoped and all the doctors remained clueless.

Royes's sister visited Charles and then sat in the conservatory with Florence who gave another moving speech: 'We've been very, very happy and Charles has said he's never been so happy in all his life. We've never had a word together.' But she didn't mention poison or coppery pans. She was every bit the devoted wife, hanky in hand but strong now in the face of crisis.

Florence's brother and mother arrived at teatime on the Wednesday and at 6.30 p.m. another doctor added his advice. This was Sir William Gull, a medical man famous at the time for curing the Prince of Wales, whom Florence had sent for. Gull spotted the symptoms of poisoning immediately but Charles still insisted that he had taken only laudanum and added, 'I wish to tell you now that I've told the truth and nothing but the truth.' He had got the laudanum from Florence's bottle and if there was anything else in the bottle he hadn't realised. And with this he became hysterical, 'I've taken laudanum before. God, I've taken only laudanum. If it wasn't laudanum, so help me God, I don't know what it was.' Gull left and that evening all the closest members of Charles' family gathered around his bed and prayed together. At 5.30 a.m. on the Friday he died.

So what had happened to poor Charles?

No one could believe that bluff, burly, jolly Charlie could have taken his own life. His denials had been uncompromising and it was only Jane's tale of the poisoning confession that kept prompting thoughts of suicide. Even Florence could not suggest any solution to the mystery. She said it would 'always remain a mystery'. But the law doesn't like mysteries and so a post-mortem had to be carried out.

Mr Theodopulus Redwood, Professor of Chemistry at the Pharmaceutical Society, was given some of Charles' internal organs to examine. Meanwhile, an inquest took place and, on Florence's request, was held at the Priory.

Jane told how Charles had said he'd taken poison and how she was sure she had told Dr Harrison. Dr Harrison duly said she hadn't told him but that was the only event that led to a disagreement of evidence.

Royes Bell, Mary Ann and Dr Byrne, who had performed the post-mortem, all spoke. But finally Redwood appeared having performed his investigations on Charles's organs. 'I detected antimony in the vomited food. Antimony is a poison not commonly used as a poison. In all the articles delivered to me I found evidence of antimony. There is one form alone in which antimony could have been administered, and that is emetic tartar. It is soluble in water and tasteless. The effect of antimony is to produce prostration and vomiting generally from half an hour to an hour after taking. Upon the analysis and evidence my opinion is that death arose upon the taking of antimony into the body, and in sufficient quantity to cause vomiting.' And with that Dr Redwood sat down. But Redwood neglected to say that antimony is quite hard to come by. You don't keep it in your average medicine cupboard. It is used to de-worm horses – a very strong poison. It made accidental death seem almost impossible – it had to be wilful killing.

The only other important note came from Frederick MacCalmont who had dined with Charles on that Tuesday. He described how cheerful his friend had been that day and how well he was getting on with Florence and said that Charles was highly unlikely to have killed himself.

The inquest ended with the verdict of death by poisoning from antimony but the jury said that they had not sufficient evidence to say under what circumstances it came into his body. It was a most unsatisfactory conclusion and made it clear that the matter could not just rest there.

And there was no doubt too about the way the inquest had been carried out – Mr Carter leading the proceedings had been all too keen to draw a conclusion of suicide and had not given the doctors or Florence an opportunity to speak. This may have suited her and Mr Campbell, Florence's father, but it didn't bode well for justice.

Charles was buried on 29 April. He had been dead just over a week, but Florence was too distressed to attend the funeral and went down to Brighton four days later. She was virtually inactive, apart from writing twice to Charles' stepfather about financial matters, and once to pass on Royes Bell's thoughts that Charles's death must have been suicide – Florence claimed he must have been under pressure to give money to his young lady in Maidenhead. But surely that would not have driven him so suddenly to suicide. And was it not rather vulgar to be checking up on money especially if she'd been too upset to even attend the funeral. However, suicide, though disturbing, was certainly less harrowing than murder and all the attention that would go with it. If Florence had hoped to avoid a scandal by pursuing the suicide theory she failed, because by the second week in May the newspapers bulged with the story. There were minute details about the meal that had been eaten on that last Tuesday as well as an account of the comings and goings of servants, doctors and relations. There was even criticism of the way the inquest was carried out.

The case was endlessly discussed in all circles – Florence's life was no longer her own. The poisoning in posh suburbia had aroused everyone's interest and the word on the scandalmongers' lips was 'murder'. Florence received anonymous letters accusing her of participating in the dreadful act and, in an effort to ward off speculation about her own guilt, placed an advertisement for a reward for information about the poison. She suggested to her own family that perhaps the antimony had come from Charles' own family home, Palace Green, as she knew it was kept in the stables there.

As Florence struggled with public and familial hostility, the jury men from the inquest had become worried about the way the case had been handled. They got together to discuss the matter and they were particularly concerned about the way Mrs Cox had been questioned – why if Charles had really talked of poison at ten o'clock did she tell no one till 2.30 a.m. And Charles' barrister friends, men in influential positions, felt that the inquest had been a shabby affair. Questions were asked in the House. Down in Brighton, Florence realised that her life was about to become very public indeed and Dr Gully was all too large a part of that life. Jane too was worried – she wrote to Dr Harrison trying to remind him of what had been said that evening. On the matter of the poison she said, 'I did not tell Dr Moore because I was expecting you every moment and I quite thought that he [Charles] would recover from the effects of the chloroform, and he would be so angry at my having told he had said he had taken poison.' Well that made sense – even if she found it hard to believe that Charles had taken poison she would certainly not want, at this precarious time in her employment, to incur his wrath in the likely event of his survival. But not to tell anyone as the man got sicker and sicker was indeed odd. Harrison wrote back with vague words of comfort.

Even if she had mentioned the poison earlier it would not have helped Charles. But Mrs Cox knew others would not be so lenient. She would be suspected of being untruthful for sinister reasons of her own.

Public concern was growing as was that in official circles. The Treasury Solicitor, after questions in the house, had made his own inquiries down at the Priory. But no one from the Solicitor's office asked Jane or Florence to speak, though in an attempt to clear their names they came forward to give their own statements voluntarily. Florence went nervously that day to the Treasury Solicitor's office. But she had the sturdy and ever calm figure of Jane Cox beside her. Would nothing shake the woman? They were asked no questions but read out the statements that they had prepared with the help of Mr Brooks, the family solicitor. The two women painted a black picture of Charlie – Florence spoke first. She described his jealousy and his temper:

> He was a very passionate man and short-tempered to the last degree. He once struck me because his mother was interfering in my household arrangements, requiring me even to put down my maid... Mr Royes Bell, who had attended me in my miscarriage, had recommended me change of air, and he said it was a useless expense.
>
> When we got to bed that night he continued very angry, and at last jumped out of bed and threatened to cut his throat. He rushed into the dressing-room, and I went after him and got him back. His words were: 'Now I will go and cut my throat!' – And he actually left the bedroom for the purpose... A compact between us before marriage was that Dr Gully's name should never be mentioned, as I told him, and requested him to tell his family, of my attachment to him. This attachment was quite innocent and nothing improper had ever passed between us. But, although I never saw, heard of or from, or spoke of Dr Gully after our marriage, he was continually, morning, noon and night, speaking of him, always abusing him, calling him 'that

> wretch' and upbraiding me for my former acquaintance with him.

Suddenly it seemed that Florence had every reason to dislike her husband – but would such incidents have driven her to murder? People have killed for less certainly. Charles wasn't the perfect man we had believed him to be – he was violent tempered and obsessed by Dr Gully – no one had suggested that of him. Even his best friends doubted that side of him. But even more bizarre was Mrs Cox's statement. She claimed that Charles had said, 'Mrs Cox, I have taken poison for Dr Gully, don't tell Florence.'

And she reiterated what we had suspected: 'I did not like to tell Dr Moore, thinking suicide from such would cause a scandal. Mr Bravo's temper was so violent. Had he recovered as I thought he would if it was only chloroform, he would have been so angry.'

Jane claimed that on an earlier occasion Charles had called Florence 'a selfish pig' and that he wished he was dead and that if he was dead she could go back to Gully. But he was as quick to cool down too according to Jane and on the same evening, he said to her, 'You love Florence, and you do the best you can for me, I thank you for it.' On another occasion, he left the house and Jane followed him down the drive begging him to come back. She told Mr Stephenson in the Treasury Office that 'these passions seemed to overtake him, because at other times he was quite pleasant'. So Charles was a complex changeable character, but he hadn't deserved to die.

After the statements had been carefully taken, Mr Stephenson at the Treasury Office showed the ladies out of the room. No one had mentioned a Dr Gully before and here was Charles the domestic ogre, a far cry from the man the official story had presented. But Florence had been in a very difficult position – she had been forced to mention Gully in an attempt to suggest a motive for suicide but now her shameful story would have to become public – and just as Gully's existence could suggest suicide, so could it suggest murder – Florence had unwittingly led herself and Jane lamblike to the slaughter. A new inquest was ordered with a new jury and suddenly instead of a domestic tragedy it seemed that a murder with three possible murderers was being investigated.

The second inquest placed even more pressure on the delicate Florence and the public and press couldn't get enough of the story. The event was held in the Bedford Hotel, Balham, and the public had to be forcibly held back from bursting into the gallery. It was to be a dreadful time for Florence – her most intimate affairs were paraded through the papers and Gully's reputation was destroyed – a fine payment for years of devotion.

At the inquest endless witnesses were ordered to appear. Almost everyone had a nugget of information about this or a suggestion about that but we shall deal with events subject by subject.

First, could Charles have killed himself and, if not, why would anyone want to murder him? He had a host of devoted supporters. Mary Ann, his maid, claimed that Charles 'was always a man who had a quiet word for everybody and he always tried to save trouble. Everyone was very fond of him.' She seemed genuinely moved by his death. Amelia Bushell, the wrinkled family retainer, who had arrived at Charles' sick-bed with his mother claimed, 'He was the very last person to commit suicide.' All his friends, MacCalmont, Edward Hope and Edward Willoughby said the same, although Hope claimed that Charles had said that Mrs Cox must be costing him £300 a year. But that was hardly provocation for Mrs Cox to kill her employer. Florence's mother, Mrs Campbell, talked too of his 'money mania'. He was always speaking of the cost of things. Had his meanness driven his wife to desperation point or had Mrs Cox seen that she was not welcome in the house? But even her opinion of his money fixation would not lead Mrs Campbell to say that he was suicidal, nor that he was a bad husband: 'I saw no trace of jealousy or bad feeling towards his wife.'

Only one man said Charles had been downright unpleasant. Mr Brookes the solicitor claimed that when he offered congratulations to Charles on his marriage he had replied, 'I only want the money.' A tasteless remark if ever there was one!

Charles' affair with the woman from Maidenhead was examined. But it transpired that he had borrowed money from the woman's sister rather than the woman bleeding him dry. And letters provided proved that the financial transaction was perfectly amicable and it didn't suggest anything as drastic as suicide.

What of the relationship between Florence and Charles at the time of death. Well, apart from the strange testimony given to the Solicitor General, the doctors all agreed that Florence had treated Charles with the utmost kindness as he lay in his sick-bed. Amelia Bushell agreed with this. And going back a little further Mary Ann had never heard Gully used as a source of rancour between husband and wife and she added, 'Mr Bravo always treated Mrs Bravo with affection.'

Ann Maria Bell – Dr Royes Bell's sister – told another tale of the devoted wife when she described a conversation she had had with Florence during Charles' illness. Luckily Ann Maria remembered

Florence's exact words, 'We've been so very, very happy and Charles has said he's never been so happy in all his life. We've never had a word together.' Her devotion seemed genuine still. But on another occasion to Mary Ann and Amelia, Florence had suggested that poisoning was possible if a 'coppery pan' was used. Was Florence attempting to hide her own guilt by suggesting another possibility? Perhaps. But when the death finally came, Florence was heard to remark to Ann Maria that the whole thing was 'very mysterious' and would 'always remain a mystery'. Was this an innocent remark or really Florence pathetically trying to push the whole affair under the carpet?

The subject of Gully of course provided a great deal of interest. He provided a possible motive for murder if indeed Florence was still in love with him. But could he be the murderer himself, the spurned lover taking his revenge? It seemed unlikely. For a start he hadn't seen Florence for months. Rowe, the butler at the Priory, had never heard mention of Gully. Mary Ann of course said that Gully had been a frequent visitor before the marriage but never since, and Parton, employed by the Bravos as the new coachman since February, had never seen Gully at all. Royes Bell's sister Ann Maria had never heard his name mentioned.

Gully was calm and dignified on the whole. He spoke clearly and unemotionally. Only once did he lose his dignity. He had been forced to say out loud, 'There came a time when she sacrificed her honour for me.' His downfall was total. But there followed more questions about the affair. Gully lost his composure. 'I don't see the relevance of these questions,' he snapped. His vulnerable position was totally apparent when the coroner barked, 'You are a witness, sir, and not a judge of the relevancy of questions.' He told of his instructions to Pritchard when Florence's engagement was announced: from then on neither Mrs Cox nor Mrs Bravo were to be admitted to the house under any circumstances. But even this had not enabled Gully to sever all ties. Pritchard said that he knew Mrs Cox had seen Dr Gully since the marriage if only by accident at the station. Had there perhaps been more to it than that – had Gully and Mrs Cox seen each other for some unknown reason?

Now it was Florence's mother's turn to reveal yet more uncomfortable secrets about Gully. He had sent laurel water, via Mrs Cox, to Florence for her second miscarriage. It was to help her to sleep but was never used as Florence managed to sleep without it. But Mrs Cox had never mentioned the laurel water to the Treasury Solicitor and strenuously defended Florence's virtue. Mrs Campbell also claimed that Mrs Cox had sought out Gully's advice when Charles had fallen so ill. He had recommended spinal mustard plaster, cold water applications and arsenicum and we know that Florence had asked the doctors attending Charles what they thought of such remedies. As a result Charles was given the spinal mustard plaster but not the water applications.

And then Griffiths spoke, the sacked and bitter ex-coachman. The room buzzed as his link between Florence and Gully became clear. He had been recommended as a good servant to Florence by Gully himself. Griffiths even claimed that he had driven Mrs Ricardo (as he insisted on calling her) in the company of Gully up until the last two or three months, which was totally incorrect as she had stopped seeing him in December.

His garbled, often contradictory story got every journalist in the place reaching for their notepads. The dismissed coachman, inarticulate, of erratic memory and shifty, was the teller of the strangest story – he regularly gave his horses tartar emetic for worms and even though he no longer worked for the Bravos he had always treated their horses in the same way, using the dreaded tartar. Everyone in the courtroom strained to get a good look at the rough figure of Griffiths. He had used the antimony he claimed between May 1875 and January 1876 when he left Florence's employ after driving her too fast in New Bond Street.

He had kept a vast amount of the stuff at the Priory in solution locked in a cupboard in a bottle marked 'poison'. He had always used the stuff when he had worked for Dr Gully but he swore that Gully had not ordered him to purchase it. He had poured all the solution down the drain when he left the Priory and he was certain that Florence had no idea it was there. He claimed that all the antimony he had ever bought was put in solution, but careful examination of the amounts he had purchased meant that he would have had gallons of the stuff in the stable. Had he left some, still in powder form, on view somewhere, in a place where anyone could get hold of it?

But Griffiths' confused garble did not make him a terribly impressive witness even though what he said caused a considerable stir. Only one thing was clear. He blamed Mr Bravo for his dismissal. But did he blame him enough to commit murder and would he have been capable of such an act?

As an added finale to Griffiths' dramatic testimony, the conversation in the very same hotel on the day of the wedding was suddenly brought to the attention of the jury. Did Griffiths remember saying that Bravo wouldn't have long to live? Stringer, the barman Griffiths had said it to, was brought in to prove that

that was indeed what Griffiths had said. Suddenly the stableman had not only a motive but perhaps the inclination to commit the act too.

But now he must turn to the method of poisoning. How did Charles come to swallow the stuff. It couldn't have been in the supper – Jane and Florence ate it too and it would have started having an effect earlier in the evening. It could not have been in the burgundy – again Charles' symptoms would have appeared long before bedtime. The poison would have also shown in the wine – it was only in water that the stuff was tasteless *and* invisible. Mary Ann supplied the clues – she filled Mr Bravo's bedside drinking bottle every evening. She said there was usually only a little of it left in the morning.

A friend of Charles', a Mr Atkinson, testified that when they had been at Oxford together Charles had been in the habit of taking a long draught of cold water before sleeping. Mary Ann had filled the bottle as usual that night. Had someone somehow had the opportunity to add a little 'something' to the water during all those pre-bedtime comings and goings? A little glass of marsala had been sent for by Florence that night. Had she had enough time to slip into Charles' room and add a little powder to the bottle? Mary Ann had no reason to do such a thing – only Mrs Cox and Florence had the opportunity and a possible but still sketchy motive. And what of Mrs Cox? How did she present herself on that terrible day in the Bedford Hotel, Balham?

Two things became clear as Jane gave her testimony. She had met up with Gully purely accidentally on four occasions since the rift between he and Florence had come about. Was this really accidental or was she trying to drag him back into the affairs of the Priory, to exacerbate Charles' jealousy? And jealousy there was according to Jane, particularly over Gully. On one occasion he had demanded to read some of Jane's mail because it looked as if it was in Gully's hand. It innocently enough contained a description of treatment for Jamaica fever but the incident illustrated the degree of Charles' obsession about Gully.

But Jane's testimony did not stretch to maligning Charles completely. She explained that he had been kindness itself when she had been asked, on urgent family matters, to visit relatives abroad. 'I will take care of the boys while you are away and I shall be very glad to see you here when you return.' But it was in Jane's interest to show Charles' affections towards her – it gave her no reason to kill him. Was she telling the truth?

As for the events of Tuesday she described how Charles had said he'd taken poison. Remember that at first she said he had taken the stuff; next, during her Treasury Solicitor statement, came the idea that he had done it 'for Dr Gully'. Now in the courtroom there was more. She said Charles had asked her on his deathbed why she had told the doctors. She had replied, she told the inquiry, by saying, 'I was obliged to tell them. I could not let you die.'

But this was nothing to what came next. Jane was questioned savagely, as the court sat spellbound, about the nature of Florence's relationship with Gully. 'Did you know that Dr Gully was her lover – Mrs Ricardo's lover?' A silence. Then a tiny whisper, 'Yes, I think I did.' Now it was almost irrelevant whether Florence had done it or not. Her reputation was totally and utterly ruined. Jane was forced to give details of trips, visits, presents and even kisses that were exchanged. The humiliation was total.

Fortunately Florence had not had to watch the proceedings – only to see them paraded through the papers from the comfort of her own home. But as Jane wriggled, a picture emerged – she insisted and her demeanour supported such a theory – that what lies she had told she had told only to protect Florence. She had omitted to mention Charles' poison 'for Dr Gully' in order to protect her employer. She had told the Treasury Solicitor that Florence and Gully were 'just friends' only to protect Florence. If Jane was to be believed, her every act was selfless. Her descriptions of Florence's excessive drinking were the only indications of a morally reprehensible act. 'I did what I could to check her and restrain her from this habit of drinking but not with success.' Jane had been through a huge ordeal and done well.

But nothing Jane could do would protect Florence from the ordeal she had to face alone. In the so-called courtroom she was forced to admit to 'intimacy' with Gully and an ensuing miscarriage. She wept uncontrollably in front of all those unsympathetic faces. The nature of their relationship was of course vital to the case but how the court relished squeezing every last detail out of poor Florence. The 'occasions of intimacy' were listed in all their sordid ugliness.

Florence claimed that Charles had mentioned separation because of Gully on that very Tuesday. This had not been mentioned before. Could it be true? Florence denied knowing anything about poisons or antimony. Florence's obvious suffering in court gained her some sympathy, but this was weighed against he once close friendship with Jane – now over according to Florence. But if Florence *had* been so close and if Jane was implicated so too was Mrs Bravo – the friendship that had supported Florence so well might easily drag her down into the mire.

Finally the verdict came. Charles Bravo, said the jury, 'was wilfully murdered by the administration of tartar emetic; but there was not sufficient evidence to fix the guilt upon any person or persons.' The courtroom went wild. The whiff of murder was in the air but there was no one to pin it on. The police had no clues either. They issued a half-hearted reward for information and closed the case in all but name. Whoever had done it had got away with it – or had they?

Our main protagonists looked a sorry bunch now. Florence sank quickly into drunken oblivion. She moved to Southsea away from everyone and everything she knew – she died of alcoholic poisoning just over a year after Charles' death. Gully lived until 1882 hounded from every reputable medical board and club. Whatever they had all done, it had surely not been worth it to sink so tragically into death or exile.

So what had really happened? Theories have never stopped flooding in. Perhaps, as has been suggested, Charles had made a fatal error in dosing Florence with tartar emetic to stop her drinking. Perhaps, whilst in truth taking laudanum or chloroform for his tooth he had become confused in administering the tartar. But surely he would have confessed in order to save himself? That it was Charles' error seems unlikely.

Griffith, the only man who had means and motive, had been miles away in Herne Bay at the time. Gully was indeed the spurned lover but he displayed no inclination towards revenge and there was no one else – Charles' ex-mistress in Maidenhead? Ridiculous.

Everywhere we look we find ourselves glancing in the direction of Jane and Florence. They acted alone or in concert to get what they wanted. Florence spun a constantly changing tale at the time – it was coppery pans and mysteries one minute, suicide due to mistresses the next. Murderess or not she gave unreliable testimony. But did she really loathe Charles enough –

perhaps his jealousies, his meanness, his sexual demands, her fear of death in childbirth had made her grow to despise him? Perhaps she wanted him dead – wanted her life all to herself once more.

And Jane would help her. Both could contemplate such an act, but only one would be capable of carrying it out. Those nights, sharing a bed as Florence recovered, gave them ample time for discussion. Did Jane encourage Florence? She was cleverer than Florence. Perhaps she could mastermind the whole thing and still walk free.

And perhaps there was something else too – maybe Jane did not care what happened to Florence. The woman had everything: wealth, looks, devoted admirers (one of them her own sweet James Gully) and husbands whom she had been stupid enough to choose unwisely. Maybe the devoted companion wanted to see Florence fall. Or maybe it was Jane and Jane alone who wanted Charles out of the way so as to preserve her comfortable life at the Priory and the income it gave her to educate her sons.

Two years after the death of Charles in September 1878, a small article appeared in the *Standard* about the death of Alexander Ricardo. 'It was said by his wife [ran the piece] that he died of drink; but peculiar symptoms were, as it was afterwards suggested, not at all incompatible with slow antimonal poisoning.'

The *Echo* in July 1876 had stated that the authorities had applied to have Ricardo's body exhumed – what did they think they would find? Unfortunately the papers relating to the exhumation were destroyed. Did the police really think that Charles was the second of Florence's spouses to die by antimony? If they did they never said so, but there were obviously some who had very strong feelings on the subject.

Florence had known that antimony was used to cure alcoholism and that too much could be fatal. Had she been slipping a gradual dose to Alexander in an effort to bump him off? Then he went off to Copenhagen and drank himself to death. The antimony she had already administered made the effects of drinking bouts all the more severe. Whatever the circumstances Alexander had conveniently died.

Florence had the opportunity to poison Charles. When Jane came to bed that night, Florence could already have slipped the tartar emetic into the water-bottle. She had had enough time when Jane was fetching the marsala. Or was it Jane who crept unobserved into Charles' room that evening? Whoever put the poison into the water, it was Jane who stalled for time by sending for a doctor from Streatham, and it was Jane who pieced together her ill-conceived suicide story over the next few days and weeks. Jane had saved Florence but their friendship was over. They could no longer be seen as bosom friends whilst the finger of suspicion suggested their joint guilt.

But surely all this is too dramatic – an unhappy catalogue of accidents is more likely. After all, we only know that nothing could be proved. Perhaps it was a case of confusion reigning on that night. Perhaps Charles had indeed used tartar emetic to keep down Florence's drinking. And perhaps, unknowingly, Florence had added a touch of tartar emetic to his water and not for murderous purposes either. Tartar emetic was known to suppress those animal appetites in men that Florence, with her medical history, found hard to stomach. It would only take confusion on Charles' part as to where he placed the fatal dose and a tot too much in the water from Florence to have produced an horrendous and unwitting disaster. But surely, if their aims had been so very innocent and so very far from murder, one of them would have spoken out. Neither did.

Did Florence and Jane act in unison merely to stop Charles' marital demands or was it all just a nasty accident? If Florence had sinned she was certainly punished severely – one life taken unceremoniously for another. And what of Jane? Let us hope that her days were happy and that here nights were blessed with blameless sleep and the sweetest of dreams. After all she had nothing on her conscience, did she?

2: No Smoke without Fire

Lesley Stevenson

Everyone agreed. Seventeen-year-old Peter Luckhurst was not a violent boy. Except, by his own admission, when it came to shooting rabbits. In 1981 he was found guilty of murdering a woman he regarded as 'like a mother to me' and was ordered to be detained at Her Majesty's pleasure. Twelve years on there is still little prospect of his release. No date to look forward to. No days to strike off. No time to get done. Except perhaps the rest of his life.

There is one way out of this hell. Peter Luckhurst, now a thirty-year-old adult, knows the way. He refuses, however, to walk that particular path to freedom. He refuses to admit to a crime he states he did not commit.

It was a particularly violent crime. Seventy-nine-year-old Gwendoline Marshall had been beaten about the head and dragged dazed and bleeding around her home. Her killer then slit her throat before pinning her to the ground with the single prong of a hayfork.

The news shattered the usual peace and quiet of Pluckley, a small village deep in the Kent countryside. Over the years Pluckley has received its fair share of attention. Its claim to be England's most haunted village made it much better known than other Kent villages. Visitors were more likely to have visited the place to catch a glimpse of one of the twelve Pluckley ghosts than to admire its prettiness.

Swarms of journalists descended on Pluckley when the body of Gwendoline Marshall was found in her potting shed in 1980. It was only a matter of time before the hauntings and the murder were linked in newspaper headlines. 'Witchcraft death riddle', 'Spinster murdered in evil village', 'Pitchfork killing in haunted village', were the predictable headlines splashed across the nation's newspapers.

Two days after the killing a *Daily Mail* reporter wrote:

> It is the occult theory which is now worrying many people. In the rich Kent countryside where superstition is rife, country folk are only too aware of the ancient witchcraft rite of the autumn sacrifice to give thanks for a good harvest. Traditionally, the blood of a virgin of good standing must be spilt – with the victim pinned to the ground by a pitchfork.

Was Gwendoline Marshall the autumn sacrifice in the village of Pluckley in 1980? There is no evidence that such a sacrifice has ever been made in the past or since.

More recently, Pluckley hit the headlines again when it was chosen as the setting for the TV series *Darling Buds of May*. Newspaper readers were reminded that the 'perfick' picture-postcard village had spawned a savage murder. Peter Luckhurst was dubbed the 'Buds Killer'. But, eleven years after the murder, questions were again being asked: Was a seventeen-year-old country boy responsible for the killing? Was the right man behind bars? Had the real killer escaped undetected?

Gwendoline Marshall had lived in the village for forty-five years. Her home, Enfield Lodge, was built in the thirties by her parents. The tiny, frail old woman had never married and lived alone with Sophie, a King Charles Spaniel. Villagers thought her somewhat eccentric because for years she had preferred her own company to theirs.

Miss Marshall rarely ventured out except to make what appeared to be mysterious trips to London. In fact, unbeknown to the villagers, she had property there and went to collect rent. This small private income helped protect the independence she was determined to retain, despite her old age.

Her time was spent painting, playing the piano and tending to the six acres of land which surrounded Enfield Lodge, where she grew carrots, cabbages, spinach and runner beans for her vegetarian meals. Her only regular visitors were her part-time gardener and a seventeen-year-old local youth she called Master Peter.

Miss Marshall allowed Peter Luckhurst to shoot rabbits on her land. In return he would run errands for her or do odd jobs around the garden. When she was alive, Peter's mother Joyce had encouraged her son to help the old lady.

Joyce Luckhurst had been Miss Marshall's cleaner until she died of TB when Peter was only twelve years old. Miss Marshall's kindness and listening ear helped fill the gaping hole left when Peter's mother died. His father, Dennis, did not find it easy to bring up his young family alone and sought solace in the local pub.

Peter's youngest sister, Tracy, battled to keep on top of the housework and put a meal on the table for her father and two older brothers. But there was only so much a fourteen-year-old schoolgirl could do. Peter's peers taunted him about his scruffy appearance. He was a sad sight as he trailed the other village boys around the country lanes of Pluckley. He rarely changed his clothes or washed. And once, when his own shoes were beyond repair, he wore his sister's Cuban heeled shoes. With his bobble hat and dirty old coat he was an unforgettable sight.

Is it any wonder he played truant from school? He was snubbed by his fellow pupils because he smelt and did not have a uniform. When he skipped lessons at his new school in Ashford – the nearest big town to Pluckley – he was likely to be found hanging around the gates of his old junior school where he had received so much support and sympathy from the headmistress.

But he was well-liked by the villagers of Pluckley, rich and poor alike. For Pluckley is a community divided by wealth. The big houses sit at the top of Forge Hill on Smarden Road, the main road running through the village. The village proper sits at the top of the hill with its Norman church and 'olde worlde' pub facing the village school. At the bottom of Smarden Road is the Thorne estate, the small council estate where Peter and his family lived. Enfield Lodge, Miss Marshall's home is more or less halfway between the two.

Class, however, was never an obstacle when it came to helping Peter. Knowing that Peter habitually scouted around for bike parts and tools from which to make a few bob, some of the villagers left food for Peter on their dustbin lids. After his mother died, it was often the nearest thing he got to a square meal. As his former social worker said: Peter had more problems than he knew what to do with. And, more than any other single individual, Miss Marshall listened to his problems.

The day before Miss Marshall was murdered Peter called at Enfield Lodge to have his elderly friend sign a form for a shotgun licence. October 7 1980 was a bright autumnal day. The apple trees in Miss Marshall's garden were heavy with fruit.

Peter claims he arrived at Miss Marshall's house at around 1.00 p.m. In return for putting her name to the form for a shotgun licence and allowing him to shoot on her land, she asked him to pick her some cooking apples. They then chatted on the front step as she peeled and cored the fruit.

As they sat in the glow of the weak autumn sun, Miss Marshall suggested to Peter that he should have a haircut if he was thinking about looking for work. As he left, Peter reluctantly consented to her booking him an appointment at her regular salon, Yvonne's of Charing, the village next to Pluckley. Peter claims this was the last time he saw his friend alive.

On 9 October 1980 at 2.30 p.m., forty-eight hours after this brief encounter, Peter Luckhurst was arrested, taken to Ashford police station and questioned about the murder of the old woman. For a while he was simply one of the chief suspects. Within hours the police put out the word that they had their man. Peter Luckhurst was charged with the murder of Gwendoline Marshall.

The body of Miss Marshall could easily have gone undiscovered for many days, but for the first time over a long period there were visitors to Enfield Lodge, other than Peter and the gardener, on the afternoon of her savage killing, the afternoon of Wednesday, 8 October 1980.

Lucy Wilson lived across the road from Miss Marshall, although their relationship was limited to exchanging a few words on the weather.

Mrs Wilson also did not know any of the people who interrupted her afternoon's gardening at around three o'clock that Wednesday afternoon. A woman pushing a pram came rushing up the drive. She told Mrs Wilson that her family had been invited to Miss Marshall's home to gather up windfall apples, but they had arrived at the Lodge to find the kitchen door open but no sign of Miss Marshall. Lucy Wilson, a trained nurse, followed the woman across the road.

The woman's name was Dianne Dryland. In the

grounds were her mother and father, Edwin and Rose Marden, her brother, Michael, and her husband, Alan. The Drylands and the Mardens all lived at the bottom of the hill in a farmer's cottage.

Mrs Marden had already been inside the house, but had seen the blood near the kitchen sink and had run back out again.

Lucy Wilson went into the house, following a trail of blood which led from the kitchen, through to the sitting room, and upstairs to the bathroom. Unable to find Miss Marshall anywhere in the house, Lucy Wilson called the police. Before the police, CID and dog-handler arrived, Sophie, Miss Marshall's dog was found cowering in the garage. Three hours after Lucy Wilson had been alerted, bloodstains were found near the locked garden shed. Police immediately used a pair of garden scissors to prise off the padlock.

There on the floor amongst terracotta pots and garden equipment, dressed in gardening clothes and black wellingtons, lay the body of Miss Marshall. There was no obvious motive for the killing. The house showed few signs of a disturbance. The only clues were a small loge which bore ominous red stains and a cheque book sticking out of a handbag which suggested it had been hurriedly searched. The police surgeon estimated that Miss Marshall had been dead only a few hours. He also said that her killer would be covered in blood.

A package, ready for posting, on the hall table gave the police a means of making contact with Miss Marshall's family. The package was addressed to Juliette Marshall, Miss Marshall's niece by marriage. In fact, the news was broken to the family via a radio news report. Juliette Marshall, a magistrate, heard it on her car radio. She immediately made contact with other members of her family for fear her father-in-law, Miss

Marshall's brother, should have the misfortune of hearing about his sister's death in the same way.

Peter Luckhurst claims he first saw the news on the television. He was at the house of a friend, Bruce Watts, who lived just across the road. The family were watching Southern News. At the end of the murder report Peter said to Bruce's mother, Mona Watts, 'I suppose they'll get me for that as well.' He went on: 'Mrs Watts, supposing it was murder up the road and I was involved why I'd get twenty-five years, I'd be an old man by the time I got out.' Mrs Watts replied, 'Why, Peter, you've done some silly things in our time, boy, but you'd never do anything as silly as that.'

Peter then began talking about the after-life and how he thought people were still around after they had died. Mrs Watts comforted him as she thought he was thinking of his mother's death. But she went cold at the thought of Peter having been involved in the killing. Even as she spoke the police were looking for Peter.

Sergeant Eric Peacock, who had helped in the search for Miss Marshall, had stopped to question one of Peter's friends about his whereabouts that day. Nikki Mannouch told the sergeant that he had been with Peter around 2.30 that afternoon when Peter had put Miss Marshall's dog back in the grounds of Enfield Lodge after finding it on the road. Sergeant Peacock found Peter near the top of Forge Hill and set about questioning him about the incident. He then warned Peter that someone would be calling on him to make a statement. 'I'll be around,' Peter promised. With that Peter and his friend Nikki rode off together on their bikes.

The next day, Peter was returning to Pluckley by train after having his hair cut in Ashford. Despite the fact that there was still no evidence to connect him or his friend with the murder, a number of police officers were waiting on the platform to take Peter and Nikki Mannouch to Ashford police headquarters for questioning. Twenty-four hours later Peter Luckhurst was formally charged with the murder of Gwendoline Marshall. The police had a signed confession which Peter had insisted on writing himself.

Peter had a habit of confessing to crimes he did not commit. It was part of village folklore that whatever happened, Peter would take the blame. Once, he had confessed to and was fined for vandalising a parked car. But everyone in Pluckley knew Peter was not the culprit.

It had been the same at school. When Peter was eleven or twelve years old, some of the other pupils broke into the metalwork shop. Peter told the headmaster he had done it, to stop the others from getting into trouble. He was caned. He always took the rap. He wanted friends. On one occasion his innocence was proved when one mother found that her son was to blame for something Peter had admitted to. She told the headmaster and Peter was caned again for telling lies. It was the same story outside school – so that, whenever anything happened in Pluckley, the police found an obliging suspect in Peter Luckhurst.

Peter's social worker Ann Colwell knew only too well that Peter was prepared to confess to anything to gain acceptance amongst his friends.

She arrived at Ashford police station soon after Peter had confessed to the murder of Miss Marshall. The detective in charge of the operation waved Peter's confession in front of her, saying it was no good getting upset: 'He's done it. He's confessed to it.'

She was then allowed to see Peter. She asked him why he had confessed before speaking to anyone, especially a solicitor. Peter told her that the police had been interrogating him for so long that he was completely confused. He believed that by confessing he would be allowed out of the police station to find her or someone else who would help him.

No one was more surprised at the speed with which the police had 'got their man', than Miss Marshall's niece, Juliette Marshall. When she arrived at Maidstone Crown Court on the first day of Peter's trial in June the following year, she was greeted by a senior police officer who enthusiastically boasted, 'We've got him.' She thought it amazing that the officer should be so confident of securing a conviction before the trial had even started.

There were many inconsistencies in the confession Peter signed. A forensic scientist told the court that Peter Luckhurst could not have made such a statement unless he had committed the murder or been there when it happened. But is it not strange that Peter made no mention in his confession of cutting Miss Marshall's throat with a knife?

When Peter made his handwritten confession the police too were unaware that a knife had been used. It was a detail that did not emerge until after a post-mortem had been carried out. The interrogating officers however, did know that a log with red staining had been found in Miss Marshall's hallway. In his confession Peter Luckhurst claimed he hit Miss Marshall over the head with a log.

In fact, the red staining on the log turned out to be paint.

In his confession Peter described how he dragged the bleeding woman from room to room. But he neglected to mention the downstairs toilet which had blood smeared on one of its walls. When asked about this omission in court, Peter claims he did not know of the existence of this room.

There were other anomalies that could not be explained. For example, the police surgeon said Miss Marshall's murderer would have been covered in blood. Peter Luckhurst was arrested wearing the same clothes he had worn and slept in all week. They were not covered in blood. Peter was alleged to have carried home the knife he had used to kill his victim and hidden it in a kitchen drawer at home. But how did he carry the knife? There was no trace of blood in any of his pockets. And, why would a killer take a murder weapon back to a place detectives were bound to look first – his own home? Especially if there was no time to wash the offending article.

Before the trial Peter withdrew his confession. He told the court that he had arrived at Enfield Lodge after the murder. He claimed he followed the blood trail around the house and into the garden and down to the shed where he found the body. He said he prodded her with his knife and pulled the hayfork from her neck to see if she was alive. On seeing there was no sign of life he replaced the hayfork, locked the shed door and fled. This version may explain why he knew so much about the bloody state of the house. And, how he managed to get blood on his boots and trousers.

But the jury were not convinced. The trial lasted five days. Not a single character witness was called. Villagers convinced of Peter's innocence sat in court throughout the trial, itching to say a few words of support, aghast at his inadequate defence. Even Miss Marshall's niece, the magistrate, could not believe that Peter had carried out the murder by himself. Juliette Marshall to this day believes there was insufficient evidence to convict him.

Ken Batchelor, Peter's former employer, and his wife

Hazel; Eileen Pollard, his junior school headmistress; his social worker Ann Colwell; the village aristocrat Lady Spens; his neighbours Rosemary Davies, Moira Kirke and Gladys Dry – all of them were anxious to have their say, but their wait was in vain. The verdict was unanimous. Guilty.

Mr Justice Stocker ordcred that Peter Luckhurst be detained during Her Majesty's pleasure. Sentencing Peter, he said, 'You are totally lacking in compassion or pity, nor have you shown any signs of remorse for what you have done.'

The jury believed Peter Luckhurst had killed his friend and confidante in order to rob her. The villagers knew better. Money was the last thing Peter would kill for, if indeed he was the killer. Peter and his former neighbours continued to press his innocence. But Kent Police were adamant the case was closed.

The fast and efficient clear up of crime was considered quite a feature of policing in Kent in the late seventies and early eighties. For example, after an inquiry in 1987 one officer was sacked and action taken against thirty-four others accused of clearing the books by getting criminals to confess to crimes they had not committed.

The Peter Luckhurst case is apparently not one of those cases, and so far as we know, no disciplinary action was taken against any Ashford policemen or women because of it. But as far the people of Pluckley are concerned the speed of Peter's arrest and conviction was far too quick, considering half of them had not been interviewed by the police.

The extensive house-to-house inquiries the police claimed had been carried out had not been as thorough as local people had at first thought. Many villagers soon realised they were not the only ones the police had failed to call on. In fact, some of the villagers believed information they had given police had been simply ignored.

On the day Peter Luckhurst was arrested, one villager told police about a man she saw running through her orchard on the afternoon of the murder. She described the man as a well-dressed gypsy. Earlier in the day he had called at her house offering to tarmac her drive. The police told her the incident had 'nothing whatsover' to do with the murder of Gwendoline Marshall.

Hers was not the only lead the police ignored. On the day Miss Marshall was so savagely killed, Gladys Dry was blackberry picking with her daughter on the Smarden Road. At around twenty past one she saw a man pass her on a bicycle, heading in the direction of Enfield Lodge. About an hour later she saw him again heading the other way. This time as he passed, his eyes were bulging from his head. He looked petrified.

The next day, after hearing about the murder, Gladys Day telephoned the police. She was told that her information did not concern the person they had arrested and therefore there was no need for the police to visit her or take a statement. That man no longer lives in Pluckley, but police know who he is.

It was concerns like this that prompted villagers to campaign for Peter Luckhurst's release. NOT OUR BOY PETER! read the headline in the local paper, the *Kentish Express*, a week after the verdict.

One of its journalists, Dudley Stephens, had read the court copy and was struck by the lack of evidence and inconsistencies in the Peter Luckhurst case. Three months later the Peter Luckhurst Defence Committee was formed to raise money for a new lawyer for Peter and to campaign for an appeal.

Dudley Stephens began work on another article

entitled: 'The unanswered questions of the Pluckley Murder'. It was never published. The newspaper campaign which had begun so enthusiastically petered out.

Nonetheless, there was still some hope. Newsman Dudley Stephens introduced members of the Peter Luckhurst Campaign Committee to a former Metropolitan police officer, turned private detective, Brian Ford. Ford interviewed many villagers whom the officers had failed to speak to, despite police claims that extensive house-to-house inquiries had been made in the village. He spent many hours sifting every detail of the case, trying to uncover fresh evidence for an appeal.

It all came to nothing. The campaign committee were hard pressed to meet a solicitor's bill for initial work to re-open the Peter Luckhurst case. There was little more they could do. The villagers of Pluckley did not believe the police had 'got their man'. Many of them pointed the finger elsewhere.

There was one man feared by many in the Pluckley community, not least his own family. Despite their fears, people bravely spoke up. The day after Gwendoline Marshall's murder this man was seen building a fire in his back garden. His neighbours, an elderly couple, were convinced that he was 'burning the bloody evidence'. The fire was contained in a forty-gallon drum. The man watched over it until the flames and thick black smoke had subsided and there was nothing left but ash. 'He was certainly making sure whatever it was he was burning was well and truly destroyed,' said the neighbours, who told police they had never before seen him build a fire. But the couple claimed the police did not want to know. The police response had a family ring – *they had got their man.*

Gladys Dry was also hounded by this man after giving evidence in court about his activities on the day of the murder. He laughed in her face and began riding his bicycle around her house. Sometimes when she was working in her garden she would look up to find him just standing there, staring at her. The man was the same man she had seen cycling from Enfield Lodge on the day of the murder. The man with the bulging eyes.

Anyone who has met Gladys Dry knows she is an intelligent, kindly, no-nonsense sort of woman. The kind of person who minds her own business, who would not make a fuss over nothing, but is not afraid to tell the truth when she sees it. Did the man who stared at her through her hedge as she pruned her petunias know this?

Did vital evidence go up in smoke on that October afternoon just over twenty-four hours after Gwendoline Marshall had been murdered? Peter Luckhurst has now spent twelve years in jail at Her Majesty's pleasure for the murder of the elderly spinster who he claimed was like a mother to him.

'At least he'll be getting three square meals a day now,' joke the villagers. But, there is no laughter in the words. They shake their heads in disbelief and sadness.

3: The Jewel and the Magpie

Sian Penlington

The Midway café and service station at East Hornden in Essex on the main London–Southend arterial road was a busy watering hole in the late 1960s, where salesmen, lorry drivers and holidaymakers could stop for an ice cream, a cup of tea or a plate of steak and chips. Today it is a deserted shell fenced off from the road, windows broken, bits of old boarding rattling in the back draught from traffic belting up and down the A127. Opposite is its 90s equivalent, a bright red Little Chef.

In the early summer of 1968 on a warm Whit weekend Tony Sargeant was working at the Midway as a part-time chef. Staring out of the side window into the little car-park he saw a large brown labrador dog sniffing at the passenger door of a Jag. Sargeant had noticed the car almost a week before, as it was quite distinctive, a Sherwood green mark X Jaguar, registration number MCC 932. He had parked his humble Cortina next to it the previous Monday. It was not unusual for a car to be parked for that length of time, as the Midway was a meeting place for all sorts, but Sargeant wondered what the dog found so interesting.

He peered through the driver's window and noticed a large bundle on the passenger seat, from which some grey hair protruded. He pulled on the door handle, and the door clicked open.

The bundle was covered with a blue yachting tarpaulin, and when he lifted up the corner the smell hit him. He could see a man's legs. Sergeant called the manager, a Mr Bines, who telephoned the police and then morbidly went for a look himself.

They had found the rapidly decomposing remains of Anthony John Maffia. His body had lain stuffed down in front of the passenger seat of his own car for five very warm days, with his head resting on an old cement bag by the door, feet near the gear stick, and his smart suit jacket neatly folded on the driver's seat. He had been shot through the head twice. He was thirty-seven. In the pockets of his dark blue suit were £110 in fives and tenners, cheques worth £633 and two gold sovereigns dated 1931 wrapped in pink tissue paper in mint condition.

In 1968 Maffia was reputedly the biggest 'fence' or buyer of stolen property in Britain. With the profits from small-time beginnings buying and selling dodgy car batteries, he set himself up as a 'fence', first dealing with hijacked lorry loads, then moving on to handle millions of pounds worth of stolen paintings, coins and jewellery. He hid behind the respectable front of fifteen company directorships and an upmarket bungalow in Buckhurst Hill, Essex. The mark X Jag looked well amid neighbouring Bentleys and Daimlers. It was said Maffia would deal with anyone and anything and thought nothing of handling £100,000 worth of loot one day and selling a stolen ring for a tenner in a pub to pay for his light ales and whisky chasers the next.

He lost many friends through petty thefts, as he had an irresistible habit of picking up anything that was lying about. He once stole a man's lighter and tried to sell it back to him. For this he got his nickname, the 'Magpie'. The violent gangland world he moved in was dominated by the Krays. When one of the twins made salami out of Buller Ward's face in the gents of an East End pub one night after an injudicious insult, it was

Maffia who took the unfortunate to hospital. Maffia had stayed in the car business, owning a dealer, the Justice Motor Company, in Stratford, East London. When it was visited by protection racketeers wanting a £1,000 'donation to help a friend' Maffia not only refused to pay up but threatened the strong-arm man with a gun. Tough and violent, the Magpie was also a cunning bird driven by greed. It was greed that did for him in the end. But who pulled the trigger?

When he departed this life so prematurely the Magpie had been planning to leave the nest. He was selling up and getting out. The bungalow was up for sale at £12,000. One boat, the *Southern Skye*, had been sold and his six-berth cabin cruiser, the *Calamara*, was now on the market. She was in dry dock at a boatyard on the River Crouch at the edge of the Essex marshes.

Maffia had a huge stake in a £100,000 hotel venture in Jersey with long-time friend, renowned 1950s jail breaker Alfie Hinds. Maffia served a year in prison for his part in Hinds' daring escape from the Law Courts in 1957. Now they were business partners, in the car firm, the hotel and a copper mine in Portugal. Maffia had been making frequent trips abroad keeping in touch with his investments, his eye on ever bigger deals with richer rewards.

The police inquiry, headed by Detective Superintendent Kenneth Drury of Scotland Yard, took four days. Alfie Hinds and Maffia's brother spent three and a half hours at the incident room in Brentwood. Hinds had been going spare because Maffia hadn't banked any money for four days and had £2,000 cash on him. He had been suggesting Maffia had set up his own disappearance after a whisper that the police were on his trail, but finding the body solved that mystery.

On 3 June, Drury travelled to Manchester to

interview a man who had been with Maffia on the day of his death. The man was brought to London in a blaze of publicity on 4 June. At 5.15 p.m. on 5 June Stephen Leonard Jewell was formally charged with Maffia's murder. 'It was fully expected. I expected it, but I'm entirely innocent,' he said.

Steve Jewell was not the brightest of diamonds. He left school at fourteen and was apprenticed to a Manchester engineering works. This was in 1938, the year of his first foray into crime, stealing a bicycle. At fifteen he joined the Merchant Navy and served throughout the war on the oil tankers, dangerous work. In 1945 he was in trouble again for stealing some tools. In 1952, now married, he fell foul of the American police when a drunken night ashore ended in a factory break-in with crewmates. Jewell left the merchant fleet in 1954, by now a ship's bosun, and got a job as a rigger in Salford Docks. His conviction in 1957 for stealing copper lost him his job and changed his life.

He was sent to Stafford Prison, along with Tony Maffia who was spending time at Her Majesty's pleasure for helping Alfie Hinds escape. Maffia and Jewell struck up an acquaintance. When Jewell, down on his luck, looked Maffia up nine years later the latter didn't immediately remember him. Maffia was now big time, Jewell still a small-time crook dreaming of easy money.

It was 1967. Having been a lorry driver, a coal merchant and even gone into the nightclub business for four months Jewell was unemployed and decided to seek out his former cellmate. He thought he had a forgery deal he could use Maffia for. He had bought four ten-pound notes off a man in a Salford casino who said they were forgeries and was interested in buying £32,000 worth for six thousand pounds. Jewell thought if he could get Maffia interested and up the asking price a bit he could be on for a quick profit. He paid the man in the casino £45.

In November Jewell went to Maffia's car site in London but Maffia was out so he wrote down the number on the sign outside and went back to Manchester. Exact dealings between the two men between November 1967 and early 1968 are unknown. Some say Maffia went to visit Jewell in Manchester, others that Jewell got Maffia to fence stuff for Manchester gangs and the forged £10s were just the latest deal between the two men. Some phone calls were about the sale of Maffia's boat, the *Calamara*. The two went to see her in dry dock at the boatyard; she'd been involved in an accident and the side was being repaired.

Meanwhile talk over the forged tenners continued. Jewell showed him one and Maffia told him to bring the other three down when he came next. They always met at Justice Motors. Maffia told Jewell he needed to check with a 'business associate' to raise the cash. £8,000 was a lot of money but he was part owner of some gold sovereigns that he could sell.

Jewell used to brag to his mates in Manchester about being well in with one of London's biggest gangsters, and it was said Maffia liked him. He profited from their deals and he felt safe around Jewell who had no reputation for guns or violence. Maffia was also interested in his friend's skills as a former bosun. Jewell thought he was going to make £2,000 out of Maffia, but he was out of his depth.

There was one thing Maffia needed to get out of the country before himself and his family – bullion. On 1 May 1967 a ten-man gang had pulled off one of the biggest bullion raids ever carried out in Britain. Dressed as security guards they attacked the three-man crew of a

Rothschilds bullion van in Bowling Green Lane, Clerkenwell, as it made a delivery of grain silver to a printers. Inside the van sat 140 gold bars worth nearly a quarter of a million pounds and weighing a ton and a half. The thieves sprayed gas into the crew's eyes, took their place behind the wheel, and having beaten them up, bundled them in the back with the gold and sped off. The rest of the gang drove in a protective convoy. It was one of the most daring and professional raids of the time.

The lure to the underworld of gold is its value, not just monetary, but the fact that once it is melted down you cannot trace it. A priceless characteristic. When gold is made liquid the refiner's assay mark goes with it. This outweighs the two main difficulties with gold. When gold is stolen, Customs and Excise immediately watch all ports for its attempted illegal export, so smuggling must be ingenious. Problem number one, it's hot. Problem number two, it is very heavy. Each bar weighs 27.5 lbs. In the Bank of England strongroom, on a reinforced concrete floor, it is only allowed to stand eleven blocks high. Loading must not exceed 784 lbs per square foot. The Clerkenwell gang needed to shift and hide a ton and a half, melt it down to a manageable size and get it out of the country fast.

The Sunday papers reporting Maffia's demise on 2 June stated that police were investigating business deals in Portugal and Jersey and had re-opened files on a series of London robberies. Detectives had found twenty safe-deposit-box keys and were now hunting for the vaults that held the Magpie's hoard. Only three were ever found. One contained stolen antique coins, another miniature paintings from the eighteenth and nineteenth centuries, the third held currency and a gold ingot cut up into eighteen pieces. It was part of the Clerkenwell haul.

After the murder trial, Maffia's former girlfriend revealed in the newspapers how in the October after the Clerkenwell robbery she became curious about the contents of a brown parcel on the dining-room table. It was too heavy for her to lift. Maffia opened it to reveal several gold bars about a foot long and a few inches thick. He showed her a package containing dies for making counterfeit sovereigns. The girl explained to the reporter that sovereigns were worth more than the value of the gold they contain when sold abroad. Maffia had big plans.

When Maffia arranged to meet Jewell on Monday, 27 May, he told him not to go to the car site. Jewell should get to London then phone him for directions to his house. Jewell stopped at the Midway café for a cup of tea; he had been there with Maffia before. He called the house and Maffia's son gave him directions to Buckhurst Hill. Jewell had brought the other tenners and they were going to take another look at the boat. Jewell's mate Ted Murphy was to have gone down with him but had a big night on at the social club where he was a steward so dropped out at the last minute. Jewell was alone and, unusually, armed. Maffia had asked him if he had a gun as he 'could use it'. Jewell had a Browning automatic which he'd meant to hand in at the amnesty; although he had no ammunition Maffia told him to bring it anyway.

When Jewell arrived, Maffia was just having his breakfast. Maffia's girlfriend made Jewell a cup of tea and as they sat at a table just off the kitchen, the girl was in earshot. Maffia talked about how much he was asking for the house and showed Jewell an estate agent's handout. Jewell got the impression Maffia was trying to annoy his girlfriend by talking about it. He took the leaflet anyway and stuck it in his coat pocket. To talk real business they went into the front room. Maffia told Jewell about the *Calamara* being repaired and how he was planning to sail it to Jersey on the following Wednesday. There was also talk of the mine in Portugal.

Jewell produced the three ten-pound notes and Maffia recognised them as the genuine article immediately. 'You've been done,' he said and told Jewell that he'd just been double-crossed by a bloke hired to print ten-shilling notes for him in Belgium. Maffia checked Jewell had brought the gun with him. 'Have you got any trouble, Tony?' asked Jewell. 'No trouble I can't handle,' said Maffia and went upstairs to fetch ammunition. Maffia called a man at the car site from the phone in the kitchen to say he was going to the boatyard and would be down later. Jewell and Maffia left the house.

They drove in separate cars to the Moby Dick pub, a well-known underworld haunt of the time, left Jewell's car there and drove off towards Southend in Maffia's green Jag. They hadn't gone far when Maffia asked about the gun. Jewell had left it in his car, Maffia turned back to get it.

As they drove to the boatyard he handed Jewell a fistful of bullets, .22 with a hole in the nose. The Browning magazine clip takes nine rounds. Jewell loaded the magazine and gave the rest back. When he started playing with the magazine clip, flipping the rounds back out with his thumb Maffia got annoyed: 'Oy, leave that in, leave them in, now, put them back.' Jewell put the bullets back in the magazine clip and put it and the detached gun on the wide leather arm rest between the front seats. He covered them with his coat to stop them sliding about.

What follows is the story according to Jewell. It is not the story he told at the beginning but the one that emerged as his despairing counsel prepared for the trial some five months later. It is the story he swore by to the end.

As the green Jag sped down the main road to Southend, a maroon Jag, same model, passed them going towards London. It was flashing its headlights and Maffia pulled into a layby and waited. The maroon mark X drew up behind them and the two men who got out were angry and so was Maffia although he acted friendly when they came to the car.

'You should have been at the site. You arranged to be at the site to see the boss this morning. Why are you coming this way?'

Maffia replied, 'I've got some business with Steve. I'm going to show him the boat. Tell the boss I'll be back at 1.30.'

The men were not satisfied. 'We want you there. The people are waiting for you. You promised to be on the site on Monday morning.' Maffia asked Jewell if he minded going to the boat later. Jewell certainly did and told Maffia he could drop him back at his car and he would come down another day. Maffia got the men to follow him to a phone box nearby and the three went off. When they came back the mood had changed. Everyone was now happy, and Maffia asked Jewell to hand him his gloves.

The earlier cups of tea were starting to tell so Jewell got out of the car and, as he walked to the bushes past the boot of the green Jag, he saw Maffia lifting up a black-painted ingot. Knowing better than to ask he carried on behind the bushes. When he got back, to his alarm Maffia was behind the wheel of the maroon Jag. The green car, the two men and the gold had gone. Maffia explained they had been transferring some 'gear' but it had been easier to change cars. Jewell wasn't bothered about any gear but he was deeply concerned that his overcoat and his gun had gone off in the green Jag. Maffia was unmoved; he would get them back when they swapped cars again later on.

On the way to the boatyard in the maroon Jag, Maffia revealed his wider plans. Jewell claims he told him he had £200,000 worth of gold bullion he needed to get out of the country. He could not go himself as Customs and Excise were breathing down his neck. He wanted Jewell to sail the *Calamara* with her precious cargo over to Calais. There would be someone else with him who knew the ropes on the French side. The plan was then to sail her to St Malo where Maffia would meet them. Afterwards Maffia would get a knock-down price on the boat; he did not want to see Jewell again until they were across the Channel.

The boat had been painted blue. Maffia was angry that the navigation lights had been painted round instead of being removed first. They got a ladder and went aboard. Maffia showed him how to fracture the fuel line, which would be the reason given to the coastguard to get them to allow the boat to limp into Calais. Maffia made Jewell go back to the car and get a screwdriver out of the boot to take the lights off, and when that was done they sat in the cabin.

Inside was a bottle of Black and White whisky; Maffia gave Jewell the bottle and poured himself a cup. Despite it being very warm Jewell drank some. 'Do you know how long that's been there?' 'No,' Jewell said. 'Eight or nine months,' Maffia laughed. They lowered the dinghy off the boat and carried it into the shed. Jewell wasn't feeling very well, probably the whisky. He started retching but couldn't be sick. Maffia stood laughing at him. Jewell was easy to make a fool of.

Meanwhile, the trail was hotting up for the

Clerkenwell bullion. By March 1968, two months before the Magpie's demise, police had already charged eleven people either caught in possession or trying to smuggle bullion out of the country. Some of the methods were ingenious, other attempts merely comical.

The first smugglers to be picked up were arrested at Newhaven Docks two months after the raid. A man nicknamed 'Split' and his fiancée had been under Customs and Excise surveillance for weeks. Officers were interested in the comings and goings from a flat above a bakers' shop in North London; they also watched as Split worked on his fiancée's Triumph Herald car at her father's farm in Berkshire. The couple were booked to sail to Dieppe on the 7.00 a.m. ferry and left the farm in the Triumph in the early hours of the morning, just another couple travelling to Dieppe to start a summer holiday.

At Newhaven the car was stopped and searched. Nothing. Split stood by nonchalantly, irritating the officers leading the search who knew he had hidden something somewhere. The car was stripped down to its chassis. Nothing. Still Split was unperturbed at seeing the car reduced to its parts. Then one young customs officer going over the chassis noticed a tiny hole. Someone got a thin piece of wire and he stuck it in; as it emerged on the tip was a small thread of material and a tiny fleck of gold. They smashed off the end of the axle and pulled out what looked like a string of woollen sausages. Tied together in pairs of old socks were melted down ingots worth £10,000.

Detectives got a tip-off that a further £60,000 worth had been buried. They spent an hour digging up Split's innocent mother's garden and found a neatly filled-in square hole in the middle of the lawn.

At his trial Split revealed he was taking the car over to be delivered outside the King George V Hotel in Paris.

Another smuggling trip to Paris caught two more. A tip-off indicated that more gold was due to flee the country aboard the Golden Arrow boat train to Paris from London's Victoria Station. As officers scanned passengers coming up the platform they saw a familiar figure walking rather gingerly towards them. Instead of searching him they asked him to lift up his foot. So heavy was his burden he fell over backwards and they had to help him back up. The cause of his instability? A corset with gold nuggets worth £10,000 sewn into the lining. This second smuggler, a man called Michael Kenrick, proved more useful to police than leading them to some of the Clerkenwell bullion. In 1968 he turned Queen's Evidence against the Krays, whose trial was to begin at the Old Bailey just as Jewell's case was being hard in the next courtroom. At Christmas 1967 a man was jailed for eight years having been caught trying to smuggle a further sixteen Clerkenwell bars into Switzerland. In the New Year five more bars were recovered in a raid on the twenty-bedroomed home of an Essex businessman. In March Split was given four years having been found guilty of illegally trying to export £10,000 of gold, possessing dies that could make half crowns and £5 gold pieces, and possessing two rifles, three pistols, two sub-machine guns and ammunition. Maffia could not wait much longer with however much bullion he was sitting on.

There were two people who saw Maffia and Jewell at the boatyard, the painter who got shouted at and the boatyard manager. Maffia had complained to him as well. The manager thought Maffia's pleas of poverty were a bit rich considering the car he was driving, though the latter had said, 'It's not mine, I've borrowed it from my business.' The manager also noted that Jewell was scruffy and looked more like a workman than a prospective buyer of a cruiser like the *Calamara*.

Maffia and Jewell went off for lunch at the nearby Ferryboard Inn. Maffia bought.

According to Jewell, as they headed back towards the A127 and his car at the Moby Dick pub, the green Jag, driven off earlier by the two men, returned. Maffia was annoyed: 'Not these bastards again.' This time there were three men: when Maffia recognised the third man he looked shaken. One stayed in the green Jag while the other two approached Maffia and Jewell.

'Clever little bastard aren't you?' said the third man to Maffia. 'Get out. We want you in your own car, you're going back to London to see the boss.' The man looked frightening. Six foot tall, a deep cleft on the right side of his neck as if from an operation. Jewell thought he had part of his neck missing. The second man wore a long black chamois leather jacket over a dark shirt and white tie and had on a beret. His small thin weedy face was unshaven that morning. He leaned in at Jewell's window and asked his name. He spoke with a foreign accent. Possibly French Jewell thought.

Maffia seemed nervous. 'He's all right, he's just the man thinking of buying the boat,' he told the man with the scar. 'I'm taking him back to his car at the Moby Dick.'

The man ordered Maffia out of the car. As he got to his green Jag the man behind the wheel got out and gave Maffia a shove into his car. The two men got in with Maffia and drove off. It was the last Jewell saw of Maffia dead or alive and his gun and coat were still in that car. The driver of the other Jag got in beside Jewell. He told him his name was Langdon. 'Maffia's no good,' he told him. Jewell listened in horror as the man elaborated. Langdon was to have been the other man on the boat. In between Calais and St Malo he was instructed to shoot Jewell and dump him in the sea. Langdon had to stop the car while Jewell threw up. There was more. Fearing the same fate awaited him on the other side Langdon told someone about Maffia's plan. Unfortunately for Maffia the person he told was part owner of the gold. The gold belonged to several people and Maffia was trying to keep it for himself. Jewell was now being taken to London to meet the other people and back up Langdon about the trip to France because they hadn't really believed him.

Jewell was now very frightened. They were on the A13 heading towards London, and he was convinced he was going to be killed by the gang. Up ahead he spotted Maffia's green Jag parked in a lay-by. Langdon pulled in ahead of it. Shortly afterwards a man climbed into the back seat bleeding from a wound in his shoulder, and said Maffia had knifed him. He was in pain and dropped his briefcase on the floor. Jewell turned to help him pick it all up and met with a gun. 'You're as bad as that other bastard.' The man directed them to an address where he could get his shoulder patched up. When they dropped him off Langdon said, 'I thought you'd f***ing had it when he pulled his gun. When you get to London tell the rest of the lads the truth.'

Jewell had to get away. He suggested a cup of tea. They were now on the A127, up ahead was the Midway café. As Langdon parked the car Jewell made a run for it, up the slip road on to the A127.

Monday 27 May was a bright sunny day. Retired shipmaster John Andrews and his wife decided to go out for a drive around the country lanes to Bulpham. They stopped for an ice cream and headed home in time to beat the rush-hour traffic. It was about half past three.

As the blue Hillman Minx drove along the A127 the sun was in Mr Andrews' eyes so he pulled over to get his sunglasses off the back ledge. He was just getting back in the car when there was a knock at the rear side window and a man was opening the back door. 'Are you going to London?' They weren't. 'Are you going past the Moby Dick? It's along this road somewhere, will you take me as far as you're going?'

The man was in his forties, fat scruffy and sweating. His face was a bit flushed and he was in a hurry. Mr Andrews looked at his watch; it was 3.40 p.m. The man told the couple he had had a puncture and his lorry was back at the Midway, but his mate had pulled out before him and he had the puncture kit. Mr Andrews couldn't understand as they were driving to catch up a lorry in front why the man was permanently staring out of the back window. Mrs Andrews didn't like it. She whispered to her husband to stop and let the man out at the next garage. This they did. Jewell couldn't thank them enough. He managed to hitch a lift to the Moby Dick and fled up to Manchester.

Fred Coppin was in his early seventies. A retired plasterer, he had recently been ill and was taking forty winks in the afternoon when the sound of a car door slamming woke him up. Looking out from his little window at Rectory Cottage on the A13 at Vange, he saw across the road a green mark X Jag parked on the verge facing towards London. A man stepped out of the car and although he was alone walked round to open the passenger door. Taking what appeared to be a large rag he began wiping down the bottom of the door and inside the bottom of the car. He seemed quite calm and was there for about ten minutes. Mr Coppin watched as he threw the rag into nearby bushes. He came back to the driver's door, tried the handle as if to get in but walked to the boot, checked inside and then drove off. When Mr Coppin took his dog for a walk that evening he looked into the bushes and saw it wasn't a rag but an overcoat with quite a lot of fresh blood on it. He called the police the following Sunday when he read of Maffia's death in the *News of the World.* He couldn't remember the exact time or the day but he thought it was either the Monday or the Tuesday between three and half past.

Tony Sargeant, the chef at the Midway, remembered times and dates. Having found the body on the Saturday he recalled seeing the car before on the previous Monday evening. The Midway café is set slightly off the road. There is a car-park at the front and next to that is the petrol station. At the back of the café there are ten parking spaces, six directly behind the café building and four behind the petrol station. A boundary fence marks the end of the car-park and there is a grass verge in front of the last four spaces, separating them from the petrol station.

Tony Sargeant got to work that Monday evening, the 27th, about 6.00 p.m., and parked his Cortina in the bay nearest the café at the back of the petrol station. There were three empty bays between his car and the boundary fence. At about 7.20 p.m. he went out to the bins at the back of the café to tip some rubbish out and walked into the car-park for a breath of air. He saw a green Jag drive into the space next to his. There were two men in the front seats. He didn't see them get out. The car parked facing the grass verge, the same direction as Sargeant's car. At about 7.50 p.m. Sergeant went to move his car to behind the café and the Jag was still there; it appeared empty although he didn't look inside. When he left work at 10.50 p.m. and as he drove out he noticed the Jag was now in the bay next to the boundary fence.

On his way back to Manchester, Steve Jewell stopped off for several strong drinks. He arrived at the Switchgear and Cowans social club in Stretford, where his mate Ted Murphy was steward, at about 9.20 p.m. on the Monday night. He told Murphy some garbled half-drunken tale about going to see a boat in London and how two men in a white Jaguar had clobbered the man he had gone to see and had told him the man was no good, but also that he had lost his coat. Though Jewell saw Murphy every day up to the Sunday the incident was not mentioned again.

On the Wednesday, the 29th, Jewell says he was still expecting a call or a letter from Maffia to give him details about sailing the boat. Maffia had noted down Jewell's phone number in his small green diary. Jewell was at home at about 10.30 on Wednesday when the phone rang.

'Is that Steve?' said a voice.

'Yes.'

'Are you fond of gardening?' Jewell said he did a bit.

'If you don't keep your f***ing trap shut about the 27th, you'll be pushing up daisies quicker than that!' said the voice and the phone went dead. The next day Jewell's son answered the phone and a man who gave his name as Langdon told him to tell his dad not to forget what he'd been told.

On Sunday 2 June Jewell read with horror the *News of the World* headline: 'GANG DEATH – BODY IN CAR'. He decided to go to the police. This was around 10.00 a.m. He got to the end of the avenue when he was stopped by a man standing beside a Hillman car. 'Are you Steve Jewell? You're in a bit of trouble.' Jewell thought the man and his companion in the car were the police and told them he was on his way to the station. They said they were not the police. Someone was coming to Manchester to see him the next day and he was to keep his mouth shut. If the police picked him up he was to say nothing about the gold and nothing about where the third man had been dropped off. Jewell was terrified and that afternoon called Scotland yard asking to speak to anyone to do with the Maffia case. He arranged to meet someone at the end of the M1 but was too scared to go alone.

By then the trail was leading police to him anyway. The papers said detectives were 'anxious to trace' a northern businessman seen with Maffia on the Monday. Thanks to Fred Coppin they had been led to the Crombie overcoat discarded in the bushes at Vange. In the pocket was an estate agent's leaflet about Maffia's house, one about the boat, a cheque book for a branch in Manchester and a .22 bullet. In the well behind the driver's seat of Maffia's car was a spent .22 cartridge, discovered by the man leading the murder hunt, Detective Superintendent Kenneth Drury, later Commander Drury, head of the Flying Squad. When his career ended in 1972 he had received twenty-three commendations. The story after 1972 was less glorious. He was suspended on corruption allegations following a holiday in Cyprus with a notorious Soho porn king and jailed for bribery in 1977. His role in the murder inquiry of a Luton sub-postmaster in 1969 was also to be discredited.

The police did not find Jewell, he came to them. In the early hours of Monday 3 June, Detective Constable Ronald Charlton, on duty at Platt Lane police station in Manchester, was telephoned by a terrified Steve Jewell. They arranged a meeting point and drove out to some waste ground behind Stretford police station. Charlton described Jewell as a 'very frightened man'. He was convinced he was being followed and was very nervous.

He talked of three men who were after him. Jewell said he had been the man with Maffia on the Monday. Charlton went to phone Scotland Yard, at about 2.00 in the morning. Drury told Charlton they were aware of Jewell and to take him to Platt Lane.

An officer was sent to fetch Jewell's car from the city centre where he'd left it, another was sent to guard Jewell's home and Jewell went to Platt Lane. Charlton stressed it was for his own protection, he was not under arrest. Drury arrived with great ceremony at Ringway Airport later that morning along with his sergeant, Charlie Body. Drury was an imposing figure, not tall but big and full of his own importance. He swept into Platt Lane and took charge of Jewell. The next time Charlton saw him was in court.

Jewell didn't do himself any favours. The story he told Ken Drury was a mixture of truth, lies and pure fiction. He claimed later to have been frightened of what the gang would do to him if they found out he had spilt the beans to the police. The tale was certainly garbled. The cars were different, there was one ambush not two and Maffia had been driven off leaving him with the green Jag which he dumped, empty, at the Midway café. His one consistent line throughout regarded the three men. He gave quite detailed descriptions of them. All three, especially the supposed Frenchman, should have been known to any underworld sources of note if they did exist at all. Drury repeatedly told Jewell that the police had no knowledge of them.

After nearly eight hours of questioning he was brought down to London that night. Reporters were on hand when he stepped off the scheduled BEA flight, guided by Drury, his head covered in a blanket. As he was led into Brentwood Police station he banged his head on the door. The next morning, Tuesday 4 June, with the Fleet Street pack in full chase, Jewell along with Drury and six other officers made a fifty-mile round trip of the key sites in a minibus. Head covered with a jacket he visited the boatyard and was photographed with Drury pointing to the *Calamara*. Next stop was the pub where Maffia had eaten his last ham sandwich, then on to the bushes opposite Fred Coppin's cottage and finally to the Moby Dick pub. 'He is helping us voluntarily,' said Drury. Jewell was taken back to Brentwood.

Apart from the long interview on the Monday there is only one further recorded interview with Jewell before he was charged. At 3.10 p.m. on 5 June he identified the pocket contents of the discarded overcoat as his. He was formally charged at 5.15 p.m. the same day and made a final statement about two lifts he had hitched on the day in question.

Jewell made further appeals to Drury as he sat in Brixton prison awaiting trial: 'Have you found those three men, Mr Drury, you've got to find them.' He started making allegations about Alfie Hinds and how he was going to 'blow the whole thing wide open' if something wasn't done. As he languished in jail, police started to uncover Maffia's hoard. On 10 June they opened the box containing the cut up Clerkenwell ingot and the currency and assorted jewellery. On the 20th the antique coins valued at £100,000 were uncovered.

Around this time Jewell was threatened in prison. He told his solicitor a note from Langdon had been given to him threatening reprisals on his family if he did not tell him where the 'loot' was hidden. To his counsel's distress he destroyed the note, as instructed, by flushing it down the toilet. The second letter survived. It was typed and sent at the end of August to Jewell's wife at their home in Manchester. It was post-marked London NW1. The command of English was interesting.

> 'WE KNOW THAT YOUR HUSBAND AND TONY MAFIA [sic] WERE GOING ON A TRIP IN MAFIA'S BOAT. IT IS THIS INFORMATION THAT WE NEED. IF YOU FURNISH US WITH THESE FACTS, ENOUGH INFORMATION WILL REACH THE POLICE TO ESTABLISH YOUR HUSBANDS INOCENTS [sic] IN THE MURDER OF MAFIA . . . BE REMINDED NOT TO DO ANYTHING SILLY AS IT IS YOURS AND YOUR HUSBANDS FUTURE YOU ARE DEALING WITH.'

Forensic examination drew a blank. The police were unimpressed.

Stephen Leonard Jewell was brought to trial at the Old Bailey on 11 November 1968. Next door in Court number one the complicated proceedings against the Krays were getting under way. Few were interested in why a petty crook from Manchester should have wanted to murder a big time East End villain like Tony Maffia. They were even less interested in looking for clues that might prove his protesting innocence.

The case for the prosecution was simple. Following 'some sort of argument' Jewell, standing outside the green mark X Jaguar, had shot Maffia twice through the head. The body fell to the passenger side and Jewell pushed it down into the well and drove it to the Midway café, pausing only to throw his bloodstained overcoat into the bushes at Vange. He hitched two lifts back to his car at the Moby Dick pub and came back to Manchester. They had no murder weapon and could prove no motive. Jewell pleaded 'not guilty'.

The defence despaired of their client. He had now changed his story so much it was barely recognisable compared to the version of events he had given

Detective Superintendent Drury at Platt Lane police station. The one thing he had said that fitted with the other witness statements concerned the overcoat. In this original statement he said he'd driven the empty green Jag to the Midway café (Maffia having been taken off by the gang) and then stated, 'I got out of the car and did a foolish thing. I took my overcoat out of the car and threw it in the bushes.'

Drury asked, 'Opposite were two bungalows?'

'I didn't notice,' replied Jewell.

Jewell was now claiming to have been told what to say if police picked him up by the men who had threatened him that Sunday in Manchester. Victor Durand QC only had his client's word for it but agreed the whole overcoat episode was distinctly 'fishy'. Jewell had not noticed the two bungalows opposite, which was strange as they were the only two buildings on that road for some distance. Not only was the coat dumped in full view of the only two buildings in sight, this vital piece of evidence was left complete with personal cheque book to assist in tracing the owner and a rather incriminating .22 bullet. Then there was the time of day. Fred Coppin was not sure of the exact time, between 3.00 and 3.30 p.m. he thought. On either Monday or Tuesday. The man had been there about ten minutes and had seemed 'quite calm'.

At 3.40 p.m. Jewell was given a lift by Mr and Mrs Andrew several miles away, who described him as 'definitely worried' and hot and flustered. Then there was Coppin's actual identification. At committal proceedings in June he said, 'The man was 5 feet 8 or 5 feet 9, stocky, about fiftyish. I think I can identify him. I think it is the defendant.'

In November the man had been 'about thirty, medium height and he seemed quite calm'. Re-examined he said, 'I am pretty certain it was him. I do not think there is any doubt in my mind. It is a bit confusing.'

Jewell claimed that when he was at Vange with police on the 4 June minibus trip, Drury had let the jacket covering Jewell's face slip and Fred Coppin had seen him. Asked why there was never an identification parade, Drury maintained that as Jewell had incriminated himself by leading police to the exact spot anyway it was pointless.

This Jewell also denied. He claimed the minibus had to turn round and come back to the place opposite Coppin's cottage, and he hadn't known where they were. It was the word of a petty thief against a senior police officer with a string of commendations under his belt from a force as yet unsullied by the corruption allegations of the 1970s. None of it helped Jewell's case.

The jury were as confused as old Mr Coppin. Having heard his original story from Drury, when Jewell tried to tell the court of the ambush and swapping gold and the maroon Jag they did not know what to think. Victor Durand assured the jury that while his client was a 'histrionic liar' this did not make him a murderer. It was hard going.

Central to proving Jewell had been telling the truth in his new version of events was the colour of the two Jaguar cars. If the Jaguar at the marina could be verified as being maroon then the story of the gang swapping cars held water. If not, then his first story of turning up there in the green Jag was correct. Both the boatyard manager, who had joked with Maffia about the Jag, and the ship painter said in their statements that the car was maroon.

The prosecution tried to discredit the evidence by revealing that Mr Clements the boatyard manager was colour-blind. In his summing up, the judge, Mr Justice

McKenna directed the jury thus, 'Mr Clements suggested the colour was maroon. We know that Mr Clements is colour-blind, mistaking greens for reds.' He further suggested that Mr Trussell, the painter may have 'borrowed' the description of the maroon car from the colour-blind Mr Clements. Neither was the case. Mr Trussell had made his statement about the maroon car before the boatyard manager. On the question of colour-blindness to mistake red for green completely or vice versa is rare. After the trial Steve Jewell wrote to Moorfields eye hospital asking if it *was* at all possible that Mr Clements saw the green car as maroon. Charles Cook FRCS, Consultant Surgeon replied, 'It would be a unique condition if a patient became colour defective solely between red and green. If there is a colour defect then confusion between two tone green *or* two tone red is possible.'

The jury were concerned about the cars. After four hours trying to reach a verdict they returned. They wanted a transcript of Mr Coppin's evidence about the man at the green Jag, but this was not possible. They also wanted a transcript of the evidence of the boatyard manager and the painter, again not possible. They also had two questions. As Maffia had said the maroon car was not his but belonged to his business had police established whether Justice Motors possessed a maroon Jag? They had not. Was a maroon Jag owned by anyone else at the marina on the 27th? This had not been investigated. There were other questions about the green Jag that remain a mystery. Who drove it into the rear car-park at the Midway Café at twenty past seven as the chef was emptying rubbish when Jewell was halfway back to Manchester? Even more puzzling, who moved it to the end bay near the fence later that night? If Jewell was at the Midway café at 3.40 that afternoon who was the man calmly wiping down the green Jag several miles away outside Fred Coppin's cottage?

The jury came back again unable to reach a unanimous verdict, and were told the court would accept a majority verdict. They came back at 5.55 p.m. having found Stephen Jewell guilty of murder by a majority of ten to two.

Apart from lack of motive there was an alarming lack of forensic evidence linking Jewell to the crime. If Jewell stuffed Maffia's bloodstained body below the passenger seat and mopped up blood with his overcoat why were there no bloodstained fingerprints either on or in the car? Jewell's clean fingerprints were found only on the passenger side and rear bumper. If Jewell had driven the car and body to the Midway why were there no fingerprints, clean or otherwise on the steering wheel? The fingerprints on the passenger side and rear bumper were the only fingerprints on the car. Not even Maffia left a trace. The judge suggested Jewell may have 'taken precautions'; but Jewell's clothing was not bloodstained either. The clothes he had been wearing that day were still in the house when police searched it a week later.

Following his conviction and sentence of life imprisonment Jewell set about trying to prove his innocence. Something one of the prison officers said to him as he was taken down set him thinking. The officer was a member of a shooting club and told Jewell that the firearms expert John McCafferty had been wrong in his evidence about the gun.

The prosecution case was that Jewell had stood outside the driver's window and shot Maffia twice with his .22 Browning Automatic. McCafferty explained that this gun ejects spent cartridges to the left which explains the one found behind the driver's seat by Drury. When questioned in court he had been quite certain.

'Ejects to which side?'

'On the left.'

'Is that always the case with the Browning Automatic?'

'On this particular model.'

'There are other models which might eject to the right?'

'Yes.'

The Belgian firearms dealers L. Le Personne & Col. Ltd replied to Jewell's query: '... the calibre .22 Browning Automatic pistols eject the empty cartridge on the right-hand side, and I think that we can quite safely say there have never been any Browning pistols with left-hand ejection.' Gun manufacturers Parker-Hale were of the same view: 'So far as we are aware all Browning pistols have right ejection.' When Jewell tried to bring the matter up at his appeal he was told a transcript of McCafferty's evidence would not be ready in time.

At his appeal Jewell tried to add weight to a serious allegation he had made against Drury at the trial. On the way back from their tour of the Essex marshes on 4 June the minibus and accompanying journalists stopped at the Moby Dick pub. When Jewell asked for a drink he claimed Drury returned with four flagons of beer and made him drink them all on the way back to Brentwood police station. They even had to stop round the corner while he finished the last one off before going inside. It was by then early evening and Jewell went to sleep on a camp bed. Drury dismissed the claims as rubbish at the Old Bailey, and when his sergeant was cross-examined on the point he said, 'Not to my knowledge, sir, certainly not in my presence.'

Jewell's friend Ted Murphy was perturbed by this because it did not fit with a chat he had had with that sergeant outside the court when he came down to give evidence on the second day of the trial. The two were talking about the journey from Manchester. Had he managed to grab any lunch? No, he would make do with a pie and a pint later on. 'I bet your friend Jewell could do with a pint right now,' joked the officer. Murphy said beer did not bother him but he was a chain smoker and he would be going berserk for a cigarette. The sergeant was surprised to hear Jewell was not bothered about beer because he had seen him drink four flagons straight off when he was out with them. Murphy only remembered the conversation because he had wondered what a flagon was. For Jewell's appeal he swore an affidavit.

Many years later, writing his account from prison, Jewell threw more light on the incident. Describing what happened back at the police station at Brentwood:

> I was not only tired and exhausted but drunk as well. Then a night of utter misery and shame began, I was shaken awake time and time again, statements were taken. I know I would have agreed to anything to be left alone to get some sleep. I was not allowed to go to the toilet, till I could hold on no longer and I wet myself.'

No statements or interviews from that night have ever come to light. Jewell's appeal failed.

So what about 'those three men'? A figment of a fertile imagination? Tales of a 'histrionic liar'? He had described a weedy looking man, small face, dark hair and complexion, wearing a black chamois leather jacket and beret, with a foreign accent. Drury denied all knowledge of this to Jewell but police did take a statement from a man at Justice Motors who thought one description rang a bell:

> I have seen a man on the site whom I would describe as fragile looking, he is very thin, has a pencil moustache. Whenever I have seen him he has always been wearing a cap and I consequently do not know the colour of his hair. I know this man as 'Joe' and believe him to be a printer; in fact, when Tony changed the name of his firm to Justice Motors I believe Joe printed the billheads, etc. He speaks in a foreign accent.

In the interview of 3 June at Platt Lane, Jewell talked about the forged ten-shilling notes Maffia had shown him, and of a man who was being financed to work with him. Drury was interested.

'Did he say where this individual was going to operate from?'

'No.'

'Did he mention Belgium?'

'No, not then, this was mentioned later.'

'Did he tell you the name or nickname of this man?'

'No.'

'Did he ever, in connection with these notes mention "Joe the Printer"?'

'No.'

This was in the first hour of the interview. Yet that afternoon Jewell went on to describe Joe the Printer quite accurately, as one of the mystery men involved in the ambush. Scotland Yard found out more about Joe the printer in the month following Maffia's murder than they ever let on. The information is contained in three letters held on file in Belgium. In late June Scotland Yard requested details of a trip Maffia had made to

Ostend Airport five days before his death. He had met a man called 'Joe the Printer' about some forged ten-shilling notes. By early July more information on 'Joe' had been gleaned courtesy of an associate, André Craye from Ypres.

Craye had met Joe in May 1968 at the Hotel du Nord in Bailleuil, where he was seen spending a lot of money. Craye accompanied him on four trips to meet an Englishman, Maffia, who each time would hand Joe £50. Craye thought it concerned counterfeit money and fake British driving licences because Joe had told him the Englishman was looking for printers. They went to Calais twice, once to Zeebrugge and once to Ostend. At the last meeting at Ostend Airport, Maffia and Joe had had a fight. Soon afterwards Craye said Joe had gone to England. He returned to France at the end of June and proudly showed Craye some newspaper clippings. 'Look, the guy from England is dead now,' he said. Craye told the police that Joe had admitted involvement in the murder.

Joe was arrested at Lille in early June 1968, whence he phoned London daily asking for money. He denied any knowledge of the murder in England adding that he had already been interviewed by British police. The letter that contains this information also states that a photograph of Joe was already with Scotland Yard and one of Craye was sent in July. Other letters contain Joe's real name, along with his other alias 'Calcutta Pete', referring to his Indian birthplace. He is still alive and has a criminal record dating back to 1947. This includes convictions for firearms offences and forgery. His last prison term was in 1989 for fraud. While he was serving time in Wandsworth in 1969 for forging ten-shilling notes a bizarre thing happened. He met Steve Jewell.

Jewell wrote an account of the conversation. He claimed Joe told him he'd been arrested at London Airport in early June 1968, and interviewed by Detective Superintendent Drury. He was asked to explain why his fingerprints were all over Maffia's car. He was told his prints had been found inside the car, outside on the windows and on the side. Joe denied any involvement in the murder. No such fingerprint evidence was produced in court, nor any statement, and Joe was never called to give evidence about the mysterious events of Monday 27 May.

When I investigated this case more than twenty-five years after the event, Scotland Yard were unwilling to reveal details of Joe's involvement in the Maffia murder. The old murder file was hauled up from the vaults and a reluctant officer informed me that, yes, Joe had been interviewed by Drury and there was a statement but I could not see it and he would not read it out to me although I could ask any questions I liked about what was in the statement. Yes, there had been a meeting at Ostend airport, but there was no fight and Maffia returned to England. It was stressed that Joe had nothing to do with the murder. There were no letters to and from Belgium and no photographs of Joe or Craye. Case closed.

Ken Drury was proud of the Maffia case. At the start of subsequent inquiries, Drury, by then risen to Chief Superintendent, often wore a special tie. It was maroon with a motif of a black hand – the sign of the Mafia – holding a gold sovereign. Four years after Jewell's conviction Drury was forced to resign following corruption allegations. He was then Head of the Flying Squad. In 1977 he was sentenced to eight years, convicted of bribery and corruption. The sentence was cut to five years on appeal. He served two years and two months at Ford open prison. On release he said he had only been doing his job. Just a year after Jewell's conviction Drury headed the inquiry into the Luton sub-postmaster murder. Doubt was later cast on Drury's role concerning the chief prosecution witness who had only identified one of the men after being shown a photograph by Drury. That man had his conviction quashed. The other two were released in 1980 on the orders of the Home Secretary who cited Drury's conviction as a factor.

Steve Jewell never stopped protesting his innocence from the time Ken Drury swept into Platt Lane police station until his release from prison in 1979. On Drury's conviction, apologising for seeming to jump on any bandwagon, he petitioned the Home Office and in December of the same year got a reply at Wakefield prison. While unable to give any assurances regarding his forthcoming parole hearing, the then Under Secretary of State wrote, 'However, the Home Secretary is giving further consideration to your representations, which appear to have a bearing on the rightness of your conviction.' The Governor at Wakefield told Jewell this was unprecedented.

Sometime afterwards he was visited in Wakefield by an unnamed Home Office official who asked him whether he was thinking of going to the papers if he was released. Jewell said he just wanted to get out. Without ceremony Jewell was found a good job in a local engineering works. At the end of his shift his mates would drop him off and he would walk back to the prison. After six months he was released.

Jewell's conviction has not been quashed. He has received no official recognition of his claims of innocence and his family has had no compensation. He had served eleven years of a life sentence. During the making of the programme I traced Steve Jewell. He was living in a caravan park on the Fylde coast near Blackpool, he was sixty-eight and on oxygen to alleviate his chronic emphysema. In the few talks we had he told me he'd almost given up hope of ever being listened to. Some years ago he took all the documents up to the incinerator at the local tip but had to cart them all back home again because it was broken.

He stuck them in his shed. Jewell outlived Ken Drury by seven years. In February 1991, the day after we started filming his story I got a phone call to say that he had died peacefully in his sleep that morning. And the gold? The rest of the Clerkenwell bullion was never found.

4: Our Dearest Dear

Fiona Mackay

Britain, January 1949: austerity years still; you needed coupons to buy a bar of chocolate – or a new dress. But there was escape to be had, for the price of a ticket, in the provincial picture palaces, the music halls and the theatres. Fred Astaire's movie *Broadway Melody* was playing at cinemas up and down the country, and Ivor Novello's stage musical, *The Dancing Years*, was touring the towns and cities of drab post-war Britain playing to capacity audiences.

The Dancing Years had been the wartime hit musical of London's theatreland. It was far-fetched and sentimental. A tale of love and jealousy, of love rivals, misunderstandings and bad timing. Set against the glittering backdrop of nineteenth century Vienna, it was both romantic and tragic and it hit the right note with audiences who were starved of spectacle and glamour.

The touring version was even grander than the original. Spectacular new set-piece dances, including a masqued Viennese ball, were added. The cast of actors, singers and dancers had swelled to fifty plus. The mammoth production needed four trucks to carry the scenery alone – and took a day longer to set up than other shows, because it needed two full days for the scenery builders to construct and install the lavish sets.

The Dancing Years was news wherever it went. But in January 1949 it was to make headlines, not because of its stars or its spectacle, but because of a mysterious disappearance. Mollie Mozelle was a small-time actress and comedienne; a chorus-line dancer now working behind the scenes as an assistant stage manageress. Ironically she was to achieve fame now, not for any of her on-stage appearances, but for her backstage disappearance. For on a cold winter's afternoon Mollie Mozelle walked out to post some letters and was never seen again.

January 14 1949 started like any other day in the theatre for Mollie Mozelle. The company was halfway through a four-week run at the Empire in Sunderland, a busy port on the north-east coast. There was no indication that things might be awry as the cast finished rehearsals and collected their wages from Mollie.

Mollie was a real trouper, the sort who readily listened to other people's troubles. She was popular with the cast, the young dangers and singers. She handed out their pay, along with friendly insults, wisecracks and unsentimental advice. But she hid her own fears behind a cheerful smile. And Mollie did have problems – her life was beginning to fall apart.

Later that day she left her digs, just around the corner from the theatre. She told her landlady she was going to post some letters. It was a cold afternoon, just getting dark. The letters were never posted; Mollie never arrived at the theatre; and she never returned to her digs. The alarm was finally raised later that evening when Mollie was missing from her usual place in the wings for the Friday evening performance.

The case had all the right ingredients to make it a big news story. Mystery; an attractive woman; a showbiz background; and what seemed like a glamorous lifestyle in those drab days. Mollie's disappearance started a massive police search. The cast and theatre staff were all questioned. Detectives travelled to London and Sheffield to interview her lovers, and to Liverpool to speak to her family. A plainclothes detective was stationed outside the stage door to keep watch night after night just in case anyone should come looking for her. No one did. A fortnight later the cast and the scenery were packed up and *The Dancing Years* moved on to Hull without Mollie.

Rumour has it that the police raised the floorboards at the Empire and boarded ships leaving port. It is even claimed that detectives from Sunderland questioned Haig – the notorious Acid Bath murderer – when he was arrested later that year in the South of England. But despite all their inquiries there was no trace of Mollie Mozelle. The police clearly suspected murder or suicide but there was no note and no body.

Her disappearance excited the imagination of both the local papers and the national press. Her picture appeared on the front page of the *Daily Mail*. Wild rumours circulated in Sunderland and among showbusiness circles. Theories multiplied: she had lost her memory; she had been murdered or abducted for the white slave trade; or had stowed away on board a ship leaving the busy port of Sunderland to start a new life.

Mollie had not always been a backstage girl. Since she had left home at the age of fourteen she had appeared in theatres all over Britain as an actress, dancer and singer. She had played in serious plays and variety, pantomime and comic routines. Although Mollie was talented she had never quite made it to the top, though the married man with whom she had been involved for most of her adult life was a star.

Bunny Doyle was one of England's top comedians. In his day, he was as popular and loved as Morecambe and Wise or Tommy Cooper. He was Hull's answer to Arthur Askey: a quick-talking wisecracking comic who had been schooled hard and well in the music halls and end-of-pier variety shows of the inter-war years. His first professional engagement was as a teenage stand-up comic at a seaside show at Withernsea Sands. He recalled that the children did not even look up from their digging when his act came on. However, he survived, and, after a brief spell as a professional footballer for Grimsby Town, he became a success. He appeared regularly on radio and starred in four feature films. His mock-historica monologues were famous – and he could improvise at the drop of a hat. With a keen sense of the ridiculous, he was the self-styled Minister for Idiotic Affairs – twenty years before the Pythons brought the Ministry of Silly Walks. And, come Christmas-time, Bunny Doyle was the queen of the Northern pantomime dames.

Bunny spotted Mollie in a chorus line when she was just sixteen – and he was twice her age. For the next sixteen years Mollie was often part of his top-of-the-bill routine. On stage she played straight woman to his funny man. It would all have seemed a little corny to an audience of today. He would make jokes about Giggleswick; she would roll her eyes. He would act the errant husband; she the hen-pecking wife. Sometimes they would play castaways – who after many a *double entendre* and misunderstanding would end up in the same desert island hut. Mollie played his stooge, more often than not, his wife. Offstage, she was the love of his life.

Mollie, born plain Mary Burslem, came from the solid Northern middle classes. Her family ran a wholesale fruit and vegetable business in Liverpool. They were respectable church-goers – but Mollie, the bonny blonde baby of the family, was star-struck. She was the youngest of four children and was petted and protected by her mother, Mary. Mary had been a gifted singer and pianist herself as a girl, but when her music teacher had urged her parents to allow her to be professionally trained as a singer they had refused. She was told she 'needed a trade between her fingers' and so, the dutiful daughter trained as a seamstress instead. However, when she married and had children of her own, she was to realise some of her own dreams through her youngest daughter. When Mollie wanted dancing lessons, Mollie got her dancing lessons; and when her chance came to go into showbusiness, her mother made sure she was allowed to seize it, despite Mollie's father's reluctance.

So Mollie left her comfortable home in quiet suburbia when she was still just fourteen. She went on tour with the Liverpool dance doyenne Madame Clark's dance troupe. They danced at a series of performances across Ireland. It was hard work, and less than exciting – indeed the girls were heavily chaperoned. But Mollie had no doubt that showbusiness was her life. She worked steadily from then onwards, and was never to live at home again. Miss Mollie Mozelle may never have become a star; but she was a trouper, a professional, and she was seldom, if ever, out of work.

Mary supported Mollie, no matter how unconventional her lifestyle – even when she began living with a married man. This was twenty odd years before the permissive society and yet Mollie's family accepted Bunny Doyle and he was a welcome visitor to the family home.

Bunny and Mollie were together for almost sixteen years. But it was a romance that was to end in tragedy. By all accounts they were very much in love and very good friends. They made a striking couple: Molly was five foot six – tall for the time – and was statuesque with a danger's poise. She had the blonde permed hairstyle of the moment and blue eyes. She was stylish, sometimes wearing glamorous fur coats and sharp suits, sometimes wearing trousers – a forties' version of an independent woman, with a Black Cat cigarette permanently on the go. Bunny was shorter, a dapper little man with a wicked twinkle in his eye.

They drove around in Bunny's black Buick car which was nicknamed the 'funeral wagon'. Mollie was always behind the wheel, a fast and confident driver. Bunny, who couldn't drive, would lounge beside her, wisecracking or playing with the radio. He was useless at anything mechanical – and would surprise himself if he managed to get the radio to work.

He bought her fur coats and gold charms; she called him 'berk'. When Mollie collapsed with appendicitis in an air-raid shelter in Hull during the Second World War, she kept up the wisecracks as she was stretchered out. Later, crisis over, she held court from her hospital bed, resplendent in a Hollywood-style ostrich feather jacket. A grateful Bunny made a generous donation to the hospital, Hull Royal Infirmary, for saving her life. But he never divorced his wife; and he never married Mollie.

Bunny had married young, during the First World War, to a former Miss Hull beauty queen. He went away to fight with the Bradford Pals, and was awarded the Croix de Guerre for conspicuous gallantry. It was while he was in France that he was appointed a member of the concert party known as 'The Duds', along with stars like Hay Plumb and Leslie Earle.

The war ended but Bunny was never to return home. He left his wife to bring up their young daughter, also called Molly, alone. Although he provided for them both, he seldom publicly acknowledged the child as his daughter.

Bunny Doyle was a charming and funny man, that

rare comic who was funny off-stage as well as on. But he was also a difficult and complicated man. He was vain, insecure and careless. He was deeply afraid of growing old and never forgave his daughter for giving him grandchildren early. He was full of contradictions: although careless with his wife and daughter, he was deeply attached and attentive to his mother, brother and sister, and, although Mollie may have been at the centre of his life, he was an incurable womaniser. They were always young, blue-eyed blondes – beauty queens and chorus girls.

We do not know at what stage the charmed partnership began to sour, but eventually Mollie and Bunny split up. They loved each other undoubtedly, but the relationship was over. Bunny's family put the blame squarely on him. They believed he should have married her. Mollie did not publicly make a fuss about marriage. Perhaps at the beginning of their relationship it was far from her mind, but as she got older it seems clear that she became more insecure; Bunny's roving eye did not help.

Mollie had lived for many years unconventionally and happily. But it was hard to be an unmarried woman in your early thirties at that time. Perhaps, as the years passed, Mollie increasingly wanted the security and the status of marriage. Divorce was certainly not easy, but neither was it impossible to obtain in 1940s Britain. His first wife was not unwilling, but, as the old music-hall song goes, Bunny dillied and dallied and, in the end, delayed once too often.

Molly left Bunny for someone else. She told friends she had met a Sheffield businessman who had promised her security and marriage. She almost certainly still loved Bunny but had run out of patience. Bunny undoubtedly never stopped loving her. He was devastated.

He told his sister, 'I can't believe it, Mollie's leaving me.' But Bunny, being Bunny, soon found solace in the arms of a young dancer. However, he was never to have a relationship with another woman which lasted more than a couple of years ever again.

Meanwhile Mollie took a backstage job as assistant stage manageress with the touring version of *The Dancing Years*. It was a prudent career move for a woman who, then thirty-one, knew that her dancing days were numbered. As an assistant stage manageress she could stay involved in the theatre until her old age if she chose. However, Mollie also had other plans and so began her courtship with Sheffield boxing promoter and businessman, Walter Hattersley.

Walter Hattersley was a small, squat bulldog of a man. He ran the Alexandra Hotel in Sheffield where civic big-wigs and police chiefs rubbed shoulders with local gangsters. Walter was a typical Northern 'hard man': he was dour and more than a little ruthless. A self-made man, he had started his working life in the pits and ended up with a chauffeur-driven Bentley. He made his money out of boxing, motorcars and hotels. He was worth more than half a million pounds at today's prices.

Never a boxer himself, Hattersley began his career shortly after the end of the First World War, promoting young fighters in a backstreet stadium in Sheffield, in the days before the British Boxing Board of Control. It is reputed that his 'stable' of fighters once included the legendary Yorkshire fighter Johnny Cuthbert, when he was a young man. Hattersley later branched out into the boxing booths business, where local likely lads could slug it out with professional fighters. Later still he was responsible for open-air showpiece boxing matches at Sheffield's Hillsborough football stadium.

During this time he also entered the licensed trade and

built up a garage business dealing in early model Jaguars, Bentleys and the like. By the time Mollie met him in the late 1940s he had a sizeable business empire including the Alexandra, an imposing Victorian commercial hotel in the centre of the town. It took in paying guests, mostly theatricals and commercial travellers, and was a popular drinking haunt for influential locals on both sides of the law. Hattersley earned and commanded respect in a society still dominated by hard-faced men: civic duty mixed with sharp business. In public he was a man of influence – a generous benefactor to worthy causes, a sporting man with links not only to boxing, but with football and dog racing. In private he was something of a tyrant. It was reputed that he had bullied one of his sons into marriage because he needed a landlady for the Alexandra and that a second son had been pressurised into becoming a professional boxer at seventeen. The young lad had to step into the boxing booths when paid fighters failed to turn up.

If Walter Hattersley had a soft side, it did not show. However he was fond of the theatre and actresses. It is not known when Mollie Mozelle and Walter Hattersley first met. One story tells how they were thrown together during the Sheffield Blitz as bombs rained down on the city. Mollie may have had digs at the Alexandra whilst playing in one of Sheffield's many theatres; they may have met at one of the bars where theatricals gathered. Whatever the circumstances of that first meeting, however melodramatic or mundane, it is clear that they renewed their friendship after the war, around 1947.

Mollie stayed with Hattersley in his rooms above the Alexandra whenever her touring allowed. She was popular with the punters. She was a stylish dresser who towered above Hattersley. She told jokes, and more importantly laughed at Walter's. She could drink beer and play darts with the locals, and liked to play to the gallery. One evening she ate the heads off a whole vase of daffodils for a bet.

At first things seemed promising. Mollie seemed to have settled in her mind for life as the wife of a businessman. But the horizon was clouded. Walter's sons did not like her, perhaps they saw her as a threat, or a gold-digger. Anyway a year or more passed and marriage was no nearer.

Later, after Mollie's disappearance, Hattersley was to tell police that there had never been any plans to marry. The police believed him when he told them that Mollie had invented it all. Perhaps they thought she had been fooling herself at best, a liar at worst. For how improbable it must have seemed to the investigating detectives that this wealthy businessman, who had links with freemasons and high-ranking police officers, would have offered to wed a theatrical. He might have wanted to fool around a little, perhaps – but to marry her?

Mollie may have been wrong to believe that Walter would marry her, but it was not a fanciful invention on her part. It was clear that she had embarked on the relationship confident there was a commitment from Walter to marry. Indeed she had confided this to Bunny Doyle's own sister, who was Mollie's close friend and confidante. Walter may never have intended to marry Mollie but, if so, he was prepared to put up with the charade of an engagement party at Mollie's parents, and an engagement celebration of sorts at the Alexandra one evening in the autumn of 1948 when *The Dancing Years* was playing in Sheffield.

There was bad feeling that night – one of the sons refused to come downstairs to drink with the celebrating couple. Later yet there was some sort of argument between Mollie and Walter upstairs in his rooms. She was not there in the morning. Walter did not discuss the matter with anyone.

When Mollie disappeared for good, a few weeks later, Hattersley told police that he had thrown Mollie out of the hotel that night after finding her collapsed drunk on his bedroom floor. This brutal and degrading version of events seems unlikely – Mollie was known to be able to 'hold her drink'. It seems more likely that she had become insistent that a date for the wedding be set before the show moved on to yet another town. But by then Walter had tired of her. Anyway, Hattersley's version of events, told a couple of months later after Mollie's disappearance, was never challenged by the police, perhaps under instructions to treat this highly connected man with care and discretion.

And so the show moved on to another town, and Mollie with it. She was now thirty-three years old. When Mollie Mozelle disappeared she was the same age as Madonna is now, but in the 1940s Mollie would have been considered well past her prime. It is hard to appreciate how oppressive the conventions of the time were. Mollie had lived outside the conventions of society but now seemed to be hankering after security and respectability. Certainly Mollie would be reflective about her future and her past. She may well have decided to have a go at winning back Walter.

On the evening of 22 November 1948 she was overheard ringing Walter, who hung up on her. She was seen in tears sobbing: 'It's all over.' On the day she disap-peared she spoke of having written to Hattersley who had replied that day. Press cuttings speak of a letter having been found in her room – but the police stated it was not pertinent to her disappearance. Was it

Hattersley's reply, or did his letter disappear along with Mollie?

Walter was never to speak to Mollie again. He was not the sort to let a little bit of 'woman trouble' affect him. If, after she had later disappeared, he wondered what had happened to her, he never wondered aloud. The regulars in the Alexandra often chewed over the mystery, but nobody dared raise the subject with Hattersley. He died three years later in 1952 – already an old man at fifty-five – lame with gout.

Mollie had been part of *The Dancing Years* for nearly two years when she disappeared. The cast and production team were devastated. Leading man, Barry Sinclair, who had taken over the role from the show's creator Ivor Novello told reporters, 'Her disappearance is hanging like a cloud over the company.'

Over the next few days, in between rehearsals and shows, Sunderland detectives interviewed all the cast and the theatre staff trying to piece together her last day, hoping to come up with some leads. They discovered Mollie was vivacious, cheerful and popular, but that her personal life was less than smooth. Mollie was not the type to share her problems easily, being happier as a confidante. However there were odd clues, for example, the overheard telephone call to Hattersley before Christmas. Then, on the day she disappeared, she had had a customary lunchtime drink with the cast at the Dun Cow, a pub around the corner from the Empire theatre. There she had told one of the theatre electricians that she had received a letter from Hattersley in that morning's post. The electrician later told police that Mollie had seemed upset, but did not tell him what was in the letter. She had jollied up and gone shopping. Later that afternoon she had returned to her digs in Eden Street, just moments away from the stage door. As dusk fell she called out to her landlady Mrs Sharp, telling her she was slipping out because she had some letters she had forgotten to post.

Was Mollie merely making an excuse to slip away or did she genuinely have letters to post? Not only was it the leading man, Barry Sinclair's birthday the following day, it was also *The Dancing Years* creator Ivor Novello's birthday; and, perhaps most importantly, it was Mollie's sister Gert's birthday. Mollie did not forget birthdays, especially family birthdays. Yet none of the three was to receive birthday cards from Mollie that year. Nor were any cards found in her room, nor were they found dropped anywhere in the Sunderland streets.

Mollie left her digs wearing trousers, a blouse, jacket and a mackintosh. She did not take her handbag which was left behind in her room. Detectives found she had also left behind all her luggage, including valuable jewellery and fur jackets. And she left behind £17 in cash, a sizeable amount of money in those days. There were no clues as to her whereabouts and no suicide note.

There was no shortage of theories about Mollie's disappearance ranging from the far-fetched to the plausible. Some were made public at the time, others have come to light more recently. In Sunderland, stories circulated that she had been abducted and taken off for the white slave trade – this was one of the moral panics of the time. The old doorman at the Empire, who died a few years ago, always maintained that Mollie had been abducted by sailors and probably murdered.

The docks were only minutes away from the theatre and Mollie's digs. Could Mollie have been persuaded or forced on board one of the ships? Was she feeling fed up and agreed to have a drink on board? Did the drinking party go horribly wrong? Perhaps there was an accident?

Perhaps she was kept on board when the ship sailed and then thrown overboard when it reached the open seas? It is possible, but no witnesses ever came forward. There were no sightings, no signs of struggle, no careless talk and no body.

Could the motive have been robbery? Mollie wore a distinctive heavy gold bracelet full of charms which her family and Bunny Doyle had collected for her. Could she have been mugged and murdered? If so, what happened to her body? Mollie disappeared late on a Friday afternoon. The streets would have been dark, but not deserted and yet she was not seen by anyone. There was never any suggestion by the police that, if Mollie had been murdered, she had been murdered by someone she knew. If she was murdered, it was by chance.

There has always been a strong suggestion that Mollie had committed suicide. Did she look back on her life that winter's day and despair? She knew she was never going to be a star. She knew nothing else except show-business; but the shelf-life of a chorus girl and bit-part actress is strictly limited; indeed she was already relegated to the wings as an assistant stage manageress. Mollie had followed her dreams since her childhood, but where did she go from there? To be blunt, her prospects professionally were not bright and her personal prospects were equally bleak. As an unmarried woman of a certain age, she had little security.

She had spent sixteen years, her best years, linked up with a married man. For most of that time she had been happy enough with the unconventional lifestyle – she was an unconventional woman. But 1940s society was becoming less tolerant of unconventional women. The end of the war had seen a great swing away from the permissiveness of wartime and a re-emphasis of family values. Independent woman, the landgirls and factory girls and ambulance drivers, had been encouraged to take off their overalls land don their pinnies. Marriage, motherhood and a life of domesticity were the most powerful images for women in the immediate post-war period.

In addition, society has always tolerated racy lifestyles amongst the rich, the famous, the showbusiness set. But since Mollie and Bunny had split, she no longer shared the billing. Rather, she was in the background, backstage. Leading man Barry Sinclair spoke for the whole production when he spoke to the press about Mollie, but in reality, he may seldom have shared more than a passing pleasantry with an assistant stage manageress.

On stage each night for the past two years Mollie had seen the typically romantic and complicated plot of *The Dancing Years* played out. In it, penniless composer Rudi and operetta star Maria meet when she buys a song from him. She finds him a rich patron and he starts a glittering career. Rudi and Maria fall in love and he writes her an operetta. However Rudi does not offer to marry Maria, because he has already promised not to marry until his young friend Grete has grown up. He had half-jokingly promised to allow Grete 'first refusal', but felt unable to hurt her by not keeping his word.

Rudi and Maria live together and profess their love for each other in 'their' song: 'My Dearest Dear'. However he does not tell Maria why he will not ask her to marry him, and she is hurt. Although, at first, Maria is happy enough living with her composer, several years pass. Rudi is now an internationally renowned composer and Maria feels deeply the unacceptable social position she is in. She is in a permanent state of tension and longs for the security of marriage. Did Mollie see the parallels with her own bitter experience with Bunny?

Did she identify with Maria – who is frantic with jealousy when young Grete returns from finishing school in England as a beautiful young woman? Although, in *The Dancing Years*, the relationship between Grete and Rudi is innocent, in Mollie's experience pretty young women had come to spell pain and trouble.

In *The Dancing Years*, after a misunderstanding, Maria stages a disappearance and marries an old suitor in haste. She realises her mistake too late; Rudi and Maria's feelings remain as strong as ever – but they are destined to stay apart. Each night on stage the tragic lovers sing a reprise of 'Dearest Dear' which has become an anthem for their doomed love. In the drama being played off-stage, perhaps there was again an echo? Mollie ran off with Hattersley and, although there was no marriage, a reunion with Bunny seemed as unlikely as ever.

Bunny had let her down badly, time and time again. Perhaps her friendship with Hattersley had seemed the answer. It was certainly no love match. And Walter was no oil painting. However he was solid and wealthy and she could settle, if she wished, for comfortable, married security. Hattersley had offered her marriage and she had believed him.

We do not know when Mollie started to suspect that Walter was not going to keep his word. But by the autumn of 1948 it was clear. Walter dumped her and she was back on her own. She had kept up a brave face, but maybe it was all a bit too much. On top of all that, the show was due next in Hull, Bunny Doyle's home town. It was a place where she had spent a lot of time – she had shared secrets with Bunny's sister, drunk beer and played darts with Bunny's brother. It had been a second home. Was the thought of next stop, Hull, too painful for an already deeply disappointed woman? Did the plan to end it all form slowly over the last few days? Did it crystallise during the customary lunchtime drink that pay day Friday and later as she wandered around the dreary shops – all coupons and postwar shortages? Did she get back to her digs and decide not to go to work that evening, but to throw herself in the River Wear?

Again it is possible. Indeed it is clear that the police and some writers who have looked at the mystery over the decades have seen clear reasons for suicide. Her family, friends and her colleagues were adamant that she would not have taken her life, that she was not the type. At the time, her boss, stage manager Peter Braid said, 'She was not just an assistant stage manageress: she was one of the girls, with a strong personality. We are hoping that it is just a case of lost memory and that she will be found.'

In any event, if it was suicide, it was a suicide without a note and without a body. The docks and the river were searched at the time, but there was no trace of her. No one saw her jump. No note was ever found, and it seems likely that Mollie would have left a note. She was flamboyant, theatrical and she was bitterly disappointed. Is it not likely she would have left a note for posterity; a note for Walter or Bunny – or both? Something to explain her reasons for taking her own life, an opportunity perhaps to hand out recriminations and blame?

Or did perhaps Mollie decide that the day had come to pack it all in, not to die, but to start over again; without baggage, without history; without painful memories? Did she stage her own disappearance with theatrical flair and meticulous planning? The room left strewn with her belongings to throw everyone into confusion? She could have stowed away, or bought a passage, from Sunderland across to Scandinavia or down the British coast and then on to a destination unknown. Years later, her sister Gert tried to track down a former actor and dancer who she had heard had emigrated to Australia shortly after *The Dancing Years* tour had ended. She had been told that the man, whose stage name was André, was a good friend and confidant of Mollie's. She thought there was just a chance that she could trace him, that he might have known something – but the trail to either André or Mollie was cold by then and she was unsuccessful.

Mollie's brother, Joe, searched for her for many years. He travelled several times to Wearside. He also used the Salvation Army to try and trace her, but was told if Mollie Mozelle was still alive she was unlikely to be still in Britain.

Bunny Doyle firmly believed she had staged her own disappearance, that she had gone away for a short time to give him a shock. Indeed there were various unconfirmed sightings of Mollie at railway stations all over the country. But there are certain problems with the disappearance theory. Mollie left most of her belongings behind, including a very valuable fur coat which Bunny had bought for her. Perhaps its links with him were too painful, but it would have been a very useful insurance policy and Mollie was a sensible and practical woman. She left behind most of her jewellery, together with a sizeable amount of cash. It may be that she had other savings salted away, but it seems unlikely she would deliberately leave so much money behind.

Mollie Mozelle was, like many people in showbusiness, superstitious. Her lucky number was thirteen, the date of her birthday. Indeed she changed the spelling of her name from Molly to Mollie so that there would be thirteen characters to her stage name Mollie Mozelle.

And, since the start of the mystery, Mollie's case has always attracted the interest of psychics. During the first few weeks of the inquiry, a Lake District artist called Anne Wilson contacted the police. Whilst working on the portrait of a friend, she found herself painting the likeness of a different woman. It was only when the morning paper was mistakenly delivered to her house, with a picture of Mollie Mozelle on the front page, that the artist realised the painting bore a remarkable likeness to the missing woman. She was convinced she had received a psychic message and that Mollic was now abroad.

There is yet another theory, not made public at the time, that Mollie was pregnant and desperate and had run away to London to have a termination – illegal in the 1940s. She had then died anonymously in a botched-up back street abortion. After the 'In Suspicious Circumstances' programme on Mollie was transmitted an anonymous letter was sent claiming that the writer's grandfather had seen Mollie Mozelle on a Sunderland street on the day of her disappearance. He claimed she had told him she was suffering from morning sickness, so he gave her a shot of brandy, and she also told him she was going to London for an abortion.

Another letter writer – this time another psychic, a dowser who uses photographs and maps to try to trace missing people or objects – recounted that he had been fascinated by the mystery at the time. He believed that Mollie had gone south and had indeed died after having an abortion. He believed that Walter had broken off their relationship after she told him that she was pregnant and that Walter had claimed that Bunny Doyle was the father. He believed that Walter had met with Mollie the day she disappeared and that he had promised to post the letter she was carrying, which was to Bunny Doyle about the pregnancy.

Pregnancy could have been the reason why Walter and Mollie split up. However Hattersley was a widower and therefore had he married hastily there would have been no scandal, just an early baby. He may well have been jealous of Bunny Doyle. He may well have been suspicious; it is not known whether Mollie and Bunny kept in touch. Perhaps it was just convenient to dump Mollie, and name Bunny Boyle as the baby's father.

An unwanted pregnancy is always a tragedy. In 1949 it would have been a scandal, a shame. However it would be wrong to overplay the scale of the scandal or shame. The war had ended just four years before – and love children were not unheard of. Whose shame would it have been; a scandal for whom? As we have already said, Hattersley was a respectable and wealthy businessman, and he was free to marry her. Mollie's predicament was more an inconvenience than a disaster for Hattersley, if he had intended to marry her anyway. It would however have been a disaster for his two grown-up sons, a threat to the inheritance for which they had worked so hard.

If Mollie was indeed pregnant and Bunny Doyle had fathered the child, then there may have been a scandal. However they had lived together openly for many years and there was no real impediment to divorce. Even if Mollie were pregnant, and neither man would marry her, there were other options. Her family were a bedrock, they would have taken her in. Mollie would know that she had a safe haven where she could have the baby, perhaps giving it up for adoption as so many women did in similar circumstances; perhaps a family member would have raised it whilst Mollie went back to the theatre – such arrangements were also not uncommon. Mollie was a woman with options. It would have been a shame and a scandal, but one which could have been borne. Mollie had been having a relationship with Bunny for many years, pregnancy would always have been a possibility, and one imagines she would have often thought about the possible consequences.

Even if Mollie were pregnant – for which there is no evidence; even if neither of her lovers would marry or support her; even if she could not bring herself to return home to her family and she had decided to have an abortion, that does not explain the nature and mystery of her disappearance. If Mollie had planned to go to London to have a termination she would have needed money for the operation and to pay for somewhere to stay to recover – yet she left money behind in her room. If she was to have an abortion, why should she want to draw attention to herself? Surely she would have made some plausible excuse to get a couple of weeks absence from the show: illness, or a family crisis or whatever. If she had decided to have an operation, which was illegal and could result in prosecution, she would not have wished to stage a mysterious disappearance and spark a nationwide police hunt. Apart from anything else, she would have needed the job to go back to.

The police files into Mollie's case were destroyed in a routine clear out a few years ago. However, the journalist who had sight of them before they were destroyed makes no mention of any police line of inquiry about Mollie being pregnant. If Mollie had been pregnant then it appears she had not confided in her family, her friends or any of the cast. If that is so, why should she have 'confessed' to an acquaintance in the street?

An unwanted pregnancy may add weight to a mysterious death or suicide theory, but it must be stressed that Mollie Mozelle's personality and life was not the stuff of a Victorian melodrama. She was a resilient and resourceful woman. She may have wanted the security of marriage, but her family and friends knew she was not one to long for domesticity. She liked her work and had a steady job; and she had the support of both her family and friends, and the extended family of the theatre.

Mollie was not alone. She had people who mourned and missed her – some of them still do some forty years on. Mollie touched the lives of many people. Her mysterious disappearance has had a lasting effect: like a pebble dropped into water, the ripples have remained long after. The disappearance was a public mystery: Mollie was both glamorous and vulnerable, and interest still lives on. But there was private suffering too. Mollie's family have never fully recovered. Her mother was distraught when she disappeared. She remained adamant that Mollie had not taken her own life. Mary had received a letter from her just a couple of days before she disappeared which was cheerful and unremarkable. She made particular reference about looking forward to seeing all the family a few weeks later when *The Dancing Years* was due at Southport, and meeting her eldest nephew's new bride for the first time. She was also eagerly awaiting the new nylons (still scarce) which Mary had managed to buy from a neighbour's seafaring son.

Mary was inconsolable. Mollie's disappearance came just a few years after the death of her father. Her sister Gert remembers their mother saying that Mollie's disappearance was worse, because at least she knew where their father's grave was, but she had no idea where Mollie was, whether Mollie was alive or dead. Mary's grandson Frank, who lived in the family home in

Maghull, remembers 'Nanny' going upstairs each evening and hearing her sobs.

They all sat downstairs in uncomfortable silence. His father Joe, Mollie's brother, told him he could not turn the radio on, or expect life to go on as normal, whilst his grandmother was breaking her heart. Mollie's mother died five or six years later. But even after Mary died, her hope remained, for she insisted in her will that a portion of her estate must be saved for Mollie should she ever return.

Mollie's favourite brother, Joe, never gave up hope. He spent many years searching for Mollie. His son Frank was seventeen when his glamorous Auntie Mollie disappeared. He had a schoolboy crush on her, and idolised Bunny Doyle. He took over the search when his father died. He has followed up any leads, fewer as the years have passed. Twice he has tracked down elderly Mollie or Mary Burslems: however, one turned out to be a retired school mistress, the other a retired secretary – neither was his aunt.

Bunny Doyle never believed that Mollie was dead. Life went on, women came and went, but a part of Bunny kept waiting, always hoping. In his will he left Mollie 'my partner for many years' a third of his estate and his old Buick sedan car. But despite nationwide publicity after Bunny's death, Mollie never stepped forward to collect her inheritance.

Twelve years after her disappearance, the case took another strange twist when the badly decomposed torso of a woman was pulled out of the River Wear at Sunderland. Forensic tests revaled only the vaguest of details. It was believed that the dead woman had been aged between twenty-five and fifty years at the time of her death and that her height was roughly five feet three. Mollie was five feet six inches tall. An inquest was called and Mollie's brother Joe travelled from Liverpool to hear the evidence. The pathologist said the body could have been in the river for a considerable length of time. There was also the possibility it had been washed into the river from another resting place by heavy rains and floods. There was no means of identifying the headless torso and an open verdict was recorded on the anonymous remains. Could it have been Mollie? There is no way of ever knowing.

As the story has travelled down the years, it is the relationship between Mollie and Bunny which shines through. Vain, unreliable Bunny's love for her endured. He went downhill after Mollie's disappearance, never quite regained his old bounce, and never quite accepted Mollie was not coming back. He died in Blackpool in 1955, after an emergency appendicitis operation. His daughter Molly was at his bedside. She remembers Bunny calling out for Mollie just before he died. She said, 'I wish he had meant me, but it was Mollie Mozelle he was calling for.'

Was Mollie's relationship with Walter Hattersley a game, a gamble to force Bunny's hand into marriage? Was she still in love with Bunny? Perhaps 'in love' is the wrong expression, rather did she and Bunny still need each other? They had been at the emotional centre of each other's lives for sixteen years. They had been friends and stage partners as well as lovers. They had fitted into each other's families; befriended each other's sisters and brothers, nieces and nephews; charmed each other's mothers.

Mollie was a jealous and insecure person. She had once tackled Molly Doyle in a London nightclub about her relationship with Bunny, only then discovering she was not one of Bunny's other flames, but his daughter! Bunny was a charmer on and off stage. Gladys Laidler, the widow of the great Northern impressario Francis Laidler was to pay this tribute to Bunny when he died, 'He was one of the happiest persons I knew ... there are so many comedians who are serious and glum when you meet them ... Bunny was adored by everybody.'

Did Mollie and Bunny keep in touch after their break-up? Did the situation change from Mollie sneaking out of Bunny's house to phone Hattersley, to that of Mollie sneaking out of Hattersley's hotel to call Bunny? Did Bunny want Mollie back, did Mollie want to go back? Bunny was, by then, living with someone else.

Bunny's reaction to Mollie's disappearance, the blame he heaped upon himself and the conviction that she had staged her own disappearance to frighten him seem contradictory given that Mollie had just broken up with Hattersley, not with Bunny. Bunny's daughter remembers a phone call or visit from her father, she thinks just a few months before Mollie's disappearance, where he asked her to help him obtain a divorce from her mother. He told her that this time he really was going to marry Mollie Mozelle. However, he never pursued it further.

Had Mollie decided to stage her own disappearance – a theatrical protest to shock Bunny into action; to show both Walter and Bunny, but mostly Bunny, that she was not to be trifled with? That is what Bunny told his daughter. He said, 'Oh, she's just doing it for a game so I'll go running after her and then when she comes back we'll get married. But this time I really will marry her when she comes back because it's frightened me her running off like that.'

Why did Bunny immediately think that Mollie's disappearance was a publicity stunt against him, rather than Hattersley? Why did he still believe that Mollie wanted to marry him? Had she turned to Bunny for support when she and Walter broke up? Was Bunny giving her the runaround yet again?

But if Mollie had staged her own dramatic disappearance, it would have been temporary. Why did she not turn up again after a few days or a few weeks into the arms of a contrite Bunny? It seems inconceivable that she would not have known the effect of her disappearance on her mother and the rest of her family. Would she not have contacted them at least? Did she stage her disappearance? – intending it to be temporary – and then, by some cruel twist of fate or misfortune, was she to die in an accident perhaps, before she could stage her comeback. We will, of course, never know.

Most of the leading characters in this mystery are now dead: Walter, Bunny and Mollie's mother all died within six years of Mollie's disappearance; since then Mollie's brother Joe and Hattersley's two sons have also died.

As for Mollie, if she is still alive she will be an elderly woman in her seventies – and she will have been playing her new role – her new character – without a slip for more than forty years. Unless she chooses to step forward no one will ever know what really happened to Mollie Mozelle.

5: Maundy Money

Fiona Mackay

If all life is but a stage, then who gets to choose the character one plays? Fate perhaps, circumstance too for most of us. But every so often there are some people who create their own roles; who write their own scripts; and who fashion their own masks to face the world. Flamboyant figures, larger than life characters who fascinate their contemporaries and those who come after. They may not necessarily be centre stage; some are merely bit-part players; however, the important factor is that they are not what they seem to be, yet nobody knows who they truly are. They are more fascinating yet if there is a hint of hidden darkness, that the polished exterior masks a sinister interior.

In the years between the two World Wars, in London, there was such a man, whose name was Maundy Gregory. It is hard to say just who Maundy Gregory was – so many details about him were self-invention. He was charming, affable, and mixed with the crowned heads of Europe; yet he was a rogue who sold honours for Lloyd George; he was a flamboyant homosexual yet he shared his life for more than a quarter of a century with the same woman; he was a spy and a blackmailer, and he may just have been a killer who committed not one but two perfect murders.

Arthur John Peter Michael Maundy Gregory, was born in 1877, the son of an Anglican clergyman. His career at Oxford was curtailed when his father died, and he left without graduating. After a short spell as an unqualified teacher he then went into the theatre as an actor and stage manager. Although his time on the stage was short, acting was to mark the rest of his life. He is reported to have said, 'Acting is power, power to convince anybody of anything you like.'

He was a drinker and a dandy; a lavish spender and an impeccable dresser, even when he was a struggling young actor of slender means. He learned early the value of appearances, once saying, 'A clean silk shirt every day of the week is more of a passport to influence than a thousand pounds in the bank.'

When he became a wealthy man, and he did become a very wealthy man, his spending on clothes and accessories was reputed to be in excess of a thousand pounds a year. He changed his clothes at least twice a day and had a magnificent collection of tie pins and bejewelled cufflinks. He wore a fresh orchid in his button-hole and a monocle at his eye.

No one ever knew the real Maundy Gregory. He spent a lifetime creating and perfecting character roles which he then played out for real: the self-styled VIP; the 'Man of Mystery'; the 'Magnificent Maundy' and the 'Generous Giver'.

A small, rather dumpy man with the appearance of a dissolute cardinal, he had left the theatre after an undistinguished spell in 1908 and thereafter started his mysterious career as a backstage fixer. He was financed by the shadowy arms dealer Basil Zaharoff and was associated with Vernon Kell, the head of the British secret service. Maundy Gregory dabbled in all sorts of things, but his main business was getting to know the rich, the famous and the powerful. He spoke of having enemies and never travelled anywhere on foot. He was a man of considerable influence – a mover and a shaker – in the highest political and society circles for almost two decades.

Although he always gave the impression of affability – people who had met him spoke of his ability to 'draw people out' and take him into their confidence – he could be ruthless. His work with MI5 specialised in identifying the sexual habits and vices of various establishment figures, troublemakers, potential spies and politicians. He never hesitated in betraying a fellow homosexual if it suited his purposes, and he was almost certainly a freelance blackmailer. Maundy Gregory was therefore a ruthless man, a charming but dangerous man – but was he also deadly?

He was certainly a crook. He achieved notoriety chiefly for the role he played in bankrolling Lloyd George through the sale of honours, as we shall see. However there are also clues that the real Maundy Gregory may also have been capable of murder; indeed capable when under pressure of dispatching both enemies and friends. There is one scene played out one September evening in 1920 which may prove to be a vital piece in the puzzling jigsaw which links together three characters, all intriguing in their own right, two of whom were to die or disappear in suspicious circumstances, and one of whom may have been responsible.

British painter and naturalist George Flemwell, who lived in Switzerland at the time, was on a short holiday in England. He was painting watercolours of the Thames, sitting on the riverbank opposite Ditton Island, a small island used as a weekend retreat by artists and actors. His attention was suddenly drawn to two men in a 'new-fangled' electric canoe crossing the river to Ditton Island. One of them was someone he had once known rather well, a man called Victor Grayson. He had spent time with him in Switzerland, and had even painted his portrait, so he was sure he was not mistaken. He felt he could not pass up the opportunity to renew his acquaintance, so he found the ferryman and had himself rowed across.

He knocked at the door of the bungalow, called 'Vanity Fair', where he had seen the two men go inside. The door was answered by a handsome woman of 'Bohemian appearance'. She denied Flemwell's friend Grayson was inside. Flemwell was sure that he had made no mistake, but he also knew Grayson to be a man with a fondness for women; thinking he had stumbled upon a secret liaison with an actress or whatever, he pressed no further and left. The woman and the other man he did not know, but we do. Maundy Gregory had an electric canoe, one of the first on the Thames; he had a bungalow on Ditton Island, called 'Vanity Fair'; and he had a handsome Bohemian woman as a tenant.

Maundy Gregory was certainly acquainted with Victor Grayson. Maundy Gregory was acquainted with all manner of people: prime ministers, royalty, spies, blackmailers and a disproportionately large number of people whose names appeared in the honours list. Victor Grayson had made that connection, and he was no friend of the high society honours tout, whom he had threatened to expose.

The woman was a former small-part actress and singer called Edith Rosse. Maundy Gregory called her 'Milady', she called him 'Uncle Jim'. Their relationship was as enigmatic as they were. In the end perhaps the best description of her came to be 'victim'. Three people on an island, one who died, one who disappeared, and one who may have played a part in both their ends.

Victor Grayson was a handsome, self-destructive, spellbinding socialist revolutionary and radical journalist. Born into poverty in the slums of Liverpool, the seventh son of a carpenter, he retained a fierce passion for life's underdogs. A clever boy, he was sent by the local Unitarian minister to be educated in Manchester where he was a contemporary of Ellen Wilkinson and Lord Woolton. He later went to Liverpool University. He set out to become a missionary, but became converted instead to the cause of revolutionary socialism. He was a gifted and passionate street orator: tall, blond, charismatic, and cut a dashing figure in the inner-city slums. It is said he could move a crowd to tears one minute and to laughter the next.

He was a socialist well to the Left of the mainstream, and much disliked by the moderates. He was active in the street riots of 1904 which were sparked by massive unemployment, and was a supporter of women's rights and a friend of the Pankhursts.

In 1907 he won the Colne Valley seat as an Independent Socialist. For three years he scandalised the House of Commons; a prettier forerunner of Dennis Skinner, he was suspended from the House several times for his blunt speech. One commentator wrote that he talked 'beautiful nonsense with the tongue of an angel'. He insulted the King; called the House of Commons a House of Murderers; and he urged the workers to rise up against the ruling classes. For a revolutionary however he was something of an oddity. He adored fine clothes and thought nothing of preaching the overthrow of the old order at street corners, wearing full evening dress – earning him the nickname of 'the Bolshevik in evening dress'.

Grayson was dazzled by wealth and luxury, and when he lived in London he became an extravagant spender, living the high life. He took too naturally to champagne and whisky. He moved in society and showbusiness circles; and true socialist that he was, his womanising recognised no class divisions. He had affairs with innumerable women, ranging from countesses to chorus girls. His style and behaviour earned him the intense disapproval of the Labour leader, the temperate, cloth-capped Keir Hardie. By the time he lost his seat three years later, the promising politician had become a drunkard.

Victor Grayson was a classic case of wasted promise. He briefly dazzled then went into rapid decline. There were still flashes of brilliance, but he was dogged by alcoholism and personality problems, as well as teetering on the brink of bankruptcy. Friends sent him to Switzerland to 'dry out' where he met the artist Flemwell. Marriage steadied him for a short time and he and his wife, West End actress Ruth Norreys, went to stay in New Zealand. Come 1914, however, Grayson astonished his friends by enlisting as a private soldier. He had been a pacifist.

Grayson had what was known as a 'good war'; he fought bravely, albeit on half a bottle of whisky a day, and was honourably wounded. He survived the war, but was devastated by the death of his wife who died giving birth to a daughter in 1917.

How unlikely a boating partner poor Grayson was then for the other man in the canoe that September day – a man who had done considerably better over the years, Maundy Gregory.

The occupant of 10 Downing Street at the time of the riverside scene was Lloyd George. His party coffers were empty but he had hit on a certain method of raising cash – selling honours (the Prime Minister has the power to select those who would receive honours). Lloyd George had blatantly increased the number awarded since he came to power in 1916. In the period 1916–1923 some 25,000 OBEs were distributed and ninety-one new peers were created – for a price.

All kinds of men wanted to buy honours, and the

respectability and establishment standing they conferred; among such men were those who had made fortunes out of the war. The business just required a middleman to bring buyer and seller together; a salesman, a tout, a fixer, someone with the ear of the Government and a considerable network of contacts – and that someone was Maundy Gregory. He was not the only tout who operated in this period, but he was the most important one. It was not a very respectable trade, in fact it was a scandal. Hundreds of war profiteers were honoured during this period; including one businessman who had traded with the enemy, and another who had been convicted of hoarding food.

Victor Grayson returned from the war and was outraged. He had seen many of his comrades wounded or killed. The Prime Minister had promised the returning soldiers 'a land fit for heroes'; instead they faced poverty and unemployment. Meanwhile, those with enough 'dirty' money could buy themselves a barony. Victor Grayson took up the cause, not as a politician but as a campaigner and radical journalist. He demanded an independent inquiry into the sale of honours and campaigned with his old passion and anger renewed. It was the vintage Victor Grayson at work when, in a public speech in Liverpool in 1919, he said, 'I declare this sale of honours is a national scandal ... it can be traced right down from Number 10 Downing Street, to a monocled dandy with offices in Whitehall who organises the greatest piece of political chicanery this country has known since the days of the rotton boroughs.'

'I know this man,' Victor Grayson declared. 'And one day I shall name him.' He was, of course, referring to Maundy Gregory. Maundy Gregory, who wore bejewelled cufflinks and a monocle; Maundy Gregory, who had that same year taken plush new offices in Whitehall, just across the road from the Home Office.

What Grayson could not be expected to know was that it was a case of 'watching me, watching you'. For the same Maundy Gregory still worked as a sideline for MI5; he had a brief to watch the Bolshy Mr Grayson; and Maundy Gregory now knew that same Grayson had become a very dangerous enemy, not to the country, but to him personally.

What followed may, of course, have been just a coincidence. Sometime in the late summer of 1920 Victor Grayson was attacked and beaten by some thugs in a London street near the Strand. He was not badly hurt, but shaken enough to report it to the police. He met an old friend one evening in September 1920 for a drink and told him there were people who wanted to frighten him. He also told his friend he had begun to write a series of articles about the honours racket. Then as the two of them sat drinking in a London bar, a waiter came to speak to Grayson telling him there was a message by telephone from the Queens Hotel, telling him his luggage had arrived.

'Don't let anybody touch my drink,' he told his friend. 'I'll be back later.' He put down his glass and left, but he did not come back. His friend eventually telephoned the Queens Hotel. They denied taking any such telephone message. They knew nothing about any luggage and they had never heard of a guest called Victor Grayson.

We cannot possibly know whether that was the same September evening that Flemwell the artist saw him on the Thames. However, we can be certain that Victor Grayson disappeared and was never seen again. Now if the artist was not mistaken, the puzzle arises as to why Grayson would go with a man he despised to an island?

He would know he was putting himself in danger. Well the most probable explanation, only recently come to light, is that Maundy Gregory was probably using blackmail. Early letters to Grayson, the legendary ladies' man, indicate he may well have had homosexual leanings which left him, in those days, wide open to blackmail.

If Grayson had a secret life, Maundy Gregory would have known. Maundy Gregory had spent a career collecting useful information of that kind, both for his occasional paymasters MI5 and for his own personal gain. He milked his contacts with the rich, the famous and the powerful for information on secret vices. During the war he had run a network of informers for MI5, work which probably gave him his break into the honours racket. Is it significant that his wartime headquarters were based at the Queen's Hotel, the same hotel which claimed it had never heard of Victor Grayson?

Could the message about the luggage have been an attempt to lure Grayson to the Queen's Hotel; or could it have been a prearranged code for a meeting with Maundy Gregory? Could the 'luggage' spoken about have been the incriminating evidence that Maundy Gregory had on Victor Grayson?

So it may therefore be that Maundy Gregory was the last person to see Victor Grayson alive; and he would also have had a pressing motive to silence him. Still, if Maundy knew of Grayson's fate he had no explaining to do because nobody ever asked him. It was more than seven years before there was any official inquiry into his disappearance. Grayson was never seen again, although rumours circulated for twenty years or more – that he had run away to Russia; that he had joined the Irish Republicans; or that he had started a new life with a mysterious society lady. Maundy Gregory collected press cuttings on the mystery. The case amused him, he told a young friend.

Maundy Gregory's business prospered for another nine years or so. In his heyday, he netted tens of thousands of pounds from the sale of honours, even after Lloyd George left office in 1923; and after the practice was outlawed in 1925. His smart Ambassador Club in Conduit Street was one of the most successful and exclusive watering holes in the capital; businessmen eager for honours had their profiles written up in Maundy Gregory's society magazine the *Whitehall Gazette*.

These pieces of puzzle are interesting, but inconclusive. It would be mere speculation to implicate Maundy Gregory in Grayson's disappearance, however fortuitous for him, if nobody else in Gregory's circle had come to a mysterious end. However somebody else, one of his most intimate friends, did come to an end . . . in the most suspicious of circumstances.

Maundy Gregory and Edith Rosse were friends for more than a quarter of a century. They passed themselves off as brother and sister. There was no suggestion that they were ever lovers, but they were intimates. If Maundy Gregory had a confidante; if he ever let his mask slip to anyone then it would almost certainly have been with Edith Rosse. She also probably served, not only as his society hostess – for she could play her parts as well as the Magnificent Maundy; but she also served as a protection, a camouflage for his homosexuality.

Edith Marion Rosse was a former musical comedy actress and singer, whose stage name was Vivienne Pierpont. Her first husband, a ship's purser, had died at sea. In 1907 she married Frederick Rosse, a well known composer of musicals of the day. She met Maundy Gregory through Frederick who had worked with him at the Waldorf. Indeed she appeared in one of Maundy Gregory's productions. And she and Maundy Gregory both left the theatre at the same time in 1908.

Maundy Gregory and the Rosses were known in theatrical circles as the 'inseparable trio' and more or less lived together from the start. They all loved the River Thames and spent most of their free time boating or on Ditton Island. Maundy Gregory took 'Vanity Fair' in 1910 and installed Edith as tenant in 1911. There has been some suggestion that 'Vanity Fair' was used as a house of 'assignation' – where couples who needed to be discreet could meet.

In 1923 Frederick and Edith separated. Edith continued to live with Maundy Gregory at Hyde Park Terrace and was also a tenant at his properties in Brighton and Dorking. The reason for the marriage breakup is a complete mystery, but the Rosses never met again.

Edith Rosse was striking, rather than beautiful. A red-head with a theatrical temperament and a Bohemian streak. Maundy Gregory described her as: 'exceptionally popular because of her high spirits and amusing conversation. Her intimate friends always called her "Milady" ... she was as sharp as a needle, and her vitality was extraordinary.'

To all outward appearances Maundy Gregory worshipped Milady. He jollied her and humoured her and paid her lavish compliments, and showered her with roses and orchids.

Edith Rosse was originally from a 'good' London family. Like Maundy Gregory, she knew all about the importance of appearances. There is no firm evidence to suggest that she was his business partner, but it seems likely that she helped shape him in the early days – it was she who schooled him in the importance of stage-managing his life and his attention to detail. She may well have continued to advise him. Perhaps it was the actress in Edith which persuaded Maundy Gregory to tone down his drinker's complexion with an Elizabeth Arden preparation called 'Shine-Off'.

Under her tutelage, he became a quite obsessive snob, cultivating friendships with the rich, the powerful and the titled. He went to great lengths to befriend exiled European royalty and nobility. He was on good terms with the exiled King of Greece and often showed off the gold cigarette case the king had given him. He had in his possession a scroll, which was four feet long, drawn up by the College of Heralds which linked Maundy Gregory's ancestry to eight English kings, showing that John of Gaunt, Harry Hotspur and the Black Prince were among his forebears and that his line went back to William the Conqueror.

It is not known to what extent Edith Rosse knew about Maundy Gregory's line of business, but it is difficult to believe she did not have some inkling. She acted as his hostess entertaining his guests at the Ambassador Club. There have been suggestions, although they have not been proved, that she ran a little blackmailing sideline on Ditton Island – romantic weekends with other people's husbands and wives were kept quiet at a price. She was certainly instrumental in Maundy Gregory's decision to take offices in Whitehall in Parliament Street, almost opposite the entrance to Downing Street. They were chosen to convey the impression that Maundy Gregory and his business were part of the Government.

We do not know whose idea it was that staff call Maundy Gregory 'the Chief'; Maundy Gregory was theatrical enough to think that one up for himself. He liked his staff to tell callers he was over at 'Number 10', or that he was needed at 'Number 10'. In reality this meant 10 Hyde Park Terrace where he and Mrs Rosse lived, not 10 Downing Street. He also referred to the manager of the Ambassador Club and his business associate Peter Mazzina as 'the PM'. If listeners were confused, all the better.

Although the outer offices at Parliament Street were modest, the set was magnificent in Maundy Gregory's inner sanctum. He had a huge desk with a scarled tooled leather top and matching scarlet chair. The walls were covered with 'old master'-type paintings, including a portrait of 'Bloody' Judge Jeffreys. His desk was crammed with signed photographs and portraits from the crowned heads of Europe.

His air of mystery was enhanced by the telephone with the scrambler device, the communication system of flashing lights and the powerful wireless receiver in the corner. In another corner of his office was a safe stuffed full of brand new bank notes. Another of Gregory's flamboyant little foibles was that he would only handle money which was mint fresh. However, the days of rich pickings were to be numbered, and Maundy Gregory would be forced to become less choosy where money was involved.

Things were getting more difficult for Maundy Gregory as the 1920s progressed. Parliament had passed an Act making Maundy Gregory's line of business illegal. Not entirely impossible, but against the law. Coupled to that, the recession after 1929 had dried up the flow of interest in honours to a trickle. And the new Government wanted to stamp out the trade. He was a man under pressure.

Then, Maundy Gregory, who had for so long shaped

his own life, was hit by a series of misfortunes. A businessman who had put down £30,000 in advance to become a baron unfortunately died before the honour was bestowed. His heirs were not interested in the title-in-waiting. They wanted their money back even if they had to sue Maundy Gregory for it. In early 1932, the executors of the dead man's will indicated they would fight for the return of the money through the courts. At the last minute Maundy decided that he did not have the stomach for a legal battle. He settled out of court, and agreed to pay back the money in three instalments. However, he was a little short of funds. In fact he was on the verge of bankruptcy. Appearances were all in his line of business, but appearances did not come cheap.

Furthermore, his finances were overstretched by other demands. It must have seemed ironic to a man who had made blackmail an art that he too was being blackmailed; he needed money. He could not go to his police friends because any investigation might reveal his continued links with the now outlawed sale of honours. He asked Edith Rosse for a loan of £10,000, but she refused. Now Maundy Gregory was a generous man, and detested meanness; he had once said meanness was almost as bad as adultery – or murder.

Maundy Gregory was something of a collector, not only of gossip and secrets, but also artefacts like paintings and books. He had a secret collection of pornographic homoerotic literature, specialising in works of flagellation. He was also fascinated by the nature of vice and evil. He collected some paintings by an eighteenth-century artist called Thomas Griffiths Wainewright who was famous not only as a painter, but also because he was reputed to be a poisoner. Legend has it that Wainewright committed the perfect murder six times over, using a poison which leaves no trace.

Maundy Gregory had written an article years before about Wainewright and his poison. In fact, Maundy Gregory had become an expert on the subject; he had become acquainted during the war with the shadowy Reilly 'Ace of Spies' – an expert himself on drugs and poisons.

On 19 August, 1932, Maundy Gregory was lunching at the Carlton Hotel with the exiled King of Greece when the word came that Edith Rosse was taken gravely ill. She had collapsed that morning, her regular doctor was away on holiday and the housekeeper's husband had been despatched to find another doctor. A Dr Plummer came, who knew nothing about her. Mrs Rosse told the doctor that she felt as though something had burst in her head. He diagnosed inflammation of the kidneys and sunstroke and prescribed aspirin.

Maundy Gregory was concerned and attentive. He was at her bedside, together with the doctor and the housekeeper when Edith Rosse insisted that she make a will – in a hurry. She ordered him to fetch a paper and pen. Maundy Gregory took the menu card from inside his pocket, the housekeeper produced a pencil. He passed them to her but she waved them away. 'Write it down yourself, I will tell you what I want to say.'

Thus Edith instructed Maundy to write down her makeshift will: 'Everything I have if anything should happen to me to be left to Mr J. Maundy Gregory to be disposed of as he thinks best and in accordance with what I should desire.' Dr Plummer and the housekeeper, Mrs Eyres, acted as witnesses. It was all very unorthodox, but apparently above board.

Maundy Gregory called Dr Plummer back twice more that day; from sunstroke the diagnosis moved on to Bright's disease – a chronic affliction of the kidneys. Drinkers are susceptible and Edith was very fond of drink. Dr Plummer and then her regular physician Dr Blair attended her daily, sometimes more often until the end of August. She began to recover. On 1 September, 1932 Maundy Gregory took her for a run in the car. By 3 September, she seemed back to her old self. That night, as was their custom, she dined with Maundy Gregory in his room. The food was brought into them by the staff; the drinks were provided by Maundy Gregory. It should have been a pleasant meal but Mrs Rosse had a sudden relapse. Gregory called back, not Mrs Rosse's regular doctor, but Dr Plummer. However she did not respond to treatment. Maundy Gregory called in a battery of specialists to try to save her. Grave kidney disease was diagnosed and she died on 14 September.

The poison Wainewright is reputed to have used was Nux Vomica. It is a type of bean found in India and it contains the poisons strychnine and brucine. The effects it has on people are variable: vomiting, diarrhoea, drowsiness, numbness, mental confusion and convulsions. A victim may display any of these symptoms; Rosse had all of them. When Dr Plummer wrote Edith Rosse's death certificate he certified cerebral haemorrhage and chronic Bright's disease as cause of death. Indeed a combination of these illnesses could have plausibly accounted for the nature of her sickness and death – as indeed Wainewright could have told him. He could also have told the doctor that traces of arsenic for example will persist in human remains for hundreds, even thousands of years. Nux Vomica, on the contrary, simply dissolves away in water.

Maundy Gregory played the part of the mourner perfectly. He was insistent that he arrange the funeral and burial himself. He said he knew exactly what Edith Rosse's wishes were and that he was determined to fulfil them 'down to the last letter', particularly her wish that she be buried 'close to her beloved Thames, within actual sound of the River'.

The day after Mrs Rosse's death, Maundy Gregory toured graveyards along the Thames – though strangely he turned down the opportunity to have her buried at Thames Ditton, surely her favourite spot. He said the churchyard was not 'close enough' to the river. A donation of one hundred guineas to the parish of Bisham bought her a grave close to the water's edge, a plot which regularly flooded. He went to enormous lengths to find the churchwarden – interrupting his whist drive – in order to get the necessary papers in order.

Edity Rosse was buried by Harrods, of course. On Maundy's precise instructions she was buried shallow, the top of the coffin being a mere eighteen inches below the surface, and Maundy himself personally supervised the digging of the grave. He told the undertakers that Milady had requested just such a shallow grave, that 'she stipulated that there should be no great weight of earth above her'.

Did she also stipulate that her coffin must be lined in lead? And was it her precise wish that the top of the lead coffin should be left unsealed, a most unusual instruction? Did she realise that such arrangements would leave her body steeping in the waters of the Thames?

Edith Rosse was a good business manager, she owned or managed several properties, including some of Maundy Gregory's, and seems to have amassed a sizeable capital from modest beginnings. She was a shrewd investor and a woman of the world. When she died she left capital of £18,000.

£18,000 was useful, but Maundy Gregory was still under pressure. Perhaps he ought to have fled his creditors and retired to France then, but he stayed and tried one last scam. He made the biggest mistake of his career when he tried to sell a retired naval officer a knighthood for £10,000. Maundy Gregory, normally meticulous, does not appear to have done his homework properly this time. For one thing, Lieutenant Commander Edward Whaney Billyard-Leake RN, retired, was not as wealthy as Maundy Gregory had assumed; but far worse he was an honest man. And he went straight to the police.

It soon became clear to Maundy Gregory that his friends in high places were deserting him. The Government of the day had decided that he must be made an example of, and he became the first person to be charged under the 1925 Honours (Prevention of Abuses) Act. However Maundy Gregory knew exactly which card to play in these circumstances. He indicated that he was to plead not guilty, therefore there would have to be a full court hearing. He would call witnesses, the great and the not-so-good would be dragged through the courts. If Maundy Gregory was to go down, he was determined he would not go alone.

There was a flurry of activity in various political circles. An arrangement was made. It was decided that it would be best for all concerned if Maundy Gregory were to go away. In silence. The Conservative Party offered him a pension of a thousand a year. He held out for, and got, two thousand; enough to live well in France in 1933. It was also alleged he blackmailed at least half a dozen establishment figures at £2,000 apiece not to mention their names. But before he could retire gracefully across the Channel, there was a little business to attend to at Bow Street Magistrates Court. He changed his plea to guilty and was convicted on 16 February, 1933. He was jailed for two months, without hard labour, and ordered to pay a £50 fine for contravening the Act.

However there was trouble brewing whilst Maundy Gregory was doing his time. Edith Marion Rosse was fifty-nine years old, when she died on 14 September, 1932. When she died she had only two living relatives, a brother and a niece – who was her ward and had expected to be her aunt's main beneficiary. Mrs Rosse's niece, Ethel Davis, persuaded Scotland Yard that her aunt's death may not have been due to natural causes. The family suspected foul play and they suspected Maundy Gregory. They had not been told of Edith's death, only discovering it when they called at the house on what turned out to be the day of the funeral. Their suspicions deepened when they learned of the new will – which they did not find out about until October when it was eventually registered at Somerset House.

In February 1933 Ethel Davis was put in touch with Inspector Askew who had been in charge of the case against Maundy Gregory selling honours. He was deeply suspicious of Maundy Gregory and his suave manners. He began an investigation into the circumstances of Edith Rosse's death. He discovered that Maundy Gregory had been asking Mrs Rosse for a loan, which she had refused. Indeed it was so unusual that she had told her accountant she could not understand why he needed to borrow money. It seems clear that although they shared many confidences, Maundy Gregory had chosen not to reveal the true extent of his financial problems to Milady this time. Inspector Askew also discovered that Mrs Rosse had a very troubled relationship with her niece and ward. Ethel had lived with them from time to time, but there were frequent rows between the young woman and her highly-strung aunt, especially over money. Sometime in the July of 1932 Edith and Ethel had a further, final argument. Unbeknown to the niece, Maundy Gregory had persuaded Mrs Rosse to destroy her old will which had been in favour of Ethel.

Scotland Yard detectives became suspicious enough to apply to have Edith Rosse's body exhumed, a warrant must be issued by the Home Office. The police applied for a warrant shortly after Maundy Gregory began his prison sentence. The circumstances were ideal, as there was no chance that the prime suspect could escape before the evidence was gathered in. However there was a delay in issuing the warrant. The Home Office were inordinately slow, and it had still not been issued on the twelfth of April when Maundy Gregory was released from Wormwood Scrubs.

Whilst Maundy Gregory was in prison he was declared bankrupt and his possessions and properties were auctioned off. However it seems clear that Maundy Gregory had his French bank account in place. His shadowy sidekick Peter Mazzina, who had Maundy Gregory's power of attorney whilst he was imprisoned, would probably have removed his prize possessions to safety before the bailiffs were called in.

There was no attempt to confiscate Maundy Gregory's passport, nor to subpoena him to appear at Mrs Rosse's inquest. He was met outside Wormwood Scrubs by Mazzina and driven to the Ambassador Club for a private celebratory luncheon. Representatives from at least two political parties were present, and it was made clear that farewells were to be made. Reporters waiting outside the club were greeted with the statement that Maundy Gregory had left by car for a short holiday in the country. The statement merely omitted to tell them which country. He was, in fact, driven to Newhaven and then left on the first boat for Dieppe and exile in France.

It was to be another fortnight before the Home Office issued the exhumation order. The Home Office analyst Dr Roche Lynch, was there at Bisham churchyard to see the exhumation. The police had already been warned by experts that the likelihood of being able to detect poison in the body would be slim if it had been exposed to water. The grave had been under flood at least three times during the winter. As the coffin was hoisted from the grave, water came cascading out. Dr Roche Lynch was short and to the point. 'Not a chance,' he is reported to have muttered. 'Not a chance.'

Dr Roche Lynch and Sir Bernard Spilsbury were involved in the post-mortem examination at Paddington mortuary. Their task was an impossible one, as putrefaction had set in, and any trace of poison had long since been washed away by the rain and flood-water.

When the full inquest hearing was heard in July 1933 detailed statements from previous hearings were read out plus the new evidence from Dr Lynch who could find no conclusive evidence that Mrs Rosse had been poisoned. Sir Bernard Spilsbury added that he had examined the body and could find no evidence of either a brain haemorrhage or Bright's disease, therefore at the very least the death certificate was incorrect. Neither Lynch nor Spilsbury could identify the true cause of death.

Mrs Rosse's relatives were frustrated; they called upon the coroner to adjourn the inquest further and to get Maundy Gregory subpoenaed to give evidence. However the coroner declined, declaring that no useful purpose would come from a further adjournment: 'No poison has been found and no poison ever will be found in this body. Therefore no possible charge could arise out of this inquiry.'

An open verdict was recorded.

Until war broke out, Maundy Gregory lived comfortably in Paris and elsewhere, entertaining young men with tales of his secret service connections and spending freely. He only made a couple of trips back to England. War broke out and when the Germans occupied France Maundy Gregory was interned as an enemy alien. He died in an internment camp in 1941, aged sixty-four.

The day after the inquest, Maundy Gregory gave a newspaper interview from his Parisian hotel suite where he reminisced about his 'wonderful friendship' with Edith Rosse: 'Her friendship was the greatest and sweetest thing of my life, and I will allow no one to sully the memory of it.'

Were these words of astonishing hypocrisy and callousness, by a man who had just got away with the perfect murder? Was it Maundy Gregory the consummate actor speaking? or was Maundy Gregory, the man, speaking from, what little heart he did have, about a friend?

What lay beneath Maundy Gregory's mask? You must judge for yourselves.

6: The Name of the Game

Barry Wood

There was nothing in Freddie Mills' origins to indicate world-class boxing abilities. Born on 26 June 1919, the son of a rag-and-bone man in Bournemouth, Freddie, for most of his childhood, showed little sporting aptitude. Then, when he was eleven years old, Freddie's mother gave him a pair of boxing gloves for his birthday although she detested the sport itself.

Freddie turned his hand to a few jobs after leaving school – he was briefly a garage mechanic, then a milk roundsman. But he hated the day-to-day grind. He had a restless nature and normal routine held no attraction for him. He later admitted that he was a bit of a tearaway and said that he might have ended up in serious trouble with the law if it hadn't been for his vicious left hook which was spotted by the manager of a boxing booth in Bournemouth.

He had his first professional contest at the age of sixteen and won by a knockout in the third round. Freddie Mills was on his way. From 1936 he toured the country putting on display fights, taking on all comers and regularly knocking out his booth opponent, Gypsy Daniels, from whom he learnt most of his tactics. He was soon a big attraction in his native Bournemouth but it was not until 1940 that he began hitting the headlines. He out-pointed Jock McAvoy that year and then proceeded to cut a swathe through the country's most promising heavyweights.

A Freddie Mills' fight was not a particularly elegant sight. He made up in brute strength what he lacked in finesse. As one sports writer commented: 'No one would ever call him a boxing purist. He lunged, swung and swept in against his opponents with all guns firing and seemed to care little about the risk of taking counter punches.'

But his courage and strength were nigh inexhaustible. In 1942 Freddie beat McAvoy again in an eliminator for the British and Empire cruiserweight championship and eventually took the title from Len Harvey at Tottenham in the same year. In 1944 he fought Jack London for the vacant heavyweight title and lost. His first crack at the world title did not come until 1944 when Gus Lesnevich stopped him in ten rounds. It was a temporary setback. Undeterred Freddie came back and defeated several other heavyweights before having his second shot at a world title. Finally in July 1948 at the White City Freddie sent 50,000 fans delirious with delight when he slogged his way to a win on points over his old opponent Gus Lesnevich.

Throughout this period two characters were the mainstays of Freddie's life, providing him with encouragement and support – his wife Chrissie and his manager and father-in-law Ted Broadribb. Success came easy to Freddie Mills. He was a flamboyant boxer but had the flair of a natural entertainer. This had first come to the surface during the war when he did a successful comedy turn on the Ensa circuit.

When peace came he turned his back on show business and threw himself into the hard graft of the boxing ring. But it was not long before he discovered that he could entertain in a totally different manner – Freddie the showman was born. For example, when he was fighting Italian Enrico Bertola he seemed to spend most of his time winking through the ropes at girls in the front row. Then he would deliberately remove a non-existent 'hair' from his tongue with the tip of a glove with the languid air of a man bored with the job in hand – before turning to his opponent and knocking him out.

Although he became a world champion he maintained that he did not quit the ring with a huge bank balance. He had less than half a dozen four-figure purses and wartime service with the RAF and the pressures of raising a family cut heavily into his best years.

'No, fighting didn't make me that well off,' he told one interviewer. 'And of course boxing doesn't bring in the money for long. Before you know it you are thirty and it's time to quit. So I had to find a new career and I found it in showbusiness. I guess I've been lucky.'

Freddie Mills was at the top for little more than two years. A gruelling brawl with the American Joey Maxin in 1950 left him without teeth and title and led to his premature departure from the ring; the decision was taken by Ted Broadrib as Freddie lay flat out in the dressing room after the fight. Shaking his head and gazing down at the prone, blooded figure on the bench Ted said to reporters, 'It's no good. It just isn't there any more.' Freddie's battered face and body were wracked with weariness and pain. Brute strength just wasn't enough.

Only days before he had claimed he was good enough for two or three big fights yet. Jack Solomon, the promoter, on hearing of his biggest crowd-puller's decision said: 'I think Freddie is very wise.'

Freddie retired at the age of thirty-one having won an estimated £75,000 in purses. But unknown to him, half a lifetime of boxing had left another legacy.

For years he had been plagued with headaches. They would arrive with a blinding flash and a stab of pain that would momentarily render him helpless. Freddie dated the onset of the problem from his 1948 brawl with

Gus Lesnevich. 'I was never the same again,' he said later. 'When a fighter takes a caning like that, his fighting days are numbered.'

He also developed a twitch, spasmodic multiple blinking and sudden jerks of the arms and shoulders. In later life the problem would grow and his concentration would go. He was to suffer bouts of memory loss. After the Lesnevich fight Freddie was never able to take a hard blow in the face again without experiencing head pains and dizziness.

But boxing was a crueller and more unforgiving game then than it is now. The level of punishment then thought acceptable meant that only three weeks later Broadribb had steered him back into the ring for another battering. It is a testament to Freddie's endurance that only two years later he was back as the World Champion.

Whereas other successful boxers faded into semi-anonymity on retirement, Freddie exploded into the world of showbusiness. Boxing provided the perfect springboard for Freddie's new career. While still world champion he had grabbed the microphone in front of the strictly professional audience of the Vaudeville Golfing Society. He wowed them with his one-man impression of the Inkspots. Later, and still as world champion, he went to South Africa and perfected an act which included a few songs and snatches of sharp patter. Freddie's timing was not limited to his one-twos in the ring – he was a master of the deadpan delivery. His performing talents were noted and he was not shy about accepting offers. He appeared alongside Arthur Askey on his radio show.

When television came along it seemed only natural that Freddie would take advantage of a new outlet for his exuberant character. With his good looks, cheeky grin, pleasant voice and sense of humour he was a 'natural'. Long before Frank Bruno and Henry Cooper, the nation took to its heart a professional boxer who was a fierce opponent in the ring and a gentle entertainer outside it.

His first TV performances came in long-forgotten shows like '60-mile radius' and 'Kaleidoscope', where he sang 'April Showers' as blossoms fell around him.

He finally blossomed as a comedian in the legendary 'Six Five Special' where he played the part of a charlady in a clown act. His energy and success is hard to imagine in today's TV-saturated world. He appeared in Dicky Henderson's TV show, and he acted in seven British films, although admittedly none of them was remotely memorable and his acting abilities were modest at best. A keep fit series on the BBC was hosted by him. Turn on the radio to Frankie Howerd's comedy series and there he'd be, going through his impressions. He even became a disc jockey on Radio Luxembourg.

But one early indication of his lack of business acumen came when he tried to branch out into boxing promotion. It revealed a man for whom business pressures could be overwhelming.

'I didn't lose money but I nearly lost my sense of humour,' said Freddie later. 'What with match-making, advertising, double taxes, constant worry and spending nearly all day on the telephone I didn't get much fun out of my time as a promoter. No, television is much more fun and it pays better.'

Despite his unhappy experience he was still confident of his business abilities. The Chinese restaurant he had been running since the late forties with his business partner Andy Ho had been a great success. Situated at 143 Charing Cross Road, it was small and intimate and did well. In the early days it traded off the name of its famous proprietor.

But what could have been a more obvious progression than his own nightclub? With the bubbling personality of Freddie Mills and the pull of his pals in showbusiness, how could he fail? The small intimate restaurant was gutted and received a £6,000 facelift, though final costs were almost double. Initially Freddie had wanted to name it after his children but his wife insisted his name in lights still had pulling power. In January 1963 Freddie Mills Nite Club opened for business. It was to be his undoing.

The large star-spangled sign announcing 'Freddie Mills Nite Spot' struck an incongruous note amongst the second-hand bookshops and drab publishing offices of Charing Cross Road. The club was set away from the main champagne, lights and girls circuit and nestled only on the barest fringes of Soho. Despite girls in leotards and feathers and musical instruments the glamorous image was hard to sustain. The club was sandwiched between a surgical goods shop and the National Dairy Council. It was not particularly expensive as London clubs went; admission was one pound, a double whisky eight shillings and a double gin seven shillings. It was the 'extras' that pushed prices up to where it hurt. The company of a hostess cost five or six pounds and she would expect champagne at five guineas a bottle.

When Freddie had opened up his Chinese restaurant on the same premises in 1947 it had been a roaring success. Londoners, tired of post-war austerity, flocked to the establishment with its exotic fare. But in the two years since he had turned it into a nightclub things had not gone smoothly. The club was not doing well. Of late Mills had taken to complaining to friends and his business partner Andy Ho about the slump in takings. He blamed the Government's clampdown on tax-free entertainment expenses by businessmen. Many observers thought that because of his lack of financial expertise he had gone too far – running a Chinese restaurant was one thing but a nightclub was another.

He was also worried about police investigations into his business. Only days before his death he and his Chinese partner were each fined £50 for the illicit supply of drink and for illegally having a one-armed bandit on the premises. The club had also been at the centre of a *People* exposé into a call-girl racket. The article was particularly damning and, for someone like Freddie who was particularly conscious of his public image, acutely humiliating. It described the club as a place where a 'brisk trade in vice' was flourishing, and then went on to outline the conditions under which the 'hostesses' worked.

A 'Mr Toni', who worked at the club interviewed a potential hostess unaware she was a *People* reporter. Hostesses, he said, did not receive any pay. Nor any commission on the food and drink the customers buy. They had to get money in 'other ways' said Mr Toni:

> We expect our hostesses to tell the man at their table that they expect five or six pounds. On top of that the rate for going with him after the club closes is about fifteen pounds. Some girls are greedy and try to push up the price to twenty pounds after 3.00 a.m. but I think this is too much. We are not in the West End. Our clients are mainly middle-class English men prepared to spend around fifty pounds in an evening.

Another club employee was quoted trying to pair off

customers with hostesses saying, 'You won't be disappointed. The girls are good company. They will take you to a hotel where you can be naughty.' In his autobiography Reg Kray painted a memorable picture of the seedy side of London clubland in the sixties and the intermingling of gangsters, boxers and punters in search of glamour.

In this kind of environment it is highly unlikely that Freddie Mills' club was any worse than anybody else's, indeed it was probably a lot better. But no matter. The episode was particularly shaming for Freddie who had always prided himself on being a family entertainer. The Krays were frequent customers of Freddie's. They would arrive in their smartly cut suits surrounded by a dozen or so similarly dressed members of the 'Firm'.

Freddie's wife Chrissie was working in the club at this time and was only dimly aware of the Kray's reputation for illegal activities. One night a waiter told her of their vicious reputation and she was stunned that such people could be in her club, even being greeted cordially by her husband. She rushed over to Freddie, pulled him to one side and gasped out her fears. To her amazement and annoyance Freddie just brushed her concern to one side and returned to the side of his new 'friends'. This was the first indication that Freddie might have found his way into a new circle of friends who would inevitably lead him into trouble.

It is possible that the pressure of keeping a wobbly club on the go led to one of his own falls from the path of virtue – and onc that would for the first time threaten his marriage. Whether inside the ring or out Freddie never had any problem charming the girls. But as a boxer and when he was busy running the restaurant he was too busy to do much about it. But his nightclub was different. And the temptations were plenty. Freddie embarked on an affair with a woman he had met at the club that was to last for three years. It was to put an enormous strain on his marriage, more than boxing pressures ever had. Finally Chrissie decided she could no longer cope with his double life and issued an ultimatum. Freddie, ultimately a homely person, capitulated and gave up his girlfriend. It was one more hurdle he and his wife had overcome, but as the Swinging Sixties developed the club continued to struggle and Freddie Mills' face was looking more and more out of its time. New personalities had come on to the scene. The music world had turned upside down and the Beatles were at the top of the charts. The invitations still came in but not quite as thick and fast as before. Freddie was, to put it bluntly, becoming a relic from a bygone age.

Throughout his career the shadow of his wife Chrissie loomed large over Freddie Mills. During his fight career when Chrissie's father whispered words of wisdom at his corner she would be his strength and inspiration. Unlike the West Country boy himself Chrissie was a cockney, born and bred in Walworth. She married Freddie in 1948, the year he won his world title. She was seven years older and the age difference showed. Chrissie was a much steadier and maturer character than Freddie and he could never pull the wool over her eyes. Through her father she had become well acquainted with the world of boxing and was well aware of the seamy underside of the business.

She was kind-hearted but could be fierce and Freddie lived in perpetual fear of her scorn. No matter how many rounds he won inside the ring he could not win one against his wife. There was no doubt in the Mills' household as to who was the boss. The fights were frequent and it was not just Freddie who was the target. Waiters and hostesses at the club could also expect to feel the rough edge of her tongue from time to time. Chrissie was always giving her husband public 'dressing downs', but they seemed to bounce off the ever-ebullient Freddie.

On top of all his other problems in 1963 there occurred an event that was to shatter Freddie's confidence. It concerned one of his closest friends, a crooner called Michael Holliday. Michael Holliday was a victim of his own public image. To the fans he was a relaxed, urbane singer whose name was almost a byword for casual. But the reality behind the glitter was different. Michael Holliday was a man tortured by endless worries and numerous unnamed insecurities.

Throughout his working life he was pursued by the twin devils of depression and self-doubt. Relaxation was impossible for Michael Holliday and he never slept well. The fight to preserve his casual exterior was a daily battle which he was in perpetual terror of losing. In the end he dropped into a tunnel of despair from which he was never to re-emerge. At 6.00 a.m. on the morning of 29 October 1963, at the very summit of his career, he was found dying of a massive drug overdose at his palatial Surrey home, ironically surrounded by the very symbols of his own success, his gold records. Only a few hours earlier things had seemed completely different. On stage at Freddie Mills Nite Club Holliday seemed in terrific form. He did his Cagney and Bogart impressions then crooned, 'I can't believe you are in love with me.'

At 1.30 a.m. he had put down the microphone after having given another classy performance. He took his applause, posed for a picture with friends and then motioned to Freddie to join him. Freddie was used to his friend's depressions but his mood seemed carefree and happy enough. He joined him at the bar and after a bit of chit-chat with passers-by, Michael leant over and spoke into Freddie's ear. His words were to haunt Mills for the rest of his life.

'I'm never coming back,' he said. 'This is my last night. I'm going to end everything.'

Freddie was to describe the moment later: 'I couldn't believe it at first. I thought it was a joke. I began to argue with him seriously and told him "you must live your life to the bitter end".'

In vain Freddie pleaded with his friend. Holliday insisted he was depressed and that he had nothing to live for. Freddie wanted to take him home for the night. He and Chrissie insisted. But Holliday would not be persuaded. They eventually let him go when he said a friend would take care of him.

There certainly seemed to be little rational explanation for the death. Holliday had bookings all over Europe and a new recording contract lined up. But few knew that before his death Holliday had been discharged from hospital for the second time in two years, after a nervous breakdown. He had a severe drinking problem and the break-up of his family seemed to have been the last straw. His wife Margie had walked out on him months earlier.

The suicide of his friend devastated Freddie Mills. He immediately resigned from his membership of the counselling group, the Samaritans, in shame, saying if he could not prevent one of his best friends from killing himself how could he prevent anyone else.

His membership of the Samaritans showed another sensitive side to the bruising pugilist and brash entertainer. The local vicar at his Camberwell church later recalled how he would come and speak to 'alcoholics, people with social problems, people in distress'.

July 24, 1965 seemed much like any other Saturday in

the life of Freddie Mills. After a hearty breakfast Freddie was persuaded by his wife to do some weeding in the half-acre plot and rock garden at Denmark Hill which was Chrissie's pride and joy. At about 9.30 a.m. he began cleaning the open-air swimming pool – a hefty job as the pool had no automatic cleaning gear and had to be emptied by hand. Afterwards Freddie refilled it – again, a long job as it had to be done directly by hosepipe from a tap in the sink. These activities indicate that he intended to use it at a later date. After finishing that job he had his lunch and afterwards went down to the shops. At about 2.00 p.m. he popped into Smith's the bakers for bread and then into the off-licence next door for enough cigarettes to last him a week. That afternoon it was back to the garden and the tangled sprawl of hydrangeas at the front of the house. About an hour later he finished and, pleased with his work, called up at his wife leaning through a bedroom window, to admire the newly trimmed bushes. Later that afternoon Freddie went to bed for one of his frequent naps while Chrissie took the Mini and went out shopping, with the two girls.

A family friend, Doris Budgeon, arrived in the early evening to mind the two girls while Freddie and Chrissie went to the club together, as was their custom on Saturday evenings. In the early evening the Mills and Mrs Budgeon were treated to a 'playlet' that the small girls had thoroughly rehearsed. The three adults and the children were left hooting with laughter as it all went disastrously wrong.

As a reward for their efforts the two girls were allowed to sit up late and watch the Morecambe and Wise Show on TV featuring their favourite group, the Beatles. Shortly afterwards, a relaxed and apparently cheerful Freddie began to get ready to go along to the club. Chrissie normally accompanied him but this time she stayed behind. She had given the Mini to her son who said he would be back at eleven thirty from a party. She would wait behind for the car to return and follow on later.

Freddie Mills arrived at his Nite Club at around 11.00 p.m. The first person he spoke to was the doorman, Robert Deacon, an eighteen-year-old student, who was doing the job to pay for a trip to Russia. Freddie asked if the club was busy and was told there were only eight or nine customers. He did not look particularly concerned at this news and said that as he was not needed he would have a kip in the back of his car.

'Give me a shout in about half an hour's time, will you?' he said to Deacon. It was something Freddie had done many times before. Then he drove his silver-grey Citroën saloon, registration number 610 DLR, into the adjacent Goslett Yard. Deacon would remember later that, apart from looking a bit tired, he didn't seem any different from any other time.

Meanwhile, back at Joggi Villa, Chrissie was growing impatient with her son's lateness. He had stayed on at the party and forgotten his promise to his mum. Chrissie's son Don eventually got back to a pretty cool reception from his angry mum. To placate her he offered to drive her to the club. They got there at about 12.45 a.m. They had already set out when Robert Deacon set off for the second time to awaken the boss, as per instructions. He found him in the back seat of the Citroën.

'I went up to the car and tapped on the window. That didn't have any effect so I leaned in and pushed him on the shoulder. He still didn't move,' said Deacon later. 'I patted his face and it was then I noticed some saliva around his nostrils and his mouth.' Confused and a little panicky, Robert went back into the club and told the head waiter, Robert Grant.

Grant then rushed to Freddie's partner Andy Ho and told him he thought Freddie was ill in the car. Andy went out and could get no response from the prone figure. He tried to phone Chrissie at home but she was already en route to the club.

Chrissie continues the account:

> I got to the club about 12.55 and when I got there I saw Mr Ho. He came to the car, took me by my elbow and started to take me across the yard. He and I had had a small tiff on the phone some nights previously. But it was nothing important. I thought he was wanting to say sorry in private. I said, 'What is it Andy?' And he replied, 'I want you to come into the yard. Freddie is in the car and he is not well. You must awaken him.'

That was the first time she knew there was anything wrong. With a growing feeling of impending tragedy, Chrissie rushed into the yard and over to the car. As she approached she noticed the back window was rolled down and a flash of puzzlement went through her mind. Freddie was only just recovering from pneumonia. Why take such a risk? By the dim light of a lamp hung high on a wall in the yard she could see Freddie slumped in the back of the car. He was leaning forward and his arms hung down. She could not get a clear view of his face.

As she opened the door Chrissie told herself he was ill but it was proving difficult to fight back terrible thoughts. She climbed in and sat down beside him, started patting his face and talked to him. He didn't stir. Maybe he was just unconscious. There was a smear of blood on Freddie's collar but at first Chrissie didn't connect. Didn't think it could be anything more than a nose bleed.

Then her attention turned back to what she thought was a starting handle that lay between them beside Freddie's leg. With her hand on Freddie's brow, she began to examine it more closely and realised it was not a starting handle at all – and that Freddie was not just unconscious. Chrissie turned and screamed at the assembled knot of people, 'Call an ambulance quickly, Freddie is hurt badly.'

From the beginning the Scotland Yard detectives investigating the murder assumed suicide but were to be baffled by a number of riddles. Where and how did Britain's foremost ex-boxer spend the last hours of his life? How did three different people come across the slumped figure of Mills in his car and fail to notice that he had shot himself in the brain?

Police found two cartridges and two bullets. Was it really feasible for Mills to have missed with his first shot? How could he physically have used the rifle to shoot himself? Quickly the police discovered that Mills had left his £9,000 villa in Denmark Hill, Camberwell, at 5.00 p.m. on the Saturday to go to his club. Where had he got the gun? They quickly established it was the type normally used in fairground establishments.

Mills' friends and relatives could provide no clue as to why he should kill himself. Partner Andy Ho told detectives he had been clowning around with customers the previous night, as always. Detective Chief Inspector Wallace Virgo of West End Central Police Station called in a team of detectives from off-duty leave to carry out inquiries. It seemed cut and dry but he could not get out of his mind the possibility that there may have been a gangland connection.

A detective at the time said, 'In the soundbox of the enclosed car the first shot must have been fantastically noisy. It is incredible that he fired again after a shot like that.' And one after the other Mills' friends, relatives and business associates said they were stunned and disbelieving.

Mr Jack Solomons, the promoter who had stage-managed some of the big fights in Mills' career, told reporters, 'If it's suicide I can't believe it. He had more guts than anyone. If Freddie was in trouble he would have faced up to it. I can't understand talk of a gun.'

Edward Waltham of the British Boxing Board of Control said, 'Freddie had everything to live for. I don't think he had any financial worries.'

It is curious that despite all these reservations and without an inquest the police were quick to announce a preliminary opinion that it was suicide.

Freddie did not lack for friends at the end. At the funeral it seemed half the world of showbusiness and boxing had turned out.

Pall-bearers included Henry Cooper and other stars from the boxing world. The lesson was read by comedian Bruce Forsyth who spoke for many when he said that in his opinion Freddie was a great man and a fine, decent person. St Giles Parish Church in Camberwell was packed to the aisles. Outside police motorcyclists marshalled hundreds of silent mourners.

Not many knew of any Biblical references to boxing but the vicar found one from Corinthians for his address. 'We must run with a clear goal before us and be like boxers who do not beat the air in shadow boxing but learn to fight, in order that we may know that in the Lord our labours cannot be lost.' In his lifetime hundreds of thousands of pounds had passed through

Freddie Mills' hands. But he left the derisory sum of £387 behind.

There was an even bigger shock for his family when they went right through his finances. Freddie's debts totalled more than £4,000 and the house had been remortgaged as security on a loan. The question of where Freddie's money went still whirls around the mystery.

The inquest was to hear of a single firearm wound in the corner of the right eye which went through the eye socket and fractured the brain stem. Freddie would have died within a few minutes at the very most. But was it suicide? The Westminster coroner had no doubts. The coroner said there had been nothing to suggest a struggle of any kind. The wound was obviously self-inflicted.

Chrissie Mills, dressed in black with a black head-scarf, told the coroner that in the seventeen years of her marriage, 'I have never known anyone fitter than him. He has never been depressed or worried about anything.' In recent months, though, he had started to keep things from her because she was under the strain of having to care for their daughter who was hospitalised by illness. The only time he had ever needed medical treatment during their marriage was a fortnight before his death when he had gone down with pneumonia.

Chrissie admitted he had been worrying before his death, '... but he did not tell me a lot.' She thought it was business problems and bad publicity in the newspapers which were getting him down. Mrs May Ronaldson, the owner of a rifle range, said she had known the Mills for thirty years and was a close friend. He visited her three times in the week before he was found shot and he seemed perfectly happy. One day he said to her, 'I'm going to Esher to open a fête and I want to dress as a cowboy. Can you lend me a rifle for the pictures.'

She saw Mills a few days later when he handed the rifle back saying the fête was cancelled because not enough people turned up. He called again to say the fête was going to happen after all. He borrowed the rifle again. The next morning she had been opening the stall when her son rushed up and told her of the death. Immediately she turned to check the rounds and found three missing.

Professor Keith Simpson, the eminent forensic scientist, said that at the time of death the alcohol level in Freddie's bloodstream was insignificant. All the professionals were in no doubt. It could only have been suicide.

But from the beginning there were a number of facts which for many people did not quite fit and which have helped fuel the suspicion that Freddie was murdered. One surprise did emerge at the inquest. An ambulance attendant maintained that the rifle was 'definitely out of Mr Mills' reach' when he arrived at the scene. According to the evidence, the doorman Deacon went to wake up Freddie when he was in the back of his car, apparently asleep. Two further attempts were then made to wake him, by Grant the waiter and Andy Ho, his partner. But it was only when his wife arrived that the truth was revealed.

It seems odd, indeed almost incredible that three men on three separate occasions could try to waken Mills without one of them realising that he had been shot.

The mystery deepens once we examine what is supposed to have gone on inside the car. First of all there is the mystery of the second bullet. Two shots were fired from the rifle that night. One penetrated Mills' brain, the other went into a nearby door. The official explanation? Apparently Freddie had first tried to shoot himself while sitting in the front seat and had missed. Then he tried to repeat the exercise from the back seat. Even detectives expressed amazement at the possibility.

Then there is the rifle itself. According to Chrissie she found the rifle placed by Freddie's side. With his body slumped forward it seems the most awkward and impractical position to shoot oneself.

When he died all Freddie's prize money was gone and he was in dire financial straits. No one ever satisfactorily answered the question – where did the money go? Was Freddie the victim of an extortion racket? On that final fateful night did Freddie's inability or unwillingness to pay up exact the ultimate price?

The murder theory remains pure speculation. In her emotional state Chrissie Mills may have mistaken the position of the gun. Perhaps Mills was not killed by gangsters but by a worsening depression brought about by his position. He suffered from headaches, and the growing realisation that his name and position were gone and all that he held dear was at risk. There does remain however the small matter of the letter. It was received by author Jack Birtley after he wrote a book about the case. It is anonymous but claims that Freddie was murdered by someone called the 'Governor'. Freddie, it says, was killed because he 'couldn't pay any more'. The writer of the letter had been offered the contract himself but turned it down because he liked Freddie. Perhaps Freddie had not borrowed the gun to kill himself with but for his own personal protection. Perhaps on that final night Freddie fired the gun and managed to scare off the hitman who had been sent to kill him. That would explain the bullet hole in the door.

But then the mysterious 'Governor' turned up – somebody, the letter says, who was trying to make a name for himself 'up west'. And because Freddie knew him he relaxed. It was then, according to the letter, that Freddie made his fatal mistake and the Governor seized his chance and killed him.

A crank letter? The violent fantasy of some ex-con? As confirmation of his credentials as a murderer the writer claimed to have carried out the contract killing of a London prostitute called Black Rita who existed and indeed was murdered. Whatever the answer it is unlikely that the full truth about Freddie Mills will be revealed and that there will always be those who believe he was murdered.

7: French Leave

Fiona Mackay

Why are we so fascinated by women who kill? Although women are, by far, in the minority when it comes to the ultimate act of violence, they invariably excite extra interest. Throughout history, from Lucrezia Borgia to Ruth Ellis, women achieve an immortal notoriety whilst many of their male counterparts languish in obscurity. Is it because society sees women as creators of life, rather than destroyers, and those who kill are seen as freaks of nature? Or does the lethal woman strike a chord with secret fears that the female is truly the deadliest of the species? Whatever the complex reasons behind the obsession, female killers are always news. They are either portrayed as vulnerable victims, driven by circumstances beyond their control, or as cruel unnatural monsters, or both. And when a woman is accused of murdering her own child then fascination turns to repulsion, revulsion, hatred even. There is a special venom reserved for such women, women such as Louise Masset. In the first week of the twentieth century, Louise Masset was executed in London for the premeditated and motiveless murder of her young son. Did she commit the unthinkable and kill her own child or was she the victim of Victorian values which held that a woman capable of breaking the sexual modes of the time was capable of anything?

The murder for which Louise Masset was hanged happened in October 1899, during the twilight months of a dying century and the twilight years of Victoria's reign. Everywhere there were signs of change; the 1890s were dubbed the 'naughty nineties' by some. This was the era of the so-called 'new woman'; Victorian intellectuals argued about the changing role of the modern woman; the 1890s had seen the great marriage debate rage – no less an establishment mouthpiece than the *Daily Telegraph* investigated the current state of marriage under the headline: 'Is Marriage a failure?' Meanwhile Karl Marx's daughter Eleanor was living in a high-profile and unwedded relationship.

The stereotype of Victorian values still existed, but they were under pressure, and could no longer be seen as monolithic. Society was in a state of flux, yet as is often the case, changing moral values take time to 'trickle down'; and for the majority of the respectable middle classes living in England at the turn of the century, the prevailing social and moral conventions remained intact. Victorian society was always marked by contrasts between public virtue and private vice. There was an obsession with sex; the Victorians covered up the legs of their tables for fear of impropriety, yet had a thriving underworld of vice with female and child prostitution. But vice, or passion, was not freely available at all. Ideas may have been changing as the old century was being rung out, but they were changing slowly.

And there was still one group of people in Victorian society for whom virtue was expected and demanded both in public and behind closed doors, respectable middle-class daughters and wives. The ideal of the middle-class woman as the 'angel in the home' was still strong. Women were considered to be sweet, loving, pious and chaste. Men, even respectable, God-fearing professional men, had needs and passions – their daughters, sisters and wives did not. Although Havelock Ellis had already begun his work arguing for a new

(Above) **Mrs Bravo Regrets:** Charles Bravo, in agony after taking poison, is tended by his wife Florence (top) and her companion Jane Cox. *(Below)* **No Smoke Without Fire:** Was Peter Luckhurst guilty of the Pitchfork Killing in Britain's most haunted village?

The Jewel and the Magpie: *(Above)* Tony Maffia (centre), alias The Magpie, is ambushed by gangsters on a lonely Essex road. Did he double-cross them over stolen gold bullion, or was the ambush a figment of Stephen Jewell's imagination? *(Left)* Stephen Jewell, who fought a battle from his prison cell to clear his name.

(Above) **Our Dearest Dear:** Variety star Bunny Doyle and the love of his life Mollie Mozelle, but tragedy was to divide them. *(Below)* **The Name of the Game:** Boxing champion Freddie Mills greets the infamous Kray twins but were they friends, or foe?

Maundy Money: *(Left)* J. Maundy Gregory, the man who peddled knighthoods and peerages. Did scandal in high places lead to murder? *(Below)* Edith Rosse: did a will signed on her sickbed lead to her eventual murder?

French Leave: *(Above)* Louise Masset, a loving mother, a misunderstood woman, or the heartless killer of her young son Manfred? *(Right)* Lucas, the young lover – was a stolen weekend in Brighton the motive for murder?

Unjust Desserts: *(Above)* The Sidney family before death divided them. *(Left)* Violet Sidney: did she know her medicine was laced with arsenic?

(Above) **An Uncommon Murder:** Stinie Morrison and Leon Beron – was one also the murderer? *(Below)* **Laugh Baby Laugh:** Elvira Barney and Michael Stephen: whose hand was on the trigger the night death came to a Knightsbridge Mews?

Shadows of Doubt: *(Above)* Robert Hoolhouse, a simple lad or a callous killer? *(Below)* Farmer's wife Margaret Dobson met a savage death on a lonely farmtrack.

morality between the sexes which recognised the sexual needs of women, that eminent Victorian William Acton summed up the prevailing sentiments of the age when he said, 'Women are not much troubled by sexual feeling of any kind.' Not nice women, that is.

And one can be sure that the twelve respectable gentlemen of the jury who were shortly to decide that Louise Masset was a liar and a murderer would have their views of women more firmly influenced by the values of the nineteenth rather than the twentieth century.

The penalty for sin in Victorian times could be poverty, madness and death. The shame of giving birth to a child outside wedlock was still considerable. Women could be forcibly committed to asylums for the insane by the authorities or their families for displaying sexuality, giving birth to illegitimate children, or in some other way revealing themselves as 'moral defectives'. Fiction abounded with cautionary tales of women falling from sexual grace and facing ruination. Being an innocent victim, as was Tess in Thomas Hardy's *Tess of the D'Urbervilles* (1891), was no protection.

However there are always exceptions to the rule: Louise Masset was one. Louise was a genteel, middle-class woman; independent and singular. She was thirty-six years old, unmarried and showing no particular desire to be married. However she did have other desires and she refused to be constrained by the moral confines of Victorian society. Half-French herself, Louise had had a passionate liaison with a Frenchman which resulted in pregnancy. He returned to France some years later and Louise never revealed his identity to anyone. Despite the stigma of illegitimacy that still persisted, she never expressed the slightest sense of shame at having a three-and-a-half-year-old love child. And unlike so many unmarried mothers of the time, Louise had not abandoned her son.

Louise's little boy, Manfred, was boarded with a foster mother, a kindly woman called Helen Gentle who lived with her parents in a little terraced house in Tottenham. The boy's upkeep was paid for by his natural father in France. Louise visited the boy regularly and to all who knew her it was clear that she was an affectionate mother. Manfred had first been fostered out to Miss Gentle when he was just three weeks old, after Louise had seen her services as a nurse advertised in a newspaper. They agreed terms and she was paid £1/17/- a month. At first Louise had visited him every fortnight, but the visits increased rather than decreased with time. She was proud and loving, anxious about his future and visited him at least once a week – usually on a Wednesday – when she took him for walks and to play in Tottenham Green park.

Louise was one of three daughters of a prosperous city merchant; her father, born in France, was now dead. She was the only unmarried sister; of the other two, Leonie had married a French commissioning merchant and the other sister an auctioneer. Louise was an attractive, educated and accomplished woman, who looked younger than her thirty-six years. She was financially independent, earning a modest but reasonable living by giving music and French lessons to middle-class children around London. She was popular and respected by the parents who employed her – she had been visiting some of their families for several years.

For the past eighteen months, possibly since the time her unnamed French lover had returned to France, she had lived with her sister Leonie Cadisch, her husband and their four children for whom she was a fond and favoured aunt. She lived free of charge with them at their comfortable home in the then genteel North London suburb of Stoke Newington. She travelled by train from nearby Dalston Junction station to her various lessons around the city.

Her sister may not have approved of Louise's past, but all had long since been forgiven. Leonie had stood as guarantor for payment for Manfred's placement with Miss Gentle. Louise appears to have been free to talk to her sister about the child and his progress. Leonie supported Louise in the bleak weeks that followed Manfred's death, but both sisters wore deep mourning throughout the inquest hearing and the murder trial.

It had appeared as if Louise had escaped, largely unscathed, from the consequences of her moral lapse. Perhaps Louise would have continued to survive, to live a quiet but pleasant life in those still-claustrophobic times if she had put her past, and present, passions aside. But she did not. Desire came a-calling again for Louise Masset. Endore Lucas was, literally, the boy next door. Variously described as a medical student or a clerk he had come to live in Bethune Road in the summer of 1898. When their affair began, he was nineteen years old. They exchanged love letters and kisses; Lucas would drop love poetry over the garden wall. He would regularly meet her at London Bridge Station when she had been teaching and travel home with her via Dalston Junction and tram.

This was not a conventional romance. Neither believed they were in love. Louise had spoken freely to Lucas about the existence of her illegitimate child. But as neither saw the relationship ending in marriage, Manfred was not mentioned again. It might have been a case of a thirst for excitement in an ordered life, but Louise was undoubtedly attracted to the physical charms of the handsome, fresh-faced and youthful Lucas. He, in turn, was both flattered and enthusiastic to receive attention from the attractive and sexually experienced older woman. However, opportunities for sexual intimacy between the couple in Stoke Newington were non-existent. They wanted to have some time together and in the autumn, Louise decided they would go to Brighton for a weekend – she had worked it all out. She told him she had told her sister that she was taking Manfred to France to be with his father and they would use the excuse to steal some time together.

A woman of passion, a devoted mother, could she be both? And given her particular circumstances it was a particularly difficult question for Louise; but she was resourceful. And so on Friday 27 October 1899, Louise travelled three miles to Tottenham. There waiting for her was her son, Manfred, in his Sunday best. After almost four years, this was to be a painful parting for both the little boy and his devoted nurse. Louise had written to Miss Gentle telling her that Manfred's father had decided it was time for him to go to live in France and learn the language. He wanted him to be raised by his cousin's family.

As Manfred finally broke away from a tearful Miss Gentle, she gave him his favourite toy – some weighing scales; and she passed a brown paper parcel of his clothes to Louise. Then mother and child boarded an omnibus for London Bridge station. That was the last time Miss Gentle was to see her nursling alive. The next time she saw Manfred was to identify his body in the local mortuary. She was later to tell a juror at the murder trial that she had harboured a dread for several days before giving up the boy that something was going to happen to him.

However this was not the last sighting of Louise

Masset and Manfred together. The case against Louise Masset was to involve three railway waiting rooms: the first was at London Bridge, where she and her son were seen together for the last time; the second was at Dalston Junction, her local station, where the child's body would be found, naked and suffocated; and the third, in Brighton, where she would meet her lover and where the clothes of her dead child would be found abandoned in a parcel.

London Bridge – the busy main-line station to the South and onwards to the Continent: the first of the three waiting rooms: it was 3.00 in the afternoon. The Brighton train was to leave within the hour. Mrs Ellen Rees, the attendant, had just started what would be a long shift. She noticed a woman whom she later identified as Louise Masset, trying to comfort a small boy who was complaining. The attendant asked her if she was waiting for a train; Louise replied that they were waiting for someone who had not yet arrived. Mrs Rees reported that the woman appeared anxious; she asked the woman why the little boy was fretting and Louise replied that he had had to leave his nurse. Then she remarked that the boy might be hungry and she took Manfred by the hand and they left the waiting-room to go to buy him a cake.

This was the last sighting of mother and child together, and the last sighting of Manfred alive. At the trial, Louise Masset did not disagree with Mrs Rees's account of their first meeting. But she did disagree with Mrs Rees' contention that she had seen her again four hours later, at 7.00 that evening, alone, scrubbing her hands in the washroom. Mrs Rees also told the court she had had her suspicions about the lady and child from the first, but did not think it her duty to do anything unless forced. Louise claimed she caught the 4.00 p.m.

train to Brighton from London Bridge. If this was true, she could not have killed her son. She would have been on the train when the child was murdered.

On a busy day, and this was indeed a busy day, the washroom was used by perhaps four hundred women. Mrs Rees was insistent that she remembered mother and child, and that she recognised Louise later that evening. Mrs Rees had to wear glasses for reading and to see at a distance. That Friday she had left them at home.

At just after 6.00 p.m. that same evening a grim discovery was made in another washroom, in the ladies' waiting room at Dalston Junction. This was Louise's local station, more than half an hour's train journey away from London Bridge. Two young women on their way to a lecture found the body of a small child and alerted the station porter. In a toilet cubicle, wedged behind the door, was Manfred's body. He was naked apart from being half covered in a cheap black shawl. His body was still warm when the police surgeons arrived to carry out their examination. The little boy had been knocked unconscious by a heavy blow and suffocated. A bloodstained clinker brick, weighing almost four pounds, was found by his side. Clinker bricks were common enough bricks, but the prosecution was to make much of the fact that it was a brick identified as being of the same type as those that made up the rockery and ornamental edging in the garden of Louise's home.

Louise Masset did indeed go to Brighton. But she did not sign into her hotel until 9.45 p.m. She claimed that on arrival of the four o'clock train from London, she did some sightseeing. She made her way down to the seafront; she wondered at the splendour of Brighton Pavilion; and strolled along the magical pier. At about

6.00 p.m. she had eaten at a restaurant named Muttons and then and only then did she go to seek out her room.

She registered in the name of Brooks and booked into adjoining rooms, one for herself and one for Lucas who was joining her the next day and whom she told hotel staff was her brother. That night as she lay in her hotel room, waiting for the following day when Lucas would arrive, did she wonder also about Manfred. Or was she distracted? She was distracted enough to have left Manfred's toy scales in a bedside drawer and forgotten them.

On Saturday afternoon, Louise was back at Brighton Station, this time awaiting the arrival of Lucas. She seemed in high spirits when he met up with her, certainly she gave no indication that something terrible might have happened to her son. And so Louise and Lucas were to snatch their brief hours of love in Brighton, returning to Stoke Newington late on Sunday night.

There were to be three vital pieces of evidence against Louise – the clinker brick found next to Manfred's body at Dalston station; Mrs Rees' alleged sighting of her in the washroom at London Bridge later that Friday evening; and the most damning of all, the fact that twenty minutes after meeting Lucas, Manfred's clothes would be discovered in the Brighton waiting room.

Louise was to pay dearly for a weekend of love. The two of them returned to London on the Sunday night. On Monday, she went to work as normal. Manfred was identified in the newspapers on Monday evening. Later that night, an apparently distressed Louise appeared at the house of her second sister, in Croydon, claiming to have just read the report, and panicking that the police might suspect her of the crime. There she was arrested and charged by police.

When Louise was arrested for murder she said, 'Impossible. How could I murder my own child?'

The case for the prosecution was quite straightforward. Louise Masset was a liar. She had lied about taking Manfred to his father. She had lied about catching the four o'clock train to Brighton. Instead she had returned unnoticed to the washroom at Dalston Junction where she had suffocated her child, stripping him of his clothes and striking him with a brick around the face to hamper identification. It was a premeditated and vicious crime. She then caught a later train to Brighton where she callously spent the weekend with her lover. There, carelessly, she had left the parcel of Manfred's clothes. Once the child had been identified she fled to south London to evade capture. It was, the prosecution argued, abundantly clear that Louise Masset was a wilful, intelligent, self-possessed and shameless woman, capable of anything.

The defence asked if Louise was so intelligent, so calculating, would she have created lies so easily exposed? No motive had been shown or suggested, but in English law that is not essential. But would such a woman, even with a motive, be so unwise as to take a brick from her own back garden, kill a child in her local railway station, leave the murder weapon by his side, wash her hands in the very waiting-room they had been seen in a few hours before, and then carelessly leave the child's clothes in Brighton?

If she then panicked, would not such a resourceful woman find a better hiding place than her sister's house. Why, most of all, would a woman wanting sympathy on the death of her child choose to offend the moral codes of decency by spending the weekend in Brighton with her young lover?

Besides, Louise had her own version of events to tell.

A version which the prosecution, and ultimately the jury, considered was a fantasy, a pack of lies, a fairy-tale. She had taken Manfred from his nurse, not to take him to France, but to transfer him to a small private school in Chelsea. She was meeting the two ladies who ran the school at London Bridge station that afternoon. She had handed Manfred over before catching the train to Brighton.

Louise told the court that for some time she had been worried about what was to be done about Manfred's education in the near future. This was corroborated by her sister Leonie who gave evidence that Louise had mentioned her anxiety the previous February. Manfred's nurse, Miss Gentle, was loving but Louise was concerned that she doted too much on the boy, that she spoiled him and did not 'manage' him properly. Although there was plenty of love in the house there were not enough books. An educated and cultured woman herself, it pained her that her small son was picking up a Cockney accent and was using expressions like 'ain't' and 'look at those pins'.

She also came to express her concern to two 'perfect ladies' she met whilst playing with Manfred in Tottenham Green park in the autumn of 1899. Manfred had become friendly with a little girl of around six, called Millie, whom they had bumped into from time to time in the park. Louise came to know Millie's mother Mrs Browning – a woman in her mid-thirties – and her sister-in-law, Miss Browning, in her mid-twenties. Both were respectably dressed and well spoken.

They swapped little pieces of life stories with each other. Mrs Browning told Louise she had been widowed just six months before, and that her sister-in-law Sarah had come to stay. Louise told them she lived with her sister, and the address. They noticed she was not wearing a wedding ring and she told them that Manfred's father lived in France, that he provided adequately for him, and that she had a good nurse. Gradually they exchanged confidences. She knew the time would come, sooner rather than later, when she would have to decide what was to be done about Manfred's schooling.

The sisters then told Louise they were in the process of setting up a small private boarding school. They agreed to meet again the following week. This time they told her that they had taken a lease on a house, with a closed garden at the rear. It would make an excellent school with accommodation for six children. They had a number already, but they would welcome Manfred, not least because of his friendship with Millie. They would charge £12 a year in advance for his board and ten shillings a month for his schooling. The school was in the King's Road, Chelsea, some distance away, but Louise would still be able to visit him each Wednesday.

Louise worried about Miss Gentle's feelings, but the ladies were insistent that she must do what she felt was right for her child. They needed a quick decision. She agreed to meet the Brownings at the park in a fortnight when she would make her decision. On 15 October Louise had made up her mind. She would transfer Manfred to the Brownings' care.

It was then, she claimed, that she thought of combining all her desires in one weekend. With a small white lie to Miss Gentle she could secure Manfred's future. With another to her sister, she could equally secure her weekend of passion. She wrote to Miss Gentle telling her that it had been decided that Manfred should go to live in France with relatives of his natural father. She told her that she did not want to make trouble, and must go along with his father's wishes. She would be taking him to France on Friday 27 October. She repeated this story to her sister. She and the Brownings agreed to meet at London Bridge Station – halfway – on 27 October. Louise told the Brownings she wanted to travel over to the school and see Manfred settled in before leaving to go to Brighton. They arranged to meet at 2.00 p.m. She planned to catch the 4.00 p.m. train to Brighton from London Bridge – and that left two hours – more than enough to see her son safely installed at his new school. So a lie to Miss Gentle – Louise Masset said at her trial – to save her feelings. Another lie to her sister bought her some time alone with Lucas – or had she already planned a premeditated murder?

Louise claimed the Brownings did not turn up for their meeting at 2.00 p.m. as planned. They were more than an hour late, and Louise was getting anxious about her train. Mrs Rees, the waiting-room attendant, had indeed seen Louise and Manfred whilst they were waiting. They left the waiting room to look for the ladies and met up with them outside. Louise was agitated; as her train was leaving in less than an hour, there was not enough time to travel to Chelsea and back. She claimed that Miss Browning whisked the distressed Manfred away to see Millie, and she did not even get a chance to say goodbye. Mrs Browning assured her that everything would be all right, Manfred would settle down and Louise could visit him on Wednesday. She took the parcel of clothes from Louise and the £12. Mrs Browning briskly brushed aside any of Louise's objections; told her that school was at 45 King's Road and she would write to her with a receipt for the money and full directions in time for her visit on Wednesday.

Mrs Browning and her sister-in-law were never traced, if they ever existed. When Louise told detectives her story after her arrest the following Monday, they travelled to 45 King's Road in Chelsea. It was a dairy shop, and nobody there had ever heard of a school, or the Brownings. The two 'perfect ladies' had disappeared like shadows in the night; or like figments of someone's imagination. If they did exist they had calculatedly duped Louise Masset and cold-bloodedly killed her little boy for money.

Throughout the weeks that followed, the case of Louise Masset at turns fascinated and repelled the public. Newspapers carried detailed reports: the illegitimate child; the young lover; the stolen weekend in Brighton, whilst her child lay dead in a railway toilet cubicle. Perhaps most damning of all was Louise Masset's calm assertion that she did not love Lucas and had no intention of marrying him. An immoral woman and a bad mother, what a potent combination. She became a figure of hate to Londoners.

At the inquest a crowd of 200 gathered outside Hackney Coroner's Court to jeer and boo her as she arrived by cab. She was prevented from attending the full proceedings each day, her defence solicitor reported, because of the 'vile, filthy and disgraceful abuse' hurled at her by the largely female crowd outside. It appeared that the police were powerless or unwilling to protect her.

During her trial too she had to run the gauntlet of a jeering crowd. The case took five days; Sir Charles Matthews prosecuted. The circumstantial evidence against Louise Masset was indeed substantial: the sighting at London Bridge; the bloody clinker brick; the clothes at Brighton station. Another prosecution witness testified that a woman she later identified as Louise Masset had bought a black shawl similar to the one found draped over the boy's body. However, try as the prosecution might, they could not find a plausible motive. They suggested that Manfred might have been an obstacle to marriage with Lucas, but as Lucas already knew about the child and neither Lucas nor Louise had any intention of marrying there was no point in pursuing that line. They also suggested Louise had done it for financial gain, but all the evidence disputed this. In the end, they merely presented her as a clever and pitiless creature who had murdered for reasons best known to herself, and who had then woven an elaborate story displaying 'an iron nerve' and 'tongue of a serpent'.

The eminent QC, Lord Coleridge, defended. He tried to show that Louise Masset did not have it in her nature to commit such a crime; and furthermore that there was no possible motive. The evidence of all who knew Louise Masset was that she was a kind, sympathetic, affectionate woman. She was attached to children, and her attachment to them was specially demonstrated in her love for her own child.

'Many a woman had an illegitimate child and did not want to see any more of it. That was not the case here,' he told the jury. How improbable it was, this 'sudden conversion of a kind and affectionate woman into a fiend and a monster without pity'.

What were the jury considering when they weighed up the evidence? A highly circumstantial case for the prosecution, with no possible motive for such a crime; for the defence a highly improbable story of two ladies who disappeared. One of the big legal changes at the turn of the century was a new law which allowed defendants to give evidence on their own behalf, even women. Louise Masset was one of the first to benefit from this. But perhaps that was her undoing. Reporters at the time seemed almost to condemn her for her cool demeanour, her lawyer-like turn of phrase and cast of mind. The prosecution was keen to portray her as a highly intelligent and scheming woman, capable of more than clever falsehoods to carry out her plans. She had coped magnificently with the tough cross-examination carried out by the prosecution. They twisted this, telling the jury they regretted that her quick talent had been used to try to 'defeat the ends of justice'.

Louise would not have fitted in with their notions of modest womanhood – nor their cherished ideals of motherhood. The prosecution made much of the unthinking way in which Louise had handed over her child in her own version of events. Was it the spectre of the 'bad mother' that finally tipped the scales against Louise? Did the jury take less than half an hour to find her guilty of murder because it took only one small leap of belief to transform a careless, selfish woman, who put her own needs before those of her child, into a monstrous fiend who could murder her child on a whim?

If Louise Masset was guilty of murdering her son, then her motives were inexplicable. But perhaps Louise Masset was tried for a different crime, a crime for which she was never charged. Louise was certainly a liar in a world of hypocrisy, a temptress of young men, a woman who had apparently suffered no hardship for her past moral lapses. In a society where 'fallen' women could fall a great distance, a society of cautionary tales, and retribution, Louise was a woman who seemed to give no allegiance to the established codes. Were the jury themselves guilty of punishing her as a warning to others? Was that the factor that weighed most heavy on the scales of justice?

Louise Masset had retained her composure for most of the week-long trial. However she had to be supported by warders as, half-standing, half-swooning, in the dock she heard the guilty verdict read out. She was asked if she had anything to say and replied, 'I am innocent of the charge.'

On 18 December 1899 Mr Justice Bruce donned his black cap and sentenced Louise Masset to death. It may have only taken the jury half an hour to decide upon the guilty verdict, but there were many others with reservations, uncomfortable that Louise Masset may have been many things, but a murderess she was not.

In the bleak days that followed, the fortnight or so between sentence and her execution, during which Christmas passed without note, others were at work on her behalf. A plea for leniency was organised by a Parisian paper. The paper collected 1,200 signatures from French women, mostly governesses, and petitioned Queen Victoria for a pardon – calling for mercy from 'a great Queen who is always a perfect mother to have pity for the unworthy mother who killed her child'.

Others were convinced of her innocence. Many, including respected establishment figures, argued for a reprieve. The Home Secretary of the time, Sir Matthew White Ridley was petitioned; it was argued that the highly circumstantial evidence presented at her trial did not warrant a guilty verdict.

Then on 4 January 1900, just days before the execution date, dramatic new evidence was revealed which would seem to corroborate part of Louise Masset's story and provide her with an alibi. Mr Arthur Newton, Louise's solicitor, reported that the proprietor of Mutton's restaurant in Brighton, together with a waiter, had come forward to testify that she had indeed eaten in the restaurant on the evening of the murder. He asked the Home Secretary for a stay of execution in order that the potential witnesses might travel to Newgate prison to positively identify Louise Masset. The request was accompanied by a petition signed by a thousand people. The Home Secretary turned down both petitions and ordered that the execution go ahead.

Louise Masset was hanged on 9 January 1900 at Newgate. Despite a heavy early morning mist a crowd started to gather before 7.00 a.m. By the time the prison bell started to toll at 8.45 a.m. between two and three thousand people were waiting. A report of the time states that the official executioner Billington entered the prison at 8.57 a.m. The newspapers reported that the hangman 'pinioned' Louise. However Louise offered no resistance whatsoever and walked without assistance to the scaffold. A drop of 7ft 8in was allowed and death was stated to be instantaneous. A black flag, signalling that the execution had been carried out, was raised and was greeted with loud cheers from the crowd. They viewed her as a monster and a fiend. They also heard that the prisoner had 'confessed' to the crime. The Home Office announced that before her execution the convict had admitted her guilt and the justice of her punishment. Her last words were, 'What I am about to suffer is just, and now my conscience is clear.'

Did the Brownings exist at all? If they did then were they the murderers? Had they carefully picked their victim, a young unmarried mother concerned about her child's education? Had they taken a few simple precautions to protect themselves and to throw the blame on her? A brick from her garden left conveniently by the body and then perhaps a little outing with a small parcel of clothes to Brighton Station.

Louise's explanation seems implausible, her behaviour rash to the point of neglect. However at that time there was a huge traffic in unwanted babies and children. Illegitimate children were fostered out for money. Often the mother would then abandon the child and the nurses had to decide what to do with the child, when the money dried up. Many babies simply died from malnutrition or incorrect feeding, sometimes unintentional, sometimes intentional. Others were handed over to the authorities. Baby 'farming' was a scandal which had been made public in the 1890s by a Royal Commission. It was well known that unscrupulous men and women took babies and young children, ostensibly to look after them for a fee, but sometimes murdered them to maximise their profits.

Mrs Dyer, a notorious baby-farmer from Reading, was known to have killed more than twenty babies and small children. It is an interesting thought, is it not, that the next woman to hang at Newgate was Ada Chard Williams, executed for the murder for profit of a two-year-old illegitimate child which had been fostered out to her by a young unmarried mother. Ada Chard Williams was finally convicted of murdering a two-year-old whom she had adopted for money. However she was linked with the murder of many more children, some of whose bodies were found in the River Thames and others buried in the back garden of houses where she had previously lived. No one raised the alarm for these children; if they were missed they were not mourned.

A still stranger twist. At Thames police court on the day Louise Masset was executed there was an odd case. The magistrate was asked for help in tracing a nursling child, aged about the same age of Manfred, who had been snatched by two women from the school he attended. The foster mother had never seen him since. Against these then-common occurrences, does Louise's story still sound so implausible, so improbable?

Was Louise Masset sent to the gallows because her demeanour failed to match the all-male jury's vision of an innocent woman? Or was the real test that the jury would not believe that a prudent woman would hand over her child to two strangers; that an innocent woman would not put her child at risk for the sake of a weekend of passion?

Would she have handed over her beloved child, together with £12, to two strangers? But she argued she had met them several times, they were utterly convincing. Perhaps she felt embarrassed to insist on references from middle-class women, where she had felt able to ask for references from the humble Helen Gentle?

Was it a combination of naïve trust in respectable appearances; stupidity and an indecent haste to get away for her French leave in Brighton that caused Louise Masset to make the mistake which would ultimately cost two lives, her son's and her own? If she had any nagging doubts, she silenced them as she hurried for the Brighton train and a weekend of passion. Certainly she thought little about Manfred until the reports of the murder on the Monday.

Manfred's toy scales were found in the bedside cabinet in her hotel room. Had she realised he had forgotten them, put them away and then been distracted by other things, by other pleasures and other needs? As a loving mother, she was distraught when she realised her son had been murdered. Indeed her brother-in-law told the trial she had appeared hysterical when she arrived at his house on the Monday night. Later, after she had given herself up to the police, she begged that she be allowed to see her son's body in the mortuary. Her first two requests werc denied. Finally she was allowed to go to the mortuary, accompanied by her brother-in-law, Mr Symes. She was grief-stricken: 'Oh, my child, my poor child!' she moaned.

What of Louise Masset's so-called confession: 'What I am to suffer is just, my conscience is clear' – just punishment for what? Perhaps it was her failure that Friday afternoon in October to be a responsible mother, which was to haunt her to her end. Perhaps in the end she was her own judge and jury. Louise Masset welcomed death, because she had found herself guilty – not of murder but because she had been that most terrible of things, a bad mother.

8: Unjust Desserts

Barry Wood

In the early hours of 22 March 1929 something sinister moved amidst the eerie surroundings of the Queen's Road Cemetery in Croydon, south London. As a cold wind whistled, the light of several large hurricane lamps flickered over carved headstones to reveal the shadowy outlines of men at work behind a large canvas screen. The men were grave diggers. With them were some of Scotland Yard's most eminent detectives, and the world-famous forensic scientist Sir Bernard Spilsbury also looked on at the grim scene unfolding in front of him. And with them also was another man, Tom Sidney, who was witnessing the exhumation of the bodies of his mother and sister – suspected of having been done to death by an arsenic poisoner. That morning alerted the world to the century's most infamous poisonings – and it was to change Tom Sidney's life forever.

The setting of these horrific events was the respectable middle-class suburb of Croydon in the late twenties where bridge evenings, garden parties and the annual church panto were the main social events. That respectability was to be shattered when three members of the same family were murdered by poison. The murderer must have been someone with close access to the family and many people, including domestic servants, family doctors and close relatives were to be tainted with the smear of suspicion. Despite the suspicions the culprit was never caught. There were inquests but there were no trials and the identity of the murderer(s) has remained a mystery to this day.

The story begins with two related families, the Sidneys and the Duffs. The Sidneys were the epitome of the respectable, well-heeled middle class, descended as they were from a Lord Mayor of London. Typically, they were church going, comfortable and hard working. The family matriarch, Mrs Violet Sidney, lived in a sprawling house at 29 Birdhurst Rise together with her unmarried daughter Vera. Just around the corner in South Park Hill Road lived Violet's son Tom and his American wife Margaret and family, and a few doors away from Tom lived Mrs Violet Sidney's third child Mrs Grace Duff and her husband Edmund and their family. To all appearances the family were linked by strong bonds of affection. They were constantly in and out of each other's houses. But as the six adult members of the Sidney–Duff clan sat around the Yuletide table in 1927 they did not suspect it was to be their last together.

The first victim succumbed on 27 April and whatever anyone thought of the extravagant, rough and ready Edmund Duff it was hard to see how he could have made a murderous enemy. Major Edmund Creighton Duff was the fifty-nine-year-old husband of Mrs Violet Sidney's daughter Grace. His lack of social standing, crumpled clothes and shabby home may have made him a bit of an embarrassment to his snobbish mother-in-law but he seems to have had a happy marriage despite a seventeen-year age gap and separate bedrooms.

Every week Edmund bought his wife a carnation and a Fry's Bar – whenever he sold a magazine article he gave her six carnations and a box of chocolates. Fishing provided one of his few moments of solace in a life of dreariness and drudgery.

He had worked as a government administrator in the far-flung outposts of the British Empire but had come home to a life of constant financial struggle. The upkeep of his wife and three children on a colonial service pension, supplemented by a low-paid clerical job as a clerk in the city and the odd commissions from the *Strand* magazine and the *Fishing Gazette*, was not easy. The Duffs had five children. Two died young.

Despite being an easygoing chap, some of his in-laws strongly disapproved of Edmund. Mrs Violet Sidney was firmly of the opinion that Grace could have done much better for herself. Nor did Edmund have much in common with his brother-in-law Tom Sidney, a professional entertainer. Apparently when Tom came round to the Duff's house, to practise his comic songs on the piano, Edmund would 'bubble with annoyance'.

Despite these family tensions he was by all accounts a congenial and popular man. But money was a perpetual worry. Edmund took early retirement from the Nigerian Service with a pension of just thirty pounds a month and in 1925 he obtained employment at a City bank at three pounds ten shillings a week. At one time Duff and his wife had at least five thousand pounds in capital inherited by Grace, from her grandfather, the Lord Mayor of London, but Edmund managed to lose it all in unwise investments and never talked about the loss.

He had always been keen on the outdoors and it was a love of fishing that brought him on 23 April 1928 to Hampshire on a fishing trip with some friends from his old colonial days. Just before his holiday Duff had been feeling out of sorts and had called in at the family GP, Dr John Binning, complaining of stomach pains and diarrhoea. Could he have something that would prevent his holiday being spoiled? Dr Binning gave him some bismuth mixture and Edmund set off and spent the next couple of days on the banks of the Avon waiting for the trout to bite. He complained to his old colonial friends that he 'had a touch of the fever' a reference to his old complaint of malaria, and decided to cut short the holiday and return home. When he arrived home his wife congratulated him on looking all the better for his holiday. 'It isn't wellness,' he replied. 'It's fever.' She refused to believe it at first and remarked on her husband's appearance to the family maid Amy Clarke, 'Isn't Mr Duff looking well.' It was a description of him she was to repeat later saying he had looked 'so brown and rosy'. She continued, 'I think the first thing I said was "how well you look".' Edmund even refused to kiss his baby thinking he might pass on his illness.

At first Edmund's complaint was not taken too seriously by his wife who was used to his hypochondriac ways. She strongly suspected that a bout of malingering was more to blame. But he could not finish off a meal of chicken and potatoes and a bottle of beer – or possibly two – brought to him by the maid Amy Clarke. The beer was brought in a stoppered bottle which, as was the family custom, stood in a pewter mug. Mr Duff poured the beer himself and his wife did not notice whether the seal was intact. Edmund settled down for a good sleep but in the night his condition became much worse. His body was racked with pain and fevers which did not abate over the next forty-eight hours. The doctor was telephoned and hurried round to find that Mr Duff had collapsed. His wife was in a terribly concerned state; she knelt by his side and kissed him. One of his last requests was for a cup of tea which she made. Over the next few hours Edmund's torment increased.

After three hours of writhing Edmund fell still. Anxiously Mrs Duff leant over and asked, 'He is not going to die, is he?' The two doctors in attendance, Binning and Elwell, exchanged glances and without saying a word began giving mouth-to-mouth resuscitation. After twenty minutes they admitted it was no use, as they had known from the start.

They had done it to lessen Grace's shock. At the time the thought flashed through Dr Robert Elwell's mind that it might have been food poisoning of some sort. He asked about the meal, chicken and potatoes, and then told Mrs Duff that he was unable to write out a death certificate because he did not know the cause of her husband's death. The doctor's distinct impression was that she did not raise any objection and wanted to know this herself. The pathologist who examined the body, Dr Robet Bronte, was unequivocal. Edmund Duff had died of a heart attack. The jury returned a verdict of death by natural causes. The last thing on anyone's mind was poison.

With her warm brown eyes and ready smile, Vera Sidney, even more than her brother-in-law Edmund, made an unusual murder victim. Everybody had a kind word for the forty-year-old spinster who lived alone with her mother at 29 Birdhurst Rise, Croydon. She was a slim and sallow-complexioned woman but despite her apparent frailty led a vigorous outdoor life, winning trophies for golf, taking brisk walks and driving her own small Citroën motor car. She was close to her mother but also much loved by the rest of the family and was to be remembered as a dutiful daughter and a kindly generous woman, without, it seemed, an enemy in the world. The story of the second chapter in the family tragedy deals with Vera and begins on Sunday, 10 February 1929. On that day Vera Sidney stayed in bed with what she claimed was a heavy cold. It was deeply uncharacteristic. She had barely known a day's illness in her life.

During the whole of January, Vera, like Edmund before her, had complained of feeling below par. Then on Monday, 11 February in an attempt to shake off her illness she went for a brisk walk on a golf links and had a game of bridge with friends. It didn't work however and she returned home feeling 'rotten'. It was while she was at this low ebb that she apparently received her first dose of arsenic. At 7.00 p.m. she sat down for supper. On the table were soup, fish, fried potatoes, pudding and fruit. Her mother, Violet, never ate soup, although she kept Symingtons soup powder in her dressing-table.

But Vera tucked enthusiastically in. Unfortunately after she had some soup with her dinner she was sick all night long. The soup had been made by the housekeeper Mrs Noakes on the Sunday, as far as she could recollect, and had been placed on the saucepan overnight. Ordinarily the only person in the household who would have drunk the soup would have been Vera. But that Monday, secretly breaking a house rule, Mrs Noakes drank a little soup out of a cup and gave the rest of the soup to Bingo the cat. She became ill. The cat also was sick.

Much later it was concluded that arsenic had caused the illness. The first dose was not to prove fatal. Vera said she was better on the Tuesday and by Wednesday had recovered strength sufficiently to have a hot bath and go out to tend to her car and try to crank some life into the frozen radiator. On the way she called in at her brother Tom's house. Tom was recovering from a bout of 'flu' and was surprised to see his sister. Sister Grace telephoned 29 Birdhurst Rise and was also surprised to hear the 'invalid' was up and about.

That day the Sidneys' Aunt Gwen from Newcastle arrived for lunch. Grace met her at the station but could not stay for lunch herself as she said she had to prepare the meals for the children. At 1.00 p.m. Vera, Violet and Aunt Gwen sat down to a meal of thick soup made up of vegetables cooked over the weekend, veal and soup powder. Vera's mother ate none of it. Vera complained loudly that it was the same soup that had made her ill on Monday but still had several mouthfuls. Aunt Gwen too had some of it. It was only a matter of minutes after the meal before both Vera and her aunt fell violently ill. Vera called her sister Grace and when Grace arrived, Margaret Sidney, Tom's wife, was already on the scene.

Grace found both Vera and Aunt Gwen, sitting in the drawing room looking sick, miserable and as if they both had chills. She gave Vera a dose of castor oil, brandy and orange cordial. Both Dr Binning and Dr Elwell arrived to tend to Vera but her condition continued to deteriorate. Dr Elwell fetched a specialist who at first thought Vera was suffering from a very severe bout of 'flu' aggravated by going out in the cold on the Wednesday morning and trying to start her car. He was to say later that poisoning never entered his head. Vera's condition rapidly deteriorated despite being attended to by the two doctors and two nurses. She suffered horrible agonies and, some time around midnight on 14 February, finally succumbed.

A specialist at the time decided it was a case of gastro-intestinal 'flu' and signed a death certificate to that effect. It has been claimed that a year before Vera's death she had visited a fortune-teller but the gypsy had refused to tell what she saw after the reading because the forecast was so bad. Vera died leaving comfortable sums to her nearest and dearest. Her paternal grandfather had left her £5,000 in his will. She had no need to work but being a trained masseuse she was able to supplement her income. In all Vera left £5,530. Of that £2,000 was left to her mother, £1,000 to Tom and £2,000 to Grace. The residue of the estate was divided between Grace and Tom's children. Interestingly Mrs Greenwell was to lie ill for five days in a London hotel before taking the train back to Newcastle-upon-Tyne. She always believed she had been poisoned.

By 15 February 1929 two members of the Sidney–Duff clan lay dead and there still was not the slightest suspicion of foul play. Indeed if it hadn't been for yet another suspicious death the murders might have gone completely undetected. To the outside world Violet Sidney presented an austere and rigid exterior. She was a parsimonious, snobbish woman who had married the son of the Lord Mayor of London. She regarded herself as coming from an aristocratic background and looked down on her in-laws because they were 'in trade'. Her marriage to Thomas Stafford Sidney lasted only five years and collapsed when her husband ran off with another woman by whom he had an illegitimate son. Undoubtedly Vera was her favourite and the old lady doted on her – when Grace married Edmund Duff she could not hide her disappointment and dislike of her daughter's husband, just as she disapproved of her son Tom's American wife.

What she thought about the premature death of her son-in-law is not recorded, although she was horrified at the thought of an inquest in the family. But the death of her favourite daughter Vera shattered her. Mrs Sidney was left living alone in the house at Birdhurst Rise, and grieved terribly. Indeed her family felt she might collapse under the strain. Dr Elwell prescribed a tonic. She seemed to be recovering by the beginning of March, three weeks after Vera's death, and was even shaking off a nasty cold, although the water pipes had burst and the housekeeper had handed in her notice.

The chief visitors to the house were Grace and her brother Tom Sidney who came nearly every day. Both appeared to be deeply attached to their mother. On 4

March Tom Sidney visited his mother to discuss Vera's will. The next morning Mrs Sidney was visited by her daughter. Grace wanted to see if her mother needed any shopping done and arranged to get some butter and milk and a reel of cotton which Mrs Sidney wanted. Mrs Noakes, the housekeeper, remembered that Violet went upstairs leaving Grace in the dining-room alone – where, it was suggested, the medicine may have been kept.

Sometime that morning Violet poured two teaspoonfuls of her medicine into a wine glass of water and knocked it back. Later Mrs Noakes, the housekeeper, went into the dining-room to lay the table for luncheon. She found Mrs Sidney setting down an empty wineglass and pulling an 'awful face'.

Mrs Sidney was alleged to have said to her housekeeper, 'My last bottle of medicine has tasted nasty.' On the sideboard stood a small medicine bottle empty save for a little sediment at the bottom. Mrs Sidney had taken the final dose out of the bottle. Mrs Noakes then made some remark along the lines that perhaps Mrs Sidney had shaken the bottle too much and continued to prepare the table. As soon as luncheon was ready Mrs Sidney sat down and ate the meal, which consisted of chicken cooked a week previously. It was just after 1.00 p.m. that Mrs Duff returned from shopping and found her mother sitting in a chair 'huddled up and deathly white'.

The old woman whispered the words, 'I've had some poison,' and stretching out her hands pointed to the medicine bottle. 'It's that nasty medicine,' confirmed Mrs Noakes, standing nearby. 'She said it tasted strong and gritty.' Mrs Sidney then indicated that she felt sick and Mrs Duff rushed into the kitchen and made up a solution of salt and water. Meanwhile the doctor had been sent for. When Dr Elwell arrived Mrs Sidney had completely collapsed but he managed to revive her briefly. In her dazed state she told him her medicine tasted peculiar and gritty. Elwell and his colleague Dr Binning did what they could to revive her but she fell ill again and died later that day.

With another death in the Sidney family the cloud of suspicion that had been gathered could be ignored no longer. The two doctors refused to sign a death certificate and the police were called in. On 21 March the Home Office ordered the exhumation of the remains of Vera and Violet Sidney.

Amidst the reek of death and disinfectant in the mortuary there was little doubt in the mind of pathologist Sir Bernard Spilsbury as to the cause of death. Arsenic has known preservative qualities and both Vera and Violet's bodies were well preserved. Even the bunch of hyacinths that Vera held were still fresh. Extensive analysis of Violet's body and the contents of the house by toxicologists and forensic scientists revealed that the fatal dose must have been taken only a few hours before death. The liquid adhering to the wine glass out of which she had taken her medicine was found to be 'rich in arsenic' and there was arsenic in the sediment at the bottom of the medicine bottle. The detective in charge of the case, Inspector Hedges of Scotland Yard, now had two murders on his hands and suspicion began to mount as to the circumstances of Edmund Duff's death a year earlier.

An examination was ordered of the body of Edmund Duff. Again Sir Bernard Spilsbury undertook the post-mortem; he inhaled as the lid of the coffin was removed and the smell of arsenic was unmistakable. Again another inquest was ordered. A black carnival atmosphere surrounded the conduct of the inquests later that year. There were some twenty-six lengthy hearings.

Crowds would gather at the door to get a glimpse of the family or to queue for a seat in the public gallery. Grace Duff would always arrive looking very elegant and smart and sometimes, apparently oblivious to the gaze of the crowd, would pick daisies.

Strangely, the coroner, against the advice of the Director of Public Prosecutions, decided to hold the inquests separately which meant the juries were never able to get an overall picture of events. Although weedkiller was believed to be the form in which the arsenic was administered to the victims, the killer was also fortunate that the analyst had carelessly destroyed the contents of Violet's medicine bottle.

The second inquest on the body of Edmund Creighton Duff was opened by the Croydon coroner Dr H.B. Jackson on the morning of 5 July. One of the key questions to be answered was why did the second examination of Edmund find arsenic in the body when the first one did not. At the earlier hearing the coroner said there had been no poison in the organs and the pathologist Dr R.M. Bronte had said, 'One can exclude the possibility of poisoning.' The coroner had added that there seemed no doubt that it seemed a perfectly natural death from heart disease though he said he was puzzled by the vomiting and other symptoms.

But after the opening of the second inquest it was not long before the evidence began to point towards official incompetence as being the reason for this discrepancy. Despite his protestations to the contrary, it seemed more than likely that Dr Bronte had mixed up the organs he was examining with those of another autopsy altogether, that of an eighty-year-old woman who was being examined on a neighbouring slab. This was never confirmed for certain but the jury seemed to think that either the wrong organs were analysed or insufficient care was taken during the tests.

Either way the jury came to a completely different conclusion and decided that Mr Duff had died from acute arsenical poisoning, wilfully administered by person or persons unknown. The proceedings had been in progress for about ten minutes when Grace entered the courtroom dressed in black with a white lace collar and a large black hat. Noiselessly and with every eye in the court on her, she tiptoed to the edge of the seat kept for her at the front of the court. As soon as she sat down the coroner said he wished to bring to the notice of the jury the Home Office report saying traces of arsenic had been found throughout the body.

During the inquest relatives gave evidence that the Duff family life was happy. Amy Clarke had been working as a maid at the Duff household for about three months when Mr Duff died. She gave evidence that before the holiday Mr Duff seemed a cheerful man who did not tend to suffer from fits of depression. Mr and Mrs Duff seemed fond of each other, indeed she had never known a more united family. She had taken Edmund a bottle of beer across the top of which was a paper band which had not been broken. Dr Binning then went into the dock and said that when he first visited Edmund in the morning before he died he did not look an ill man. 'He was always a man to make the most of things.'

Edmund's life insurance had totalled £1,500 but his Colonial Office pension ceased after his death and Grace would only receive a widow's pension of one pound a week. His income would have been around £500 a year plus a small sum from writing but after he died she received around £400 per annum from relatives and other sources. She claimed that after her husband's death she lost everything: 'Without my relatives I do not know what I would have done.' He had been the only member of the family to have supper the night he came back from Hampshire. Grace was left considerably poorer by Edmund's death through loss of the pension.

Sir Bernard Spilsbury concluded that the arsenic had been placed in the beer Duff had been drinking with his meal. This he said would have caused the fastest possible reaction. The coroner was also to indicate that the bottle could have been spiked and the seal reglued. An intimate picture of Edmund Duff was given during evidence. He was described as being 'very happy' in his home life, 'as devoted' to his wife 'as she was to him'. His father never heard of him complaining of his wife or she of him though he was said to be a 'jealous man'. His children were fond of him.

Dr Binning made one claim that was to lie unsolved at the heart of the case. For he said that when he treated Edmund later that day he was now seriously ill, and claimed to have eaten chicken and potatoes and two bottles of beer. This completely contradicted the statement by Amy Clarke that she had only ever taken him one bottle.

Asked why this might be Mrs Duff smiled and said, 'I should say he snaffled it when he took the tray back to the kitchen.' She continued, 'I have no actual knowledge of it but he might do it. It would have been quite in keeping as he would have known there were extra bottles owing to his having been away.'

Another curious qucstion raised at the inquest was whether Mr Duff may have had a secret enemy. Mrs Duff said, 'If he was killed he must have had enemies,' however she did not know of one and did not think that anyone could gain from his death. Interestingly the inquest did hint at an element of discord in the Duff household before Edmund departed on his fishing holiday. Tom Sidney told the inquest that he had seen Edmund in a very angry temper with his wife. 'I understood from my sister that he was very upset and wanted a change.'

No explanation for his vile mood was given though Tom did describe another occasion when, in the company of Mr and Mrs Duff, he saw Edmund 'jump up in a frightul temper ... shaking with rage'. Tom Sidney said he did not attach any importance to the rage but before Edmund had left on his fishing trip his wife had said, 'Poor old Ted. This trip will do him good.'

Another curious feature of Edmund's trip was the mystery of the missing whisky bottle which Grace claimed to have seen in his suitcase. It was of the type that could be bought cheaply in high street shops but it never materialised and Grace's claim was never substantiated.

In the witness box Grace Duff maintained that her life with her husband was one of domestic contentment. She told the jury her husband was a good man and her marriage a happy one. Mr Duff was 'very fond' of her and she was 'very fond' of him.

The jury returned after twenty minutes deliberation with the verdict that Edmund Creighton Duff met his death from acute arsenical poisoning wilfully administered by person or persons unknown.

With his tall good looks, careful hairstyle and taste for flamboyant suits and hats, Tom Sidney cut a considerable, if dandyish, figure. His musical talent had manifested itself in his teens and he had already performed for the public before the outbreak of World War One. This talent was to become more than a hobby. It was to become his living. His profession of entertainer was to take him around the world. In fact it was while working a cruise liner coming to England from America that he met his wife. Margaret McConnell had been travelling on a European holiday but intrigued and dazzled by the loud cheerful Englishman she decided to marry in England and stay on. During the length of the investigation Tom was to behave in a sometimes erratic way that was to prove far from helpful to him.

At various times he was to suggest that the guilt for the murders lay with Mrs Noakes, his mother's housekeeper. She had the perfect opportunity he said to plant poison on his mother and sister (although she was not employed by the family at the time Edmund died). Then with the exhumation of his brother-in-law he changed his mind and decided that Dr Elwell must be guilty. Just for good measure he also pointed the finger of suspicion at the local curate's wife. The police found him a veritable fount of knowledge about other family intrigues. Finally, he pointed the finger at Grace, describing her as a homicidal maniac.

He also cast a shadow over the claim that Grace had no financial problems. He claimed she had threatened suicide because of money worries, and hinted she was having an affair with Dr Elwell, a handsome, rich bachelor. Grace denied any impropriety with Dr Elwell, who was godfather to her youngest child and regarded as a family friend. Her version of events was that Dr Elwell was a flatterer and it had been a joke between her and her husband that Dr Elwell was her 'admirer'. She claimed that after Edmund's death Dr Elwell proposed to her but she turned him down.

Tom Sidney was at the centre of stormy exchanges during the inquest on Vera's death. His tendency towards outbursts and emotional exchanges only helped to show him in a poor light. His evidence was shot through with inconsistencies, inaccuracies and misunderstandings of recollections of conversations he had had with police officers. Under examination about statements he allegedly made to the police he noisily interjected saying that 'words had been put into my mouth' by the officers. Under questioning about a tin of weed-killer found in his house he said he did not remember where he bought it or if he had signed for it. Then in reference to evidence he felt was not being examined he angrily shouted out, 'Why feature my tin of arsenic and leave out the tin which contained arsenic found on my mother's premises?'

And later Tom again clashed with the coroner on the truth of his statements to the police. Insisting that he had been misrepresented, Tom said, 'Inspector Hedges put words in my mouth; I did not think this matter was going to be brought before a jury.' The coroner then interrupted: 'Not so fast. I have to put it down.'

'I don't want it put down,' said Tom but the coroner insisted: 'It must be put down, you are here to give evidence.'

It was only the interjection of Tom's barrister Fearnley Whittingstall that was to save the day for him. Later Tom was closely questioned on his financial circumstances. He described his financial position as 'fairly satisfactory' at the time of his sister's death. He had, after all debts were paid, £5,000 in liquid cash. He owned his own house with no mortgage or debts and in the months before the deaths his professional earnings as an entertainer had been steadily increasing. But Tom's position was not helped when he was shown to be less than truthful in smaller matters.

Queried about his statement that he did not have any creditors he was faced with a letter to a private club stating that he wanted to delay his joining until 'he can look his debtors in the face again'. Tom claimed that this was merely an excuse to postpone joining because the club cost much more than he had anticipated. The coroner put it to him that it was 'strange that a man should go out of his way to say he cannot meet his creditors when it cannot be true'.

Tom's answer was inaudible and the coroner proceeded, 'Anyhow that is your explanation, that it is not true?' Sidney agreed. It was a small point on a matter not connected to the poisonings but it could have had a devastating impact on the jury by creating the picture of an untruthful man. Not for the last time Fearnley Whittingstall jumped to the rescue and helped to deflate the notion of Tom as untruthful.

Whittingstall asked his client, to laughter in court, if in applying to the club he had bitten off more than he could chew or swallow. Then driving the point home he asked Tom, 'With regard to your thoughts on March 6th did you feel the day after your mother's death in any mood to have a logical reason for every thought that came into your head.' Tom Sidney indicated that he did not. At the inquest of his mother Tom was at the receiving end of more firm questioning by the coroner about his reaction to the bottle of medicine that his mother had used. He had noticed a distinct white sediment at the bottom of it. The coroner harried him, asking when he had seen the bottle, what he had done, what he had not done, why he did it. Again Tom was becoming noticeably distressed at the line of questioning and again his QC came to the rescue with supporting questioning. At one point after four hours of questioning he turned to the coroner: 'After an examination like this it is remarkable if you don't get fed up and tie yourself up. It is a fearful strain on the memory.'

Again at the inquest of Violet Sidney, Tom had to point out to the court that although his wife had told the police there were no poisons at their house she had forgotten a bottle of 'Eureka' weed-killer and some rat poison. Tom pointed out that it was he who showed the police that he had it in his possession.

The inquest into Mrs Violet Sidney was to hear that an extensive analysis of the body and the contents of the house by toxicologists revealed that the fatal dose must have been taken only a few hours before death. The liquid adhering to the wine glass out of which she had taken her medicine was found to be 'rich in arsenic' and there was arsenic in the sediment at the bottom of the medicine bottle. At the inquest Mrs Noakes would give evidence that was to prove to be highly damaging to Thomas Sidney and place a question mark over his account of events.

'On March 5th,' said Mrs Noakes, 'the day Mrs Sidney was taken ill, this was after Dr Elwell had been and just before Mrs Sidney took her medicine, I was taking in things to get ready for lunch when I saw to my surprise Mr Sidney standing in the hall with one of his children.'

She went on to say that the front door was closed. Tom did not, as far as Mrs Noakes knew, see his mother that morning and she could not understand how he got into the house as she usually admitted him herself (Grace supported this story by claiming that she met Tom near her mother's house as she returned with the shopping). Tom's barrister Mr Fearnley Whittingstall immediately realised the danger of this evidence and in a spirited damage-limitation exercise rose to question Mrs Noakes.

Mr Whittingstall: 'Every day of the evidence have you had a long conversation with Inspector Hedges?'

Mrs Noakes: 'Yes, but not always about this case.'

'How many times has he been to your house?'

'Several.'

'What has he been there about, this case?'

'Yes.'

'When did he last go?'

'About Tuesday week.'

'What did he talk about, did he ask you anything about Tom Sidney?'

'I don't think so.'

'What questions did he ask?'

'I don't know.'

'Let me suggest to you that he might have asked you about Mr Sidney.'

'He might have done.'

'I suggest to you a large part of these conversations have been taken up with discussions of this affair.'

'Yes.'

'He must have asked you nearly dozens of times whether Tom Sidney had been to the house on that day, March 5th.'

Mr Whittingstall finally said, 'After badgering you for six weeks, all Inspector Hedges can get out of you is that you "fancy" you saw Mr Sidney?'

'I told them I wasn't sure.'

At this Inspector Hedges intervened: 'I strongly object to the word badgering. I think it is unfair.'

The coroner upheld the objection but this, taken with more close questioning, helped to completely undermine Mrs Noakes' evidence.

Dr Ryffel concluded that a dose of arsenic must have been taken about twelve hours before the victim's death. He based his opinion on the fact that arsenic is rapidly eliminated from the body. There was no evidence, through analysis of Mrs Sidney's hair that she had taken any arsenic for any longer period. If she had, the residue would have worked its way through to her hair.

Thomas Sidney told the inquest jury that Vera Sidney, his dead sister, had left £2,000 for life to her mother with the wish that after her death it should be equally divided between himself and Mrs Grace Duff.

At the inquest the jury decided there was insufficient evidence to show whether she killed herself or was murdered by person or persons unknown.

The chief suspects, Grace and Tom, were to be haunted by the saga. Tom left Croydon almost immediately after the trial and took his family to America. He never saw his sister Grace again although they corresponded. In a remarkable newspaper interview given after the verdict he talked about what it was like to have the finger of suspicion pointed at him for killing three members of his family. He writes of walking down the street 'with all eyes' on him and wishing that the earth would open up and devour him; of the macabre interest shown by those people who wanted to befriend him and of the hate mail.

He writes of one day during the inquest receiving a letter which said, '... the rope is waiting for you and you honestly deserve it ... why not get some more poison and do yourself in. It would save time and expense.' On another occasion he opened an envelope and a sample of rope fell out which the writer claimed was '... a sample of rope from which you cannot possibly escape ...'

In one telling passage he writes, 'It must be very difficult for police when they are making inquiries to get beyond that barrier known as personality which hides so much of the true inner self. Having an artistic and perhaps highly strung temperament I began, in the eyes of the police, I feel sure, to do and say just the very things I should not do and say.

'What a position! In a few hours my whole business of life which had been to portray the humorous side of our humdrum existence and to show that even tragedy has its lighter side has changed.'

What was Grace Duff – a scheming temptress with murder in her heart or a misunderstood assertive woman who made men feel uncomfortable? She certainly had a Bohemian streak in her that seemed out of place in the genteel tedium of day-to-day life in Croydon. Her strong character and assertive behaviour might seem to be suited to another age rather than one where women were expected to be docile and obedient. Either way it's difficult to explain the vitriol she attracted from observers, all of it based on nothing but the flimsiest tittle-tattle.

All this amounted to not one jot of evidence. The most salacious accusation against her, that she had an affair with Dr Elwell, was never proven, although that slight detail would not have bothered the gossip-mongers. After the verdicts Grace was to leave Croydon and, with her family, move to a south coast seaside resort where she lived out the rest of her life uneventfully. According to one reporter the move helped her recuperate: 'It is plain that her sojourn by the sea has done her an immense amount of good. Her eyes are no longer sunken and lined. She is full faced and a picture of health.' Grace died in 1973 aged eighty-seven.

The thousands of words that have been printed since the Croydon poisonings have brought us no closer to an answer to the mystery. Who might have had motive? Let us look at the main players in detail. During the inquiry the coroner received an anonymous letter saying that Edmund Duff had an affair with Tom's wife. Did Tom murder Edmund in a cuckolded rage and then poison the other two for financial gain?

Did Grace have a motive? Throughout the saga there

was a strong rumour that she was having a relationship with Dr Elwell. The inquest jury was not to hear that she sustained severe bruises as a result of her husband's violent lovemaking. And she was always short of money. Could these motives have been enough to turn her into a killer? (Some people thought Grace had been deranged by the death of two of her children though again there was absolutely no evidence for this.)

In the case of Violet Sidney, the family matriarch, the jury did not rule out suicide. Could she not bear to lose her daughter Vera? Or was she the poisoner who killed herself in remorse? She disliked Edmund, feared for Grace's financial future and thought they had too many children. Was she worried about Vera's mental health? Vera had been upset at losing the friendship of the vicar's wife because the vicar did not approve of them seeing each other.

When we look at opportunity the puzzle becomes no clearer. Grace, certainly, could have poisoned Edmund's beer. And she visited her mother's house the day the poisoned soup was eaten. It's also possible she was left alone with the medicine when it was spiked. Tom could have poisoned Edmund. The Duff home was an open house to him. He would go in to use their piano whenever he liked. Tom also first told police he had been in bed with 'flu' the day that Vera was first poisoned; in fact he had gone for a long walk. Why the lies?

He was seen near his mother's house the day she died and the housekeeper insisted she saw him in the hall. And another intriguing possibility was that none of the immediate family were to blame and that the crimes were committed by an outsider.

Tom, Vera and Grace had a half brother – the illegitimate offspring of their errant father. The Sidneys never recognised this brother. Did he set out to wreak revenge on the family that had turned its back on him?

Many people fell under suspicion but at the end of the day the main suspects were Tom and Grace, but was this because of unfortunate aspects of their character? Grace with her strong personality, Tom with his lies, excitable manner and attempt to attach blame to others. The detectives suspected Tom then Grace but the Director of Public Prosecutions decided there was no evidence or case to answer. The mystery of the Croydon poisonings remains unsolved.

9: An Uncommon Murder

Fiona Mackay

At first light on New Year's morning 1911, the body of a man was discovered near Long Path, on Clapham Common in London. This was no ordinary murder – in fact it was a most uncommon murder. The body had been carefully laid out and then strangely and elaborately mutilated. The Clapham Common murder came at a difficult time for the authorities, already dealing with trouble in the immigrant communities of the East End.

Now, the authorities always denied that there was any link between the death on the Common and the two dramas played out in the East End that winter between Russian anarchist gangs and the police and army. However, to a British public increasingly alarmed by the 'foreign troublemakers' in their midst, there was always a connection. And somebody needed to be called to account. One man, Steinie Morrison, was made to pay for the Clapham Common murder, but was he guilty or merely a scapegoat?

Britain at the turn of the century enjoyed relatively liberal immigration laws. Under Gladstone's premiership, the government was probably the most tolerant in Europe in its attitude towards political refugees. The East End of London, around Whitechapel, became known throughout the rest of Europe as a haven and place of refuge for those fleeing political or racial persecution. It provided asylum in particular for East European Jews escaping not only oppressive governments, but anti-semitism, vicious persecution and pogroms.

The nineteenth century had been a period of ferment in much of Europe. Industrialisation had led to massive movements of people from country to town; vast armies of the labouring poor were billeted in grim, filthy slums; and the social fabric of many societies was unravelling. Peasants were becoming increasingly restless and rebellious towards their feudal masters. Freedom from serfdom rarely improved their lot but brought fresh oppression from new masters. The ideas of freedom and equality which had been developed in the eighteenth century and which had infused the American and French revolutions were becoming more widespread. As the nineteenth century progressed it was not just the middle classes which demanded political rights but the peasants and workers too; they sought economic rights as well.

The spread of such ideas led to a series of worker and peasant uprisings all over Western and Central Europe, especially in large cities and manufacturing districts. The so-called 1848 revolutions were all put down, but from then on the still largely despotic monarchies of Europe were haunted by the spectre of communism and anarchism.

In the years that followed regimes used their police forces and armies to suppress any popular dissent. In Russia under Tsarist control, in some regions torture and flogging of whole communities was routine; freedom of expression and association were mostly denied. The authorities could not stamp out the stirrings of revolution but they could contain them.

Over several decades fresh waves of immigrants came to Whitechapel driven by political, economic or racial hardships. They crowded into its narrow streets, its rooming houses and its cafés, bringing with them alien cultures, new ideas and a cacophony of strange tongues.

The vast majority of poor immigrants were only intent upon making a better life for themselves in a country where they neither understood the language nor the customs. They took what work they could find, sometimes legal such as second-hand trading or sweated tailoring; sometimes illegal – many were drawn by their desperate circumstances into the underworld as prostitutes, pickpockets, burglars and fences.

Many European governments regarded London, where dissidents and refugees could meet freely and discuss political ideas, as a hotbed of sedition. Indeed it was widely believed that the plot to assassinate the French president in 1894 was hatched in London at one of several clubs for foreign anarchists – such as the Autonomie Club in the West End or the Jubilee Street Club in the East End.

The term 'anarchist' at the turn of the century came to be a catch-all expression to describe dissidents ranging from the most desperate nihilist through to revolutionary socialists and reformist social democrats; what they had in common was a desire for a new social order. Whitechapel in the early 1900s teemed with such groups. They included those who had fled from repressive regimes in Eastern Europe and came with a dream of building a new political order by the power of debate and others who believed that more violent action was needed to achieve their ends. The latter were prepared to condone political assassination and bombings to further their cause, and to carry out robberies – or 'expropriations' as they called them – to finance their various causes.

One such group was the Liesma gang, which, in 1910, shattered the fragile peace in the East End and triggered a wave of xenophobia and anti-semitism in British public opinion. Immigrants and political refugees had been largely tolerated by public opinion until a series of events whipped up a moral panic and a demand for retribution. The Winter of 1910–1911 saw both policemen and anarchists die by bullet or fire; troops were called out into the East End. The Houndsditch Shootings and the Sidney Street siege were national outrages, international events. But there were two other victims almost certainly linked to the events, who were drawn unwittingly into the tragedy by fate and circumstance. Both were Russian Jews: one ended up dead on Clapham Common and another ended up in jail – perhaps justly; perhaps because he was an ideal scapegoat – a handsome feckless foreign Jew.

It was almost midnight, 16 December 1910, a Friday night, when Max Weil, a trader in fancy goods in Houndsditch, complained to police about strange noises coming from the jeweller's shop next door. It was the Jewish Sabbath and his rest was being disturbed. The police arrived shortly after at Harris the Jewellers, a shop which had opened earlier that year and was reputed to be the wealthiest in the street. Unlike many of the other shopkeepers and traders in Houndsditch, Mr Henry Harris did not live above the shop.

The police officers, five of them, went inside the shop to investigate. They were brought down in a hail of bullets. The police had disturbed an attempt to tunnel into the jeweller's shop and its safe. Harris the Jeweller's safe at the back of the premises was rumoured to hold up to £30,000 worth of jewellery – some said it also contained Romanov treasure. But the shopbreakers were no ordinary burglars. They were members of the Russian Liesma anarchist group. They were desperate and dangerous and were willing to turn to crime to fund the revolution; and murder if necessary.

The Houndsditch massacre left three policemen dead

and two seriously wounded; one gang member was left close to death after he had been accidentally wounded by his own men in the mêlée. The gang – more than ten strong – escaped into the night and the relative safety of the labyrinth of side streets and alleyways. Three of the conspirators helped their wounded leader George 'Karl' Gardstein escape. He was to die shortly afterwards. They kept to the middle of the road, as anarchists always did, to minimise the possibility of being ambushed. They were far from inconspicuous, but no one reported them. Whether people agreed with the anarchists or not, a common history of persecution and a common suspicion of the authorities kept most lips sealed.

A huge police operation was launched to capture the anarchists who had escaped. They pressed their informants; they offered money. The cockney gangs were also leaned upon, but they too refused to co-operate seeing the police as a common enemy. It looked as though it was going to be a difficult Christmas for the police. However during the days before the Clapham Common murder they were able to arrest five members of the group. At least another three, including the notorious Peter the Painter remained at large.

The young anarchists involved in the Houndsditch shootings were from a different generation to the peaceful, intellectual anarchists who ran the Jubilee Street club – official title, the Hall of the Friends of the Workers – and whose work involved social lectures and providing community services like a reading room with Russian newspapers.

The Liesma gang, led by Karl Gardstein, were from the Baltic region of the Russian Empire. They were mainly Letts - their password was '*Brehoiba*', the Lettish for freedom. A large number of Lettish refugees had fled in 1906 after the brutal suppression of political uprisings in Riga. Many had been harshly treated by the authorities, some had been flogged by Cossacks; others had been tortured and had their fingernails pulled off by the Tsarist police. Thousands fled abroad, many to Britain. Amongst their number were some of the most militant and reckless political extremists.

A man such as Leon Beron was in complete contrast. By East End standards Beron was a man of substance. A man untouched by the bullets of revolution. Yet his ordered life was about to chance irrevocably, indeed end violently; and the turning point may well have been the night of the Houndsditch shootings.

Beron, known as the 'Landlord' was born in Russia and brought up in Paris. His family moved to London in 1894. A wave of East European Jews left France after the murder, by anarchists, of the French President Marie Francois Sadi Carnot in Lyons. Some were well-known anarchists fleeing the French authorities, others believed they would be persecuted by association. In any event there is nothing to suggest that Beron and his two brothers, David and Solomon, had any links with anarchist groups at all.

Indeed there is no evidence that Beron had any interest in politics beyond the odd discussion over a glass of Russian tea at the Warsaw restaurant, an East End café much favoured by the Russian Jewish emigrées. Beron, now in his late forties, was certainly no anarchist. If anything, as his nickname suggested, he was something of a capitalist.

His daily routine was unshakeable. In the mornings he would meet his two brothers for prayers. The rest of the time they would barely acknowledge each other. At midday he would repair to the Warsaw in Osborne Street near Brick Lane and settle down to the pressing matter of drinking tea, making small talk and admiring his celebrated watch. If Beron had achieved any fame at all, it was for his watch. It was a heavy eighteen-carat-gold English lever watch, weighing about six ounces with a heavy gold chain. From it hung a five guinea gold piece. With a trim little goatee beard, his gold watch, and his heavy overcoat with astrakhan collar, Beron gave the impression of having plenty of money.

Although he had lived in London for sixteen years he had never learned the language. He spoke little or no English, speaking only French and Yiddish. However he was firmly established in his own way. Indeed, Leon Beron appeared surprisingly affluent for a man with a small income and no occupation, normally carrying between £20 and £30 in gold in a leather wash-bag fastened to the inside of his waistcoat.

His income was ten shillings a week from rents from the nine properties he owned. He himself lived with his brother David in a rented room in Jubilee Street. They lived in a lively, noisy community, centred on the small streets and alleys that lay between Brick Lane, Whitechapel Road and Petticoat Lane in London's East End. There were all manner of Jewish shops and cafés; Jewish gaming houses and theatres, as well as the great synagogue in Fournier Street. But conditions for the majority of emigrés, many disoriented and dispossessed, were desperate. Some refugees found it harder than others. For instance the waiter at the Warsaw restaurant, Joe Mintz, was unable to acclimatise to his new country. In the two years he had been in England he had attempted suicide more than once – attempting to hang himself – and had spent three months in a lunatic asylum.

The vast majority of immigrants were poor tailoring workers, outworkers who would have to gather daily along the Whitechapel Road waiting to be hired for piece-work by the master tailors; others were stall-holders, pedlars and traders, cabinet-makers and bakers.

Steinie Morrison, who, by the time of the Houndsditch shootings, had become a new regular at the Warsaw, was altogether different. In the drab poverty of the East End Steinie Morrison cut a dash. Tall, handsome and charming, Steinie was also a teller of tall tales. He was known as the Australian because he claimed to have been born there – although in reality he was a Ukrainian Jew. Steinie claimed he had lived all over the world; that he had worked as a cowboy; as an actor; he claimed he had trained as a singer in Italy. He spoke like an educated man, in an accent that mixed Dickensian English with Eastern European, even Australian. He had lived in England for twelve years and had spent a total of ten and a half of those years in jail for burglary.

Morrison had been released from his latest spell inside in September 1910. He was twenty-nine years old. At first he had worked for a baker in Clapham, but the local police made it clear that his presence was not welcome on their patch. He was regularly harassed on his way to and from work; after seven weeks he had had enough and headed back to the East End.

In early December 1910 Steinie Morrison had taken to calling at the Warsaw. He had already charmed the owner's young daughter Becky. Steinie could generally charm women and children. He baited the unfortunate Joe Mintz – for which he would later pay dearly; and he had started taking tea with the Landlord and his interpreter Hermelin. He spent at least an hour a day deep in conversation with Beron.

After Steinie left his employment at the bakery it is not clear how he came by his money. He was a gambler, playing a game called faro for high stakes; he may still have been a housebreaker. When police arrested him, he claimed he was working as a trader in cheap jewellery. His income was erratic; he was either on a spending spree or queueing up at the sign of the three balls. In November he had managed to spend £19 in two days. He bought collars, a suit, a striking green overcoat, and a gold watch on a chain. He also bought a revolver and ammunition. A few weeks later he was back at the pawn shop.

Morrison liked to dress for the ladies; he had the wardrobe of a dandy. Conspicuous suits, a clean collar every day – courtesy of the Japanese laundry and of course his overcoat in green. Six feet three inches tall, Morrison was intelligent, witty, exuberant. He loved women; in the space of a week he was to propose to two young women and move in with a third. He was also a regular at the many brothels around Whitechapel.

He also adored children – from little Becky Snelwar the ten-year-old daughter of the proprietor of the Warsaw, whom he teased and brought presents of fruit, to the children of his landlady Mrs Zimmerman – to whom he played his flute and with whom he played games of Varney the Vampire. He lodged with the Zimmermans in Newark Street just off Brick Lane. He slept on a sofa in a downstairs room paying three shillings a week for the room plus a penny a day for a glass of warm milk for breakfast. He was a popular lodger.

New Year's Eve 1910, some two weeks after the Houndsditch shootings. Three weeks after Steinie Morrison first met Leon Beron at the Warsaw. Perhaps one tragedy was to lead to another? That morning Steinie had an argument with Joe Mintz – he was irritated he had not been served his breakfast and had shouted, 'Where is he, Mintz? Hey don't say you hang yourself again!' Mintz confronted Steinie and threatened him: 'One day I will get this back on you.'

Steinie returned that evening with a parcel, which he asked Becky to put behind the counter for him. He told her it was a flute. She handed it to Joe Mintz who put it in a cupboard.

Beron and Steinie had business that night. They left the Warsaw several times together in the course of the evening, returning to drink more tea or lemonade (the Warsaw did not sell alcohol). A little before midnight they left together. They must have appeared a strange duo – the dashing Morrison and the little, shambling Beron with his strange gait.

What follows next is a matter of some dispute. Witnesses said they saw Steinie and Beron walking the streets together until the small hours. They were spotted at a coffee stall at 1.45 a.m. Leon's brother Solomon said he saw Leon walking alone but obviously waiting for someone and obviously drunk. He called to him, but Leon did not respond. A cab driver said he had picked up the two men in the Mile End Road at about two in the morning and taken them to Lavender Gardens in Clapham.

Steinie was to claim later he was home by this time. He claimed he had gone to bed just after midnight. The Zimmermans confirmed this and said they had then bolted the front door. He would not have been able to go out again without disturbing them because of the terrible grating noise the bolt made when moved. There is no dispute however that at about 3 a.m. on 1 January 1911 there was a murder on Clapham Common. Ten minutes later a man caught a hansom cab at Clapham Cross. The murdered man was Leon Beron. Who was the man in the hansom?

The murder of Leon Beron looked simple enough, at least on the face of it. Beron's famous gold watch had gone, as well as the stash of sovereigns he kept sewn inside his jacket. And what other motive could there possibly be to murder a man like Leon Beron unless it was to rob him? But Leon Beron was not all he appeared to be. The houses he owned were slums, some were brothels. He was not averse to taking a cut from the girls' earnings. Nor was he above making use of their services. The odd walk of his may have been an early sign of syphilis. Neighbours reported that Beron seldom returned to his lodgings until 2.00 a.m.; the Warsaw closed at midnight; perhaps Beron paid nightly visits to some of the multitude of Whitechapel brothels, which also doubled up as illegal drinking haunts? Maybe it was their liking of women which drew Steinie and Beron together, maybe it was something else.

The Jews, together with the Cockneys and the Irish, played an important part in the East End underworld. The age-old Jewish stereotype of inborn shrewdness did not save many thousands of them from the miserable conditions of the squalid dives and makeshift sweat-shops. The Jews were more 'sweated' than 'sweaters', and those desperate conditions were a breeding ground for delinquency, petty crime and prostitution. The East European Jews, like other groups of poor immigrants, also gained a toehold in the second-hand market. The whole second-hand trading business was permeated with stolen goods; Jews did not have a monopoly in crime, in receiving stolen goods, but they did their fair share.

Ruby Michaels was known to be the biggest buyer of stolen jewellery in the East End, and had several front men, one of whom Leon Beron was reputed to be. Beron may have appeared to be doing nothing when he sat for hours in the Warsaw. In fact he was making himself available for business. He earned ten shillings a week from rents from his properties. He made the rest of his money as a fence, a receiver of stolen goods. Screwsmen – burglars – and whizzers – pickpockets – would take their wares to him at the Warsaw. His tariff was well known. For gold chains he would pay 27s 6d an ounce for 9-carat gold; 56 shillings for 18 carat; and about £4 for 22 carat. He might take big hauls on to someone like Michaels.

Steinie Morrison was undoubtedly an established screwsman. When he was arrested he told police he was a trader in cheap jewellery. He may well have started acting as a small-time fence himself, or as a middle man between gangs and a possible fence. As fences go Beron was not large fry, however he was successful in one respect. After sixteen years in London, he had never been caught. It was rumoured that it was because he had made a deal, that Leon Baron was a police informer. Certainly he was well-known to the police, despite his clean record. So plenty of people may have had a grudge against the Landlord – the whizzers and screwsmen he had short changed; people on whom he had informed. Steinie Morrison claimed there had been two previous attempts on Beron's life. On the last occasion he had been struck down with a spanner by two Frenchmen.

Was the motive for Beron's murder robbery, or was it revenge? Beron was reputed to have informed on Gardstein and his gang after the Houndsditch shootings. Certainly there were links. Gardstein and his fellow anarchists had been introduced at the Warsaw and the Jewish café in Sclater Street when they first arrived in London. They were frequent customers at the Warsaw. They were also regular visitors to the Anarchists Club in Jubilee Street just down the road from Beron's lodgings. Did Beron give away the whereabouts of the injured

Gardstein and the others to police in the days just before his death? Did they believe he had tipped the police off about the Houndsditch job?

After Leon was bludgeoned to death with an iron bar near some railings on Clapham Common, he was dragged by his astrakhan collar into a clump of bushes, where the killer – or killers – laid out the corpse. Leaves and grass were gathered to make a sort of pillow. His head was covered with a red and black silk handkerchief which was arranged like a shroud. Finally and most sinisterly of all the killer signed Leon's face carving two letter 'S's on his cheeks with a knife. The Chief Superintendent of Brixton Police Station noted in his official report that: 'The crime seems to be the work of a lunatic'. The pathologist who examined the body remarked, 'I thought it was extraordinary that anyone should have stopped to inflict such wounds.'

However it was well known in Whitechapel circles that, in countries East of the Elbe, treatment of that sort was often meted out to traitors. 'S' could stand for either the Russian or the Polish for false spy. The police were later to downplay the significance of the marks, even going as far as to state that they were not S-shapes, but merely random cuts. Their backtracking came after increased speculation that the murder was a revenge killing, a theory which did not accord with their case.

Their case was that the perfectly sane, ordinary criminal, Steinie Morrison had lured Beron to the Common and murdered him for his money. He was positively identified by three cab drivers who had worked the route taken by the murderer and the victim on the night of the crime.

Now it is possible that these identifications were suspect; one of them might have seen Steinie's picture in the *Evening News* – apparently a copy was left open in the interview room at Brixton police station. And we also know that the police posted reward notices all along the route, offering cab drivers the equivalent of one cold winter night's pay in exchange for information.

The evidence against Steinie Morrison was circumstantial, however there was a lot of it. Beron had been robbed, and the day after the murder Steinie was flush with cash. He met one of his girlfriends, an eighteen-year-old Jewish tailoress called Eva Flitterman. He changed a cheque given to Eva's brother for eight half sovereigns. He showed Eva some banknotes, which she had never seen before; and then he gave her two gold sovereigns to buy an outfit. Eva Flitterman was to later tell police that Steinie was wearing a gold watch on a chain, with a coin on it. Was it Beron's famous watch – or was it the cheaper version Steinie was known to have bought himself a few weeks before?

After the murder Steinie moved out of his Newark Street lodgings and stopped eating in the Warsaw restaurant. Joe Mintz told police the parcel he had handled of Steinie's on New Year's Eve was too heavy to be a flute and felt more like an iron bar – however Mintz was no friend of Steinie's. He had handed it back to Morrison before he and Beron left together. It was Hermelin and the other Warsaw regulars who put the police on to the Australian.

The anarchist outrage that Christmas gave rise to a fear among more orthodox foreign political groups and their British supporters that the incidents would be used to tighten up Britain's immigration policy, and to restrict the right of asylum. Britain was the only country where political refugees really enjoyed the right of asylum, where they did not live with the constant threat of expulsion hanging over their heads as in France, Belgium or Switzerland.

Some of the national newspapers whipped up the outrage, and started to agitate against the anarchists, against political refugees and against aliens generally. The *Daily Mail* wrote: 'Even the most sentimental will feel the time has come to stop the abuse of this country's hospitality by the foreign malefactors.'

The East End had always been a dangerous, violent and lawless place, but while East End criminals – whether local or foreign – killing each other was one thing, the murder of policemen was quite another. The case of the strangely mutilated corpse on Clapham Common added to the general public hysteria – something had to be done. The arrest of the anarchists; the successful resolution of the Sidney Street siege; and the arrest of Steinie Morrison were greeted with a collective sigh of relief from the British public.

Steinie was in a sense the ideal accused – a foreigner, a Jew and worse still he was well dressed and well spoken – too big for his fancy boots. The prosecution were unable to make a conclusive case against Morrison, being hamstrung by witnesses retracting their statements; they made great play of his former employment in Clapham; and his sudden move from his lodgings. Steinie had a simple explanation for that; he had met a young woman called Florrie on New Year's Day and moved in with her that night. He had already proposed to one woman by then and would propose to another before the week was out.

However the prosecution were able to undermine Steinie's alibi; and he was reluctant to account for his sudden change in financial fortunes so soon after Beron's death.

However Morrison's greatest misfortune was the state of public opinion – mirrored no doubt by the gentlemen of the jury. They were unlikely to be sympathetic. In the dock the tall striking Steinie spoke violently, and they heard he had just come out of prison; and, of course, he was a foreigner. He looked a desperate man – the sort of desperate man they had had to call the army out to deal with in Sidney Street.

Despite a summing-up by the judge Mr Justice Darling which indicated strongly that he considered the case against Steinie Morrison 'not proven', the jury returned a guilty verdict. Just before the death sentence was passed, Steinie accounted for his sudden, unexplained wealth. He confessed to a massive cheque fraud which had netted him £300.

So – if Beron's murder was motivated by money, as the police maintained it was, then Steinie had no motive, if the cheque fraud story was true. He told his lawyer that he did not want to admit to the fraud in court, because he thought he was going to be acquitted, and did not want to implicate himself in any more trouble by confessing. There was evidence enough to back Steinie's claim. When it was brought to light, the Home Secretary Winston Churchill commuted the death sentence to one of life imprisonment, although the authorities did not take this as indicating Morrison's innocence. However if Steinie Morrison did not do it, who did?

Most of the anarchist gang had been rounded up but police had offered a £500 reward for the remaining gang members. Then two nights after Beron's murder, the police were tipped off that two anarchists were hiding in a house at 100 Sidney Street. A thousand policemen surrounded the housc. This was no ordinary policing operation, this was war. Two squads of Scots Guards, dressed in greatcoats and armed with the new short Lee-Enfield rifles reinforced the police. Loud cheering greeted their arrival in Sidney Street. The Winston Churchill himself arrived on the scene. Two anarchists held out in a gun battle lasting more than six hours. They kept firing even after the house caught fire. There were huge crowds of spectators, some of whom climbed on to the roof of the Rising Sun pub opposite (the landlord is reputed to have charged a sovereign!).

The sightseers cheered when the house caught fire. The fire brigade arrived, but were turned back by Churchill. He thought it better to let the anarchists burn to death than risk good British lives. By the end of the siege, Joseph Sokoloff, aged twenty-seven, had been shot; Fritz Svaars had been suffocated by smoke. The police outside discussed the Beron murder. Five days later Steinie was arrested. Nine weeks later he was condemned to death. The public hysteria abated and life returned to normal, for most people.

However Steinie Morrison refused to take his punishment, now life imprisonment, quietly. 75,000 signatures were gathered for the petition for clemency; Steinie had refused to sign his own petition. He wanted to be freed, or hanged. He was not a model prisoner. He was restless, violent and raged about his innocence. He was tireless in his efforts to get the case reopened. He claimed Beron had been involved with the anarchists and had lent the gang £50 to buy equipment for the robbery.

Evidence came from all over the world. Some East End emigrées told the Australian police that one of the anarchists had admitted that the gang murdered Beron because he had informed upon them. The SS carved on his face were indeed traitor's marks.

A surprising number of people involved in the case came to be certified insane. Two of the crown's main witnesses had later to be committed to the lunatic asylum, as did Solomon Beron, the brother of the victim, and the waiter Joe Mintz. After the trial, Becky had contradicted Mintz saying Steinie's parcel had been lighter than a soda bottle.

But the authorities dismissed all the fresh evidence. Just as they had dismissed their first suspect, Leon's brother Solomon, who, incidentally, had once been charged with threatening to murder his sister and her husband in France. And if Solomon was involved, it would explain one of the central mysteries of the case, why Leon should allow himself to have been led from the safety of the East End to the relative danger of Clapham, for the Berons' elderly father lodged within four hundred yards of Clapham Common.

At Morrison's trial, Solomon burst into paroxysms of rage when he thought that the case for the defence was going well. During the closing speech to the jury by Steinie's barrister Mr Abinger he lost control. He crept from the back of the court and shouted, 'When are you going to stop?'; he then swung a punch at the barrister and was dragged away shrieking, 'He's going to get him off. He's going to get him off.' Was this a display of brotherly grief – or was it the fear that if Morrison were indeed acquitted, the finger of suspicion might again be pointed at Solomon himself?

Why was it that when Leon failed to appear for daily prayers on New Year's Day, Solomon immediately claimed that his brother had been murdered? Is it also a coincidence that the most damning witnesses in the case were friends of Solomon? It is suggested that he forced some witnesses to give false evidence about seeing Beron and Steinie together. One man withdrew his statement and did not give evidence at the Old Bailey. Another of Solomon's friends was one of the three cab drivers who did so much to damage Steinie's case. Andrew Stephens lodged in the same house as Solomon. He was the cab driver who changed his story – particularly the time that he picked up the man he later identified as Morrison – to fit neatly with the other two cab drivers. He also saw a photograph of Steinie before he identified him as his fare. Solomon Beron was carried from the Old Bailey and driven straight to Colney Hatch insane asylum, from which he never returned. This was not considered sufficient to reopen Morrison's case.

After ten years in jail, Steinie went on hunger strike. Some accounts say he starved himself to death, others that he was accidentally strangled by a prison warder whilst being force fed. His death certificate states that he died from heart disease aggravated by voluntary abstention from food. What is certain is that Steinie despaired of ever being released from prison and preferred death to incarceration.

The story in the East End underworld at the time was that Leon Beron was murdered because he was a police informer who had helped them make their arrests after the Houndsditch murders. The man who was arrested for the murder – Steinie Morrison – had acted unwittingly as a decoy, but he had neither taken part in the execution nor known it was to take place.

The Houndsditch gang were also burglars, calling themselves the 'Expropriation Committee' and needed fences to buy their stolen property. Morrison is believed to have been the go-between between the gang and the fence, in this case Leon Beron, working on commission. Morrison was told that the gang had a large haul of stolen jewellery to dispose of, but that it was highly dangerous to do business in the usual place, because of all the police activity; so Clapham Common was chosen as the meeting place, because Morrison was acquainted with the place having lived there. Morrison met Baron in the Warsaw restaurant on New Year's Eve at about 6.00 p.m. and told him of the deal. From then on he did not allow Beron to leave his sight, in case he should inform the police of the meeting place; these precautions were standard when a would-be fence was told of a meeting place.

The two men left the Warsaw and travelled to the meeting place at Clapham Common. When they arrived at the meeting place, Morrison left Beron with his soon-to-be-executioners, not knowing the fate that awaited him. The next morning he heard the news and is reputed to have said, 'so that's what they got me to "lumber him for".'

On the day Churchill commuted the death sentence, an Englishwoman living in Paris overheard a conversation between two foreigners on a tramcar. One of the men said the Clapham Common murder had been committed not by Morrison but by Gort or Cort, but it was better for Morrison to suffer than for their comrade to run the risk of detection. The French authorities could not find or identify the men or Gort, but they did identify some of the names mentioned in the overheard conversation as members of an international gang well known to the police – and they sent a report to the British police.

Morrison, it was also claimed, was framed by a man only known as X. Mrs X came forward after the trial and told Morrison's solicitor that her husband had gone out at 11.00 p.m. on the night of the murder and had not returned for three days. He then burned his blood-stained shirt in the fire and threatened to kill his wife if she said anything. He was very agitated when he heard of Morrison's arrest and said, 'There's nothing like a Jewboy for keeping his mouth shut.'

Mrs X had told the authorities that Morrison had brought Beron to see X shortly before the murder and he had also been with her husband on the night of the murder. So were X and Morrison accomplices in the murder, or did the mysterious X set Morrison up? Was X the man Gort, identified in the overheard Paris tramcar conversation as the real murderer?

These are all theories, theories that the Home Office chose not to investigate. The authorities still continued to believe that Steinie Morrison was guilty, if not of committing the actual act of murder, then at least of luring Leon to Clapham Common where an accomplice lay in wait.

The case of the Uncommon Murder has fascinated crime writers and investigators to this day; and many who have studied the case remain convinced that Steinie Morrison was innocent, his only crime being to have been in the wrong place when a scapegoat was needed.

10: Laugh, Baby, Laugh

Lesley Stevenson

Most of us have skeletons in our cupboards. For some, the bare bones of history are too gruesome to confront. Others dare not open the cupboard door for fear the deeds of their ancestors may cast a shadow over their own lives. To call up the ghost of Elvira Barney, to unlock the cupboard door may be to tempt fate. The bad luck which plagued Elvira may be standing by to seize its next family victim. Elvira believed in such things. She called it her 'hoodoo' and felt she was somehow fated to be unhappy. Did the 'hoodo' die with her?

At around 6.00 p.m. on Monday, 30 May 1932, brightly coloured sports cars began pulling-up outside the home of Elvira Barney. Elvira was twenty-six years old, but over-indulgence in drink, drugs and goodtime had put years on her. A bloated woman, looking well into her forties, greeted her cocktail-party guests.

For the next three hours neighbours watched the visitors, with loud cars and louder voices, come and go along Williams Mews, Knightsbridge, in the heart of London. At that time it was an undistinguished address. The houses were former stables and were mainly occupied by chauffeurs and their wives and children.

Elvira Barney lived at 21, Williams Mews. Her rich father, Sir John Mullens, had bought her the house when her marriage to an American singer ended in separation after two years of cruelty and humiliation.

Elvira and her younger lover, Michael Stephen, tended to the thirty or so guests who had filled the small downstairs living room at No. 21. Elvira passed round the caviar sandwiches and 'Mickey' saw to the drinks, leaving the hired hand with little to do but wash up.

Like his friends, Mickey devoted his life to the pursuit of pleasures which would bring about their early deaths. He was a delicate creature. And, like Elvira, was probably bisexual; both of them loved to live life dangerously.

Mickey served gin and whisky from behind a gargantuan cocktail bar. It was a fashionable piece of furniture, but took up most of the room and left little space for the gramophone and seating. On the wall hung a large picture. Was it modern art or pornography? – it depended on the observer.

Many of the guests were relics of the twenties' 'Bright Young Things'; actors, musicians, artists, men and women of independent means. Whilst three million people were out of work, and much of the country was ravaged by the effects of the Great Depression, these sons and daughters of the rich upper class partied, boozed and made love, with reckless abandon.

Amongst the guests was their rich American friend Arthur Jeffress. Jeffress devoted his life to his art collection and his homosexuality. He also gave his fair share of parties, always on a far grander scale than the relatively sedate shindigs Elvira threw each month.

It was after nine before the partygoers left 21, Williams Mews. They headed off in twos and threes to London's West End theatres, clubs and restaurants.

Elvira, Mickey and Arthur Jeffress sped off in Elvira's Delage sports car to the Café de Paris, near Piccadilly Circus, after closing the door on thirty dirty glasses, three empty gin bottles, two empty vermouth bottles, four empty soda siphons, a cocktail shaker waiting to be washed, and maybe one or two drunken guests. The party was voted a success. Nearly half of London would later claim to have been there.

As the cars and voices disappeared down the street and into the city, the residents of Williams Mews settled down to a peaceful night. All was quiet at No. 21 – for the moment.

One or two residents would hear Elvira and her young lover return from their night on the town. At around 2.00 a.m. they would awake on hearing the vague sounds of a cab creeping into the street and fall back to sleep when the familiar engine noise became a distant purr. Some residents would hear the young lover and his mistress arguing two hours later. They would even hear the shot that signalled the death of one of them. Still the street slept or put the kettle on.

Those residents who slept through it all would wake up to the news that their strange neighbour, the woman at No. 21, had become a murderess overnight – or at least the obvious suspect.

Elvira, Mickey and Jeffress arrived at the Café de Paris on Coventry Street at about ten o'clock, still raving about the successful soirée. The head waiter served Elvira sweetbreads and Welsh rabbit. Mickey and Jeffress ordered quail. All three drank champagne.

It was around 11.30 p.m. when they took a taxi to Soho, to the Blue Angel Club at 52, Dean Street. Jeffress, a club member, signed in his two friends. Considering the amount of alcohol they had consumed that evening, all three appeared quite sober. The threesome were still going strong after midnight when they ordered yet another double whisky each to wash down three pairs of kippers.

Elvira wandered from table to table talking to friends, some of whom had been guests at her party earlier. They included the club's piano player Hugh Wade. Hugh loved camping it up. He was notorious for his over-the-top make-up. But, women adored this twenty-four-year-old charmer.

Later on in the evening of Monday, 30 May 1932, Hugh was doing his regular stint at the Blue Angel Club, when Elvira came over to talk to him as he played the piano. She asked how he had enjoyed the party at Williams Mews. 'It has my vote,' he declared. Hugh Wade claimed she seemed sober and untroubled on leaving the club at around 12.30 p.m.

Elvira's life had not been trouble-free. Her parents, Sir John and Lady Mullens, were extremely wealthy. They owned a house in Belgrave Square, one of the most luxurious homes in London where they held lavish parties. At one infamous party guests ate dinner round an ornate fish pond complete with fountain. The family also had a manor house in Surrey.

The Mullens had earned their wealth, it was new money. Therefore, the family were never quite accepted into high society. As Barbara Cartland said: 'They were just very rich.' Sir John Mullens had been the Government broker during the war years. A trustee of the Stock Exchange, he was knighted after earning the country a great deal of money through canny investments. There were three children: Cyril, the eldest, died during the First World War; and Avril, Elvira's attractive younger sister, who outshone Elvira in everything she did and helped the family's standing in society when she married a Russian prince at the age of sixteen.

Things might have turned out quite differently if Elvira had married her first beau. The *Tatler* of 23 August 1932 announced the engagement of Elvira Mullens to Andrew Wilson. Elvira was seventeen at the time. Her elfin face peers out of the pages of the magazine. Nothing more is known of her intended or reasons for the break-up, but the couple never married.

As a teenager Elvira tried her hand at acting. She received dramatic training at Lady Benson's School of Acting, but her career never really took off. In 1925, aged nineteen, she appeared in a musical comedy under her stage name of Delores Ashley. The following year she performed in *The Blue Kitten* at the Gaiety Theatre. That was it – she started and ended her career on the stage as a chorus girl.

At the age of twenty-two Elvira married an American singer five years older than herself. John Sterling Barney performed with his group, the 'Three New Yorkers', at the Café de Paris. But it was while performing at the Mullens' home that he met Elvira. 'I was singing Russian songs and we seemed attracted to each other at once,' he told newspaper reporters on announcing their engagement.

Compared to her sister's wedding, which was a social event, involving two grand church services, Elvira's was a small affair at Princes Row Registry Office on Buckingham Palace Road. The marriage took place on 2 August 1928.

When her sister Avril had married Prince George Imeretinsky three years earlier, her parents had been generous. They bought her a flat in Park Lane, gave her a yearly allowance of £4,000 and a coronet of 'exquisite' pearls. As far as we know Elvira received no cash, property or jewellery. Perhaps her parents disapproved of her marriage to the apparently penniless performer. Neither marriage lasted long however. Avril stayed with her prince for seven years, Elvira with her pauper for less than a year.

According to Elvira, her husband physically abused

her, showed her little love and was eaten with jealousy. One of Elvira's closest friends, John Barney, claimed her husband delighted in crushing lighted cigarettes on her bare skin. Although the couple separated early on the marriage, Elvira was unable to secure a divorce until 1933.

Elvira and Mickey returned to Williams Mews at around two in the morning. By all accounts they had not spoken a cross word to each other all evening. Michael had been a most attentive escort, and Elvira had enjoyed being with her Bohemian friends. Shortly after getting home on that fateful day, Tuesday, 31 May 1932, the couple went to bed in the main bedroom above the lounge overlooking the Mews. They made love.

Elvira claimed Mickey was unhappy with her response to his lovemaking. A violent row ensued which raged on for two hours or more, only ending when one of them was dead.

Mickey – his real name was Thomas William Scott Stephen – was a handsome wastrel with not a penny to his name. He had spent most of his life sponging off women. Elvira was happy to indulge him. But she was not prepared to fund his gambling, particularly when he pursued his new found habit with another woman.

Mickey's father was a banker in the City. The family home was in Kent, although the family house 'Doubleton' no longer exists. Mickey, his older brother Francis and their younger brother Harbon, were all educated at Shrewsbury Public School. And, as is often the way with middle children, Mickey sought an identity outside the family and was dubbed the black sheep.

He worked as a dress designer in Paris and London's West End theatres. But, unable or unwilling to find suitable employment at home or abroad, he turned to his friends for an irregular income. They were generous, particularly the women.

Elvira and Michael had first met in Paris some years previously. Without notice, Mickey turned up on the doorstep of No. 21, Williams Mews, in the autumn of 1931. From that time on Elvira supported him 'almost entirely'.

For some reason or other Mickey's father had cut off his allowance. His mother occasionally gave him the odd sum of money, but not enough to satisfy his hedonistic lifestyle. Mickey's father strongly disapproved of his relationship with Elvira Barney, who was after all a married woman. The couple claimed they wanted to marry as soon as Elvira's divorce came through. Parental pleasure at such a prospect was non-existent. Whether Elvira and Mickey truly intended to marry, or wanted to give Mickey's father the impression that his wayward son had settled down to a respectable life and was now worthy of an allowance, is not known.

Theirs was a tempestuous relationship. It was a source of joy and of misery for both of them. Elvira claimed she was devoted to Michael. Their friends believed them to be in love. But a violent streak underpinned the affair. It was this that excited them and compelled them to stay together. They argued passionately and made up passionately as their letters reveal. This is one from Mickey to Elvira:

> Baby, little Fatable,
>
> Forgive me all the dreadful, horrible things I've done, baby. I promise to be better and kinder, so's you won't be frightened any more.
>
> I love you, only you, in all the world, little One's

Elvira wrote in a similar vein:

My Darling Baby,

You hand me the biggest thrills I've ever had, my sweet, and all I hope is we can go on being thrilled endlessly. I adore it when you are sweet and kind to me as I haven't had a lot of affection in my life. So you see it means a great deal and I feel like suicide when you get angry.

All my love, really all, Elvira.

Elvira had frequently threatened to kill herself. She had the means to; she kept a .32 Smith and Weston revolver illegally in a recess behind her bed. She had had the gun for nine years and had first used it to shoot rabbits on a friend's estate in Devon. The shootings took place at night; dazzled by the light from car headlamps, the rabbits were gunned down. Mickey knew about the gun. But, on the fateful date of 31 May 1932 it does not appear to have been in its usual place.

A chauffeur's wife, Dorothy Hall, lived just across the street from Elvira, at No. 10, Williams Mews. She had been kept awake all night by her baby's cries. At around four in the morning she heard a din at No. 21. She went to the window to see what was going on and noticed a light on in the upstairs room. At No. 18a, William Kiff, a chauffeur, was awakened by high-pitched screaming coming from No. 21. He too looked out of the window, but could see nothing out of the ordinary. Deciding that there was little point in going back to bed again he made a cup of tea for himself and his wife.

The quarrel over the other woman began quietly enough. By four-thirty in the morning it had reached fever pitch. Elvira was screaming hysterically. 'Get out of my house at once. I hate you. Get out. I'll shoot you.'

Police had been called to No. 21 a number of times to deal with disturbances, though the neighbours rarely called them, despite having good reason to. It was usually Elvira who summoned the police to sort out her domestic difficulties. She even kept the phone number of the local police station on a piece of paper next to the phone in her bedroom.

To Elvira, police officers were her social inferiors. The same 'bloody swine' she called to her house to get rid of unwanted visitors were expected to turn a blind eye when they saw her driving recklessly through the streets of London.

Just two weeks before the fatal shooting at No. 21 all hell seemed to break loose at Williams Mews. In the early hours of the morning a taxi pulled up outside Elvira's house. Michael got out and started shouting for Elvira. He was asking for money. Elvira appeared at an upstairs window, and yelled, 'Clear off or I'll send for the police.'

Michael needed the money to pay the taxi driver.

'Let me have some money, Vera.'

'Go fish for the money,' she said before closing the window.

Twenty minutes later Michael returned to the house. Elvira refused to let him in. She stood at the window. She was naked and was pointing a gun straight into the mews.

Michael walked across the street for protection.

'Laugh, baby, laugh for the last time!' shouted Elvira, then fired the gun. As she did so she fell backwards into the room. She claimed she wanted to make out that she had killed herself. Michael feared this was her intention. He was standing directly underneath Mrs Hall's front window when the shot was fired.

He looked up at Mrs Hall, who was looking out of the window, and apologised for his friend's behaviour. He said he feared she might kill herself if he left her alone too long. Mrs Hall had no such fears. She could see Elvira peering over the window-sill.

Mrs Hall, presuming to know her neighbour better than her friends did, said, 'She'll never do that; she is too wicked.'

Michael tried one more time to get Elvira to open the door to him. He rang the doorbell but got no reply. Mrs Hall watched him walk to the end of the road and get into a grocer's van, where he spent most of the night.

The following day Elvira and Michael emerged from No. 21. They had made up. The troubles of the night before were forgotten. But a few days later Michael was sporting a black eye.

Perhaps Elvira had been affected by the death of her brother, or constant comparisons with her successful and socially acceptable sister had embittered her. Or, maybe at seventeen she was heartbroken when her fiancé jilted her? But a model child had grown into a spoilt little rich girl with a vile temper and sharp tongue. Taxi drivers and police officers were frequent victims of her verbal abuse.

Had Michael grown tired of her vicious attacks? Had he found another woman? Was he planning to leave Elvira? Michael had recently found lodgings and no longer needed to rely on Elvira's hospitality, although he still relied on her money. He had started playing bridge for money and his partner was a married woman known as Peggy. Elvira was madly jealous, although she may not have had cause to be. Peggy claimed that her relationship with Michael was purely platonic and he had never spoken of leaving Elvira for her. She believed that Elvira and Michael were equally fond of each other.

The shot was heard at around 4.30 a.m. Elvira claimed she had intended to kill herself, that Michael had jumped out of bed, grabbed the .32 Smith and

Wesson from under a cushion on a chair by the bed. 'Well, you won't do it with this,' he had shouted as he ran towards the spare room.

Elvira raced after him. A fierce struggle for possession of the revolver took place on the landing. Suddenly, the gun went off. Michael looked at Elvira in astonishment, then went into the bathroom. Moments later he came out and suggested to Elvira that she call a doctor. This is the version of events Elvira stuck to from the time the police arrived to her appearance in court.

Dorothy Hall heard Elvira shouting at Michael to get out. She claimed she heard Elvira screaming, 'I'll shoot you, I'll shoot you.' When Michael said he was going Mrs Hall heard the gun-shot.

'Good God, what have you done?' she heard Michael say.

Michael was dead within ten minutes. The bullet had shot through his light grey cashmere overcoat, yellow woollen jumper and shirt, before piercing his left lung.

Elvira rang the doctor, but got no reply. She claimed Michael was going to tell the doctor that it had been an accident and she was not to blame. She then rang her friend, Terence Skeffington-Smyth. She demanded that he came at once as something terrible had happened. She did not say what. But, Skeffington-Smyth had heard it all before. Elvira had often called him in the middle of the night asking him to come over urgently. He knew Michael and she fought ferociously and then quickly made up. He explained to her that it was impossible for him to come.

She tried the doctor again. This time she managed to get through.

Dr Thomas Durrant was Elvira's own GP. He had last seen his patient about a year previously when he treated her for concussion after a car smash.

'Oh, thank God! Come at once, come at once! Jump into a taxi – there's been a terrible accident. A gentleman has shot himself!' Elvira shouted down the phone. By this time Michael's body was propped up on the landing with pillows from the bed. Blood was seeping through his clothes.

Elvira was beside herself. The doctor seemed to be taking an age to get there. She rang him again. This time his wife answered and said the doctor was on his way. It was 5.14 a.m. before the doctor arrived. Michael had been dead for almost an hour.

'I was so unhappy I wanted to kill myself. I told him I would kill myself if he left me,' Elvira told the police when they arrived. 'We were struggling, then I don't know what happened.'

Elvira paced the room smoking a cigarette and wearing a translucent dressing-gown which revealed the outline of her underwear as she told police what had happened. She was incoherent. The police officers tried to make sense of her hysterical outpourings.

It was decided that she should be taken to Gerald Road police station where a statement could be taken. She refused to put on the fur coat that lay on the settee in the lounge. She wanted another one to be fetched from her bedroom.

Detective Inspector Clarence Campion boldly suggested the fur one might be warmer for her down at the station.

His colleague Inspector William Winter noted: 'At this suggestion Mrs Barney flew into a paroxysm of rage and struck Inspector Campion a violent blow on the right side of his face with her fist, at the same time saying, "I'll teach you to tell me you'll put me in a cell, you vile swine."'

Just as they were setting off for the station, Lady

Mullens rang. Realising who was on the phone Elvira grabbed the receiver: 'Mummy, mummy, come round quickly, they are going to take me away, don't let them do it, don't let them do it.'

Elvira then turned to the police and said, 'Now you know who my mother is you'll be a little more careful in what you say and do to me. I'll teach you to say you will take me to a police station.'

Did her class and family influence wield any favour? Well, Elvira did go down to the police station. But, incredibly, after making her statement she was allowed to leave. She was given her liberty unconditionally.

Here was a woman whose lover had been shot at point-blank range in her presence and with no other suspects; a woman who had assaulted a police officer; a woman who kept an illegal firearm in her bedroom for fun as much as fear; and yet she left the police station without a charge to her name.

But, freedom is not so easily won, even for the likes of Elvira. Further investigations uncovered evidence that could not be ignored, and Elvira was charged with murder three days later.

The trial of Elvira Barney opened at the Old Bailey on 4 July 1932. Queues formed overnight for seats in the spectators' gallery; hundreds lined the streets for a glimpse of the poor little rich girl as she arrived at court in her father's chauffeur-driven limousine.

A pitiful figure stood in the dock. Elvira was dressed in a black coat, and a tight-fitting black cap with white rosettes, under which she seemed to be trying to conceal her fair curly hair. In her hands were a bottle of smelling salts and a handkerchief. Each day of her trial she was so overcome with emotion that she fainted.

There was no trace of the arrogant woman who could slap a person down to size with a turn of her head. A woman who could stab you with one word and leave you to mop up the wound.

'Swine!' The police officers laughed at the vulgarity of a woman of such social standing. But they were hurt, hurt because they did not know how to behave. How should they proceed with a daughter of titled parents?

New evidence uncovered against Elvira meant the police did not have to sidestep the issue for long. As far as rank and file police officers were concerned, Elvira was a condemned woman.

Elvira was taken to Holloway prison at the end of her first day in court. She was treated the same as other prisoners on remand, except she was allowed to use her own cutlery.

In fact, Elvira refused the privilege, granted to all prisoners at that time, of ordering food from a restaurant outside the jail. The medical officer at the prison reported that she had bruises on her arm, scratches and abrasions on the fingers of her left hand and a large bruise on her right thigh. In court, the medical officer claimed the bruises were consistent with a violent struggle.

The eminent pathologist, Sir Bernard Spilsbury, did not accept that there had been a tussle. When he came to examine the fatal wound he severely challenged Elvira's account of what had happened.

The gun had been fired three to six inches from Michael's body in a horizontal direction, therefore, the pathologist argued, it would have been quite impossible for the wound to have been self-inflicted.

In court Sir Bernard Spilsbury demonstrated how holding a gun by the butt in the direction of Michael's wound with his wrist bent at a most awkward angle, there was no way anyone would have enough power in the trigger finger to discharge the pistol at all. Sir

Bernard went so far as to say that Michael could not have been holding the gun at all when the trigger was pulled.

If Michael had been holding the gun by the barrel when it went off there would have been blackening and scorching of his hand, wrist and probably his clothing, Sir Bernard argued. There was none. Elvira's account of the struggle received a further blow when the evidence of the famous gunsmith Robert Churchill was given in court. Churchill said that the gun had a fourteen-pound trigger pull. He considered it one of the safest revolvers made. 'It would be virtually impossible to pull the trigger when the revolver was pointed at one's left lapel, particularly if the gun had been fired from a distance of three to six inches,' he said. With such damning evidence from such esteemed experts, Elvira looked set to swing.

There was only one man who could save her. Call Mrs Barney's defending counsel. Call the most brilliant criminal lawyer of his generation. Call Sir Patrick Hastings.

Sir Patrick was in his early fifties and at the peak of his career as King's Counsel when he defended Elvira Barney at Court Number One at the Old Bailey in 1932.

'If anyone will get her off, Hastings will,' thought the judge on hearing Hastings had agreed to take the case. Hastings had taken the case reluctantly. He had always avoided taking part in murder trials. It was his wife who persuaded him. Sir Patrick's two daughters had had the same governess as Elvira. The governess praised Elvira to the hilt for her good behaviour.

'Dear Elvira,' she would often say, would never do this or that. Sir Patrick's wife felt sorry for 'dear Elvira'. She pleaded with her husband to defend her. It is said that Elvira's father, Sir John Mullens, got down on his knees and offered Sir Patrick a blank cheque if he took the case. Hastings caved in, but he knew he would have his work cut out to achieve an acquittal.

When he reached the courtroom, Hastings was appalled at the behaviour of those who had come to watch the trial. London's smart set had fought to gain entry to the court. Some had even sought Hastings' aid obtain tickets for the trial. Counsel for the defence nervously rolled his gold pencil between his thin fingers, looked at the packed courthouse, glanced at the dome of the court, then got down to business.

HASTINGS: And then what did you hear?

Chauffeur's wife Dorothy Hall had given a statement to the police and was now promising to tell the whole truth and nothing but the truth.

HALL; I heard a struggle and Mrs Barney shouting, 'I'll shoot!'

HASTINGS: 'I'll shoot?'

'I'll shoot,' was entirely compatible with Elvira's story that she was trying to kill herself. Mrs Hall had told police she had heard Elvira shout, 'I'll shoot you.'

'I'll shoot YOU, I'll shoot YOU,' the prosecution willed her to say. But she did not. In her enthusiasm, Mrs Hall, was on a course to destroy the Crown's most damaging evidence – her own testimony.

Sir Patrick then began questioning Mrs Hall about a previous shooting in the Mews. An inch-by-inch search of Elvira's house had uncovered a second bullet, embedded in her wardrobe after apparently ricocheting off a wall. This still had to be accounted for. One shot may be an accident, two is no mistake. But when was this shot fired?

Mrs Hall told the court that she had seen Elvira in the early hours of Tuesday the nineteenth of May 1932, lean out of the upstairs window, aim a small revolver at

Michael, then fire. Elvira definitely held the gun in her left hand, said Mrs Hall.

When Elvira came to give evidence she fiercely denied shooting out of the window at Michael. But she did admit firing at random into her bedroom that Tuesday morning, in the hope that Michael would think she had shot herself.

If Elvira was telling the truth, the second bullet was accounted for; her story of accidental death began to look considerably more plausible. But Sir Patrick needed to discredit Mrs Hall's evidence completely if there was any chance of the jury believing Elvira's version of events.

A gun was placed in front of Elvira as she stood in the dock giving evidence. The court fell silent. Sir Patrick walked away from the dock towards the back of the court. Suddenly, he turned around. 'Pick up the gun!' he boomed.

Elvira immediately picked up the gun with her *right* hand.

Mrs Hall's evidence was now shot through completely.

For a man who despised courtroom drama, Sir Patrick seemed to be enjoying playing centre stage. But he still had the evidence of the experts to dispel. The gunsmith, Robert Churchill, and the Home Office pathologist, Sir Bernard Spilsbury, had both described how difficult the gun was to fire.

Sir Patrick picked up the gun and pointed it at the ceiling. He reminded the court that they had been told by experts that the gun was one of the safest on the market, that it needed a great deal of strength to pull the trigger. And, well, there was no way it could go off accidentally. He then proceeded to pull the trigger rapidly and easily over and over again.

It seemed easy. But the word around town was that Sir Patrick's thumb and finger were bruised for weeks afterwards. He had made his point, however. It was not impossible for the gun to go off accidentally.

The jury were bowled over by Sir Patrick's performance. Elvira was found not guilty of murder. Not guilty of manslaughter. She was later fined £50 for possession of a firearm.

The judge, Sir Travers Humphries, told the court that they had heard a story of two rather useless lives bound by passionate devotion and a sort of rather hysterical intimacy and affection.

A newspaper described the scene at the end of the trial: 'Ascot-gowned women left in a state of high glee at having been privileged to witness the sufferings and ordeal of a woman in a terrible plight.'

The day after the trial Elvira was seen speeding off in her blue and beige sports car. At a nightclub a few days later she is said to have shouted, 'I've shot one bugger and got away with it, so don't think I'll hesitate to shoot another.'

Elvira turned to her friend Barbara Graham after the trial. Barbara's real name was Gertrude Gamble. Gertrude had been a drug addict for fifteen years. Perhaps it was her ready supply of heroin that Elvira turned to. Three weeks after the acquittal, Elvira and Gertrude travelled to France.

Coincidentally, Sir Patrick Hastings was also holidaying in France. As he was travelling towards Paris, his chauffeur at the wheel of his car, he heard the blare of a horn behind him. A sports car raced by him at high speed causing him to swerve off the road. His chauffeur noticed the driver of the speeding car that had almost killed them. It was Mrs Barney.

Elvira never did thank Sir Patrick for saving her from

the gallows. During her trip to France, Elvira's car was involved in a collision with Countess Karolyi's. She was charged with causing bodily harm by imprudence. It was a charge she was found guilty of.

Elvira was enjoying her freedom in the South of France. She found Gertrude's inclination to take it easy tiresome, so she packed her off home. Gertrude felt that Elvira had not appreciated all she had done for her. 'I was a nursemaid, everything to you,' she wrote. Gertrude was also jealous of Elvira's relationships with other women.

She wrote to Lady Mullens describing how Elvira, a woman called Audrey Carton and Miss Carton's brother had all spent the night together in a filthy pension. Gertrude was lonely and penniless when she returned to Britain. A month later she jumped to her death from a hotel window. In her suicide note she blamed Elvira.

For four years after the trial Elvira continued to live a decadent life, although she lived in fear of her parents cutting off her allowance. She spent her time between Paris and London, reconciled to the fact that she'd never be really happy again.

She told a newspaper reporter that she had a feeling that her 'hoodoo' would step in again. 'I somehow feel that I'd not fated to be happy.'

On Christmas Day 1936 the body of Elvira Barney was found in a room in the Hotel Colisée, off the Champs Elysée. Elvira had spent Christmas Eve in the fashionable clubs around Montmartre. She returned to her hotel after telling her friends she felt ill. Sometime during the night she suffered a cerebral haemorrhage and died. She was still only thirty years old.

11: Shadows of Doubt

Barry Wood

It was a simple, unspoken ritual but for hundreds of years it had bound the men of County Durham to the land. At market time the boys of twelve and over would stand in line while the farmers and their wives did the hiring. Once a boy, a 'hind', was chosen, the farmer would slap a 'hiring penny' of a shilling into the palm of his hand and the agreement was sealed. The lad then had to honour it by working on the farm for six months. The average pay prior to haymaking was nineteen shillings a week. During haymaking the men would be paid the same amount but would receive a pint of beer and some bread and cheese at 4.00 in the afternoon and if they worked till after 7.00 p.m. they would earn another pint. It was into this world that Robert Hoolhouse was born in 1917. A world of rigid social division and obedience to authority that had stretched back for centuries.

He was the son of an ordinary working-class farm-labouring family and in all respects totally unremarkable. Rather simple, bespectacled and ungainly, his life revolved round a few simple pleasures such as pigeon keeping and football and he seemed content to spend his days seeking casual work on the farms around Wolviston or near the more recently built estates of Haverton Hill beside what is now the ICI complex at Billingham. Then, in January 1938 he was accused of the murder and rape of a sixty-seven-year-old woman. He was found guilty and on 26 May, seventeen weeks later, he was hanged at Durham Jail. He had celebrated his twenty-first birthday while awaiting trial.

It was a sordid though otherwise completely unremarkable case little noticed outside the immediate area. But, ever since, the case of Robert Hoolhouse has been the source of continuing unease for many people in the district. Opinions about the case have divided the local community and, for many in the village of Wolviston itself, mention of the story touches such a raw nerve that it is likely to provoke a hostile reaction from otherwise friendly folk.

For the fact is that Hoolhouse was convicted on purely circumstantial evidence and that not a single fact was ever established by the prosecution to prove beyond doubt that he was the murderer. Today, more than fifty years after the original crime, the evidence of the recently released files on the Robert Hoolhouse case at the Public Record Office show that those original concerns may well have been more than justified.

Over the years the people of Wolviston had learnt to exercise a certain amount of caution in their dealings with Mrs Margaret Dobson. The sixty-seven-year-old farmer's wife had a reputation for not suffering fools gladly or any other way and her tongue was kept sharp through constant use ticking off the boisterous young 'hinds' at High Grange Farm. And it was not just those she felt were getting above their station who felt her wrath. Her husband Henry, though hard working and liked in the village, had also come to know where he stood in the Dobson household.

But despite all this, to the people of the Co. Durham village, farmer Henry Dobson, his wife Margaret and their family were the very epitome of respectability. He was a 'gentleman farmer' of a type fast dying out in country areas and one of the main employers in a village that still had strong ties to the land. With her pince-nez glasses, Edwardian hats and dresses, his wife cut an imposing figure in the village High Street, 'like Old Queen Mary' remembers one resident.

But, for Henry Dobson, all that was to change on 19 January 1938, the day his world turned upside down.

The previous morning had seen the start of a typically busy day. At the crack of dawn he had been to a nearby market to order the delivery of some pigs. At about 3.15 p.m. he and his wife had eaten a meal during which she suddenly announced, as was her habit, that she was going out. He expected her back by 6.00 p.m. He said that the last time he saw her she was walking out of the farmyard at about 4.30, 'just as it was getting pretty dark', dressed in her outdoor clothes and carrying a lady's handbag.

After the pigs were delivered Mr Dobson busied himself around the farm then returned to the farmhouse and some reading. When his wife did not return by 6.00 p.m. he went down to the main road to meet the regular buses from West Hartlepool, which came through Wolviston. When his wife did not turn up he assumed she had gone to stay the night with their daughter in Newcastle fifty miles away.

The next morning, a Wednesday, he was out to supervise the 5.00 a.m. milking. The first of the threshers came at 6.00 a.m. and others arrived at 8.00 a.m. with none reporting having seen anything unusual on the farm track. Still apparently unconcerned at his wife's whereabouts Dobson left the farm at 9.45 a.m. to walk to the village of Wolviston. Halfway up the track to the main road, to where a gate in the hedge on the right led to a short cut across the fields he stopped – 'I cannot tell you why,' he was later to say in evidence.

It had been one of the most bitterly cold February nights in years and a thin sheet of frost covered the fields but as Dobson glanced across the farm track to his left he saw a dark object flapping some 150 yards away on the ploughed field right by the track. It was in a dip in the land he had just passed. Retracing his steps he found the body of his wife 'tucked up under the grass verge where it met the plough about two feet below the level of the track'. The sixty-seven-year-old woman had been raped and stabbed to death.

Stunned, the old man later described how he walked around the body from feet to head in his rubber boots before setting off to the village to get the police. Local beat constable John Chapman was stopped on the road by Dobson, and the two men then flagged down the local GP Dr Craven, then driving through the village. Together they drove up to the High Grange gate entrance and walked up the track to the body of Mrs Dobson. An immediate and intensive investigation was launched from Haverton Hill Police Station and many farm workers and other local men were interviewed.

Mrs Dobson's body had lain off the farm road in a furrow of the ploughed field fifty yards from the main road. A *Northern Daily Mail* report stated that: 'A surprising circumstance is that the discovery was not made earlier in the day. A postman, milkman and about a dozen men employed on the farm had passed down the lane during the morning...' The next day the police announced they wanted to interview the following person: Fairly tall, about thirty years of age, dressed in cap, short brown smock, breeches and leggings, has appearance of farm worker, local accent and gruff voice.

There were several sightings of possible suspects. The *Northern Echo* of 20 January reported that one 'Charles Adams' who worked on the farm said that while he was waiting to meet a bus from West Hartlepool he was approached by two men who had in their possession an ex-servicemen's card. They had tried to cadge a cigarette and then money but he told them he could only give them a cigarette. One of the men had a disfigurement of the face.

A chance meeting outside a newsagent's shop on the day after the murder led to the accusation that Hoolhouse was responsible for Mrs Dobson's murder. It was the evidence of three threshers, Herbert Collins, James Fulcher and Bertram Smith, who met Hoolhouse outside the Haverton Hill newsagent, which was to point the finger at him. They said that when they met Hoolhouse he was shifty, evasive and bore incriminating scratches. But their descriptions of his demeanour and appearance were totally at odds with that provided by other witnesses, and clear contradictions in their accounts of the meeting were never resolved in court.

According to Bertram Smith, owner of the threshing machine, he and his colleagues came upon Hoolhouse outside the Haverton Hill newsagents around 6.00 p.m. on the day after the murder. The billboards outside the newsagent announced: WOLVISTON WOMAN'S MURDER. All three noticed a number of scratches down the young man's cheek. They said he acted nervous and evasive. He told them the scratches were caused by his falling off his bike. He also said he had hurt his right shoulder.

Smith said he looked 'white, much different than usual and he could not hold himself together'. He told Hoolhouse that he looked as if he had had a shock to which the reply – referring to the fall – is supposed to have been: 'Yes it will be some time before I get over it.' After nodding to the 'WOLVISTON WOMAN'S MURDER' placard at the newsagent Smith commented that it was a horrible murder to which Hoolhouse gave an inaudible, mumbled, reply.

But Herbert Collins, the second of the thresher men

and the more forceful in his questioning of Hoolhouse outside the newsagent gave a slightly different account. Collins, a forty-eight-year-old former policeman who proudly stated in court that he had served twenty-six years as a police constable also noticed 'abrasions or scars' on Hoolhouse's right cheek. He was following a few steps behind Smith and came on Hoolhouse just as Smith asked him about his accident.

Collins, together with his colleague Fulcher, continued the interrogation of Hoolhouse after Smith went into the newsagent's shop. In a phrase loaded with implication Collins asked Hoolhouse, 'You were at Wolviston last night, were you not?' and then, 'I told him to try and think as to where he had been and who he had seen as I said the police will be interviewing [him]. He said, "I hope not."'

Collins' account of the conversation, which was to be denied by Hoolhouse, then ended with the accused saying he 'bloody well hoped' he would not have to account for his movements. Collins also admitted asking Hoolhouse if he had worked at High Grange Farm some time before.

Collins' enthusiastic pursuit and questioning of Hoolhouse was to be the subject of some interest to the defence at Hoolhouse's trial. When in the dock Collins was asked: 'Were you doing a bit of your old job, police work, on the 19th of January?' He replied emphatically: 'No.'

According to Fulcher the first thing he heard outside the newsagent was 'someone' asking Hoolhouse when he had been in Wolviston that night and hearing Hoolhouse reply, '... the only time I was in Wolviston was about seven o'clock in the evening' and then went on to say he went by one bus and back by the next. But there is no mention of this in Smith's account. According to

Smith he asked Hoolhouse about the scratchings, about his absence from work the previous day and about the 'horrible murder at Wolviston' but there was nothing about asking Hoolhouse about his movements and getting a reply about buses.

Collins' account also did not square with the others about questions, answers and sequences. He was a few paces behind Smith and arrived with Fulcher to hear Hoolhouse apparently answering a question from Smith about the accident. The first thing he said he heard was: 'Smith asked him why he had not been to work, he said he had an accident.'

An interesting subtext to the story is added by the scrutiny of the threshers' movements and by Smith's account of their relationship with Hoolhouse. In this the judge felt necessary to pin down the movements of all three of the threshers around High Grange Farm on the day of the murder. The court learned that Bert Smith had been at High Grange Farm the previous afternoon at about half past three on the 18th, the day of the murder, and had deposited the threshing machine at the farm to begin work the next morning. The men with him then were not Collins and Fulcher but two others called Irving and Coates. (They were subsequently interviews by police.)

The three had left the farm at 4.30 p.m. pushing their bicycles up the farm road and then riding down the road together to Wolviston village. Smith discounted in the village and saw the other two ride off together on the Hartlepool road. None of them saw Mrs Dobson as they left the farm.

At 7.30 a.m. on the 19th, Collins, together with Fulcher and Smith, arrived at High Grange to do the threshing. It had just come light at the time and they all had lamps on their bicycles. Nevertheless they saw nothing unusual as they cycled up the farm track. That all three had caps, clothes and bicycles similar to the accused was remarked on by the defence in their summing up. The defence's intention is not to suggest anything sinister in this but merely to emphasise the point that there were others who would have resembled Hoolhouse on that afternoon and in a case where identification was so unsure it served to underline the dangers of relying on identification evidence.

When the police went to fetch Robert Hoolhouse from his bed to the police station early in the morning the clothes that the young man wore that night and his behaviour were to become of crucial importance. The defence argued that if he was guilty then why did he go to the police station in the same clothes he wore on the day he allegedly committed the murder? Why did he not take the opportunity of disposing of them? He certainly had ample time. At any rate he told police he had no objection to an examination of the clothes he put on: blue overalls, white shirt, jacket, cap, brown shoes and a handkerchief, some of which were bloodstained.

Three policemen, Inspector Proud, Sergeant Vickers and PC Joe Hodgson arrived outside Robert Hoolhouse's home at 1.15 a.m. on the morning of Thursday, 20 January. Hoolhouse's father answered the door. Shortly afterwards Hoolhouse came down, partly dressed, and said, apparently without prompting, 'I have done nothing wrong, what do you want me for?'

These words were only heard by Hodgson, not by the accompanying inspector. The policemen asked Hoolhouse to accompany them to the station for questioning. At the police station Hoolhouse was asked to remove his top clothing. Hoolhouse was sitting on a stool while he took off his jacket, pullover and shirt without any obvious discomfort. There were no bruises or any other marks on the shoulders.

Detective Constable Crossley saw 'three distinct scratches, not the marks of a scrubbing'. Crossley and Foster also examined Hoolhouse's bicycle which had been brought from his home. It was very muddy but they could find no tell-tale marks on it one way or another. Hodgson, accompanied by Inspector Proud, returned to Hoolhouse's home the following afternoon. Hoolhouse's father was present when the Inspector removed a knife from a waistcoat hanging on a kitchen door leading into the scullery. From the waistcoat a white comb was also taken. A raincoat was also taken away.

This knife was taken apart by forensic scientists and shown in court. Despite their claims it had been cleaned there was apparently a trace of what might have been a bloodstain but it was never proved that this was blood. A curious feature of Hodgson's testimony was that he maintained that he did not at first tell Hoolhouse why he was wanted for questioning because he did not know himself. The prosecution then tried to argue that this gave Hoolhouse's words: 'I have done nothing wrong...' a sinister implication.

But does Hodgson's claim really stand up to serious scrutiny? As a beat PC based in a sleepy neighbourhood he would have spent his entire day involved on a murder inquiry which it would be fair to assume was not a frequent occurrence. He was working with a fairly small team and yet when asked to get a young man out his bed at one in the morning and take him down to the station he claims he had no idea what it could possibly have been for. Hodgson did contradict himself at one point during cross-examination saying he *did* know why he had to go to Hoolhouse's home but the point was not picked up and driven home by the defence.

At Haverton Hill Police Station Hoolhouse was asked for his name and address, cautioned, and told he was being interviewed in connection with Mrs Dobson's murder, to which he replied, 'I know.'

The statement then made by Hoolhouse went as follows:

> I was in Haverton Hill until about 12.30 p.m. on Tuesday, January 18. I then left and went to Wolviston where I stayed until 3.30 p.m. I cycled there and went to the house of William Husband whom I often visit. I saw at the house Miss Husband and Miss Lax. When I left Husband's house I cycled home via Cowpen and arrived home just turned 4.00 p.m.
>
> On the way back I had a spill on my bicycle. I was riding with one hand on the handlebars and one hand in my pocket and in trying to avoid a brick which was lying in the road I applied my front wheel brake which caused me to go over the handlebars.
>
> I hurt my right shoulder and scraped my face on the right side. About 6.30 p.m. I left by bus for Wolviston via Billingham [which] required a change of bus at Billingham and went again to Husband's house. I saw the two young ladies and John Lax. I got to Billingham at 7.00 p.m. and it was just turned seven when I got to Wolviston. I was talking to the three persons already mentioned and then Miss Lax.
>
> I caught the 7.15 p.m. bus for Billingham. On arriving at Billingham Miss Lax called at 62 or 68 Station Road with a parcel. I waited at the gate.

When she left this house we went to the second house pictures at Billingham; the picture *Between Two Flags* was showing.

After seeing the show through we left. It was then getting on for 11.00 p.m. I saw Miss Lax on to the bus for Wolviston at Billingham Green and I got a bus for Haverton Hill and I arrived home about 11.30 p.m. I had my supper and went to bed.

On Wednesday, January 19, 1938, I stayed in the house until 10.45 a.m. and then went to Haverton Hill Labour Exchange to sign the book. I then walked as far as Lloyds Bank and then went home and had my dinner.

I left home again and cycled to Wolviston via Cowpen and went to Husband's house. I arrived there about 1.45 p.m. Miss Lax and Miss Husband were in the house and I stayed with them for half an hour. I then returned home. I was in the house before 3.00 p.m. I was never out any more until 6.00 p.m. when I went to get a paper. I then returned home and was not out any more.

I did not tell Bert Smith [at this point the police were asking questions] that I was looking for the machine. Bert Smith told me that Mrs Dobson had been murdered. I told Bert Smith that the postman on Billy's Lane round had told me about it. Bert Smith had asked me about being in Wolviston. No one said anything about the police would want to see me. I did not say that I bloody well did not want the police to interview me. About five years ago I was employed by the Dobsons' farm as a hand.

The last time I saw Mrs Dobson was about a week before Christmas when I went to see if I could get a job and I have not seen her since.

Hoolhouse was then asked to explain the reddish marks, which had the appearance of blood, on the lapel of his jacket, on his handkerchief near the bottom, on the peak of his cap and on the outside and inside of his shirt. He said he had cut himself whilst shaving. He had also used his handkerchief to mop up a boil. He was also wearing overalls on top of his jacket. On the overalls, according to one officer, 'There were clear marks which I could not distinguish or say what had caused the marks.'

He was also handed a comb and asked to give some hair samples which he readily agreed to do. His bicycle was brought from his home to be examined.

Hoolhouse's problems began when detectives interviewed witnesses to corroborate his movements on the 18th. Hoolhouse had been transferred from Haverton Hill Police Station to Stockton and at 6.45 a.m. in the morning, only hours after he had been arrested, Sergeant Foster, accompanied by Superintendent Kirkup, spoke to him again. The sergeant said he had checked the times Hoolhouse was supposed to have been in Wolviston and was told he'd gone there much later and stayed an hour and a half. Immediately Hoolhouse conceded his mistake. He must have got to Wolviston about 3.00 p.m., an hour later than he said originally.

Hoolhouse then made a corrected statement which read:

> Everything I told you at Haverton is correct except the times. On Tuesday, January 18, 1938 I arrived at Wolviston at 3.45 p.m. I only stayed an hour and then went home where I arrived at about five o'clock. I did not meet anyone that I knew on the way. I travelled by Cowpen Bewley to Haverton Hill. It would take about fifteen to twenty minutes. I was wearing a raincoat and a cap, not the one you

have. I was never on the road from Wolviston to Billingham until I went along by bus at night after seven o'clock.'

If this statement was true then Hoolhouse's route home would not have taken him past High Grange Farm.

At 7.15 a.m. Superintendent Kirkup cautioned Hoolhouse in the usual manner and told him he would be detained on suspicion of causing the death of Margaret Jane Dobson at Wolviston between 4.30 p.m. on 18 January and 10.15 p.m. on 19 January.

Hoolhouse's slip of one hour was to prove crucial. For the prosecution would argue that it proved he was claiming to have got home before 4.30 p.m., the time of the murder. But this is in itself a contentious argument for the 4.30 p.m. death time is one conveniently chosen to have fitted into Hoolhouse's known movements. Other evidence suggested that Mrs Dobson could have died much later or much earlier than 4.30 p.m. Forensic evidence based on undigested stomach food suggested a time of before 4.00 p.m. Even if Hoolhouse's first story had been true he could still have killed her. But according to the evidence of Percy Swales who was delivering livestock, he saw a man near the farm track at around 5.30 p.m. If that was the murderer then the killing must have taken place later than 4.30 p.m.

Two other possibilities were not examined by the court or the investigating officers. Hoolhouse may have just made a mistake having been roused from his bed at such an early hour or having known that because of a family dispute years before he was immediately under suspicion; or he panicked and made up a story that would distance himself from events as much as possible. Five years before the murder there had been a row between Henry Dobson and Robert Hoolhouse's father, who worked at High Grange Farm. As a result father and son lost their jobs and the Hoolhouse family was evicted from their tied cottage. Mrs Dobson in particular was adamant they should never return.

But to return to the night of the murder: it had just turned 5.30 p.m. on 18 January when livestock transporter Percy Swales and his mate Tom Nelson turned their Bedford cattle truck left on to the High Grange Farm Road. They were delivering six saddle-back pigs which Mr Dobson had ordered from Sedgefield market earlier that day. It was nearly dark as they turned on to the farm track but as their headlights swept the ploughed field both men caught a glimpse of a man standing in the field with his hands above his head. As soon as the lights struck him the man dropped on to the ploughed field.

The man, who did not face the lorry straight on, would have been 50 yards away and quite close to the farm road. To Swales it seemed he wore a bluish-coloured smock, a brown coat, and it looked as if he had gaiters on. He was wearing a cap. That first glance made Swales think the man might be about thirty. He could see no glasses. Hoolhouse always wore glasses, and he never wore gaiters.

Swales had to swerve to avoid a bicycle lying by the side of the road. According to Nelson this was a 'racing bicycle'. He said he could not swear to the colour. When asked in court if the handlebars were silver he said 'pewter I think'. He thought they may have been black. When faced with Hoolhouse's bicycle Nelson eventually admitted he could not make a positive identification of it – the handlebars were silver.

When Swales stopped the truck and looked out to his right he could see the outline of a man lying on the ploughed field. Puzzled, Swales leant out of the window of the cab and shouted at the stranger to which the reply, Swales said later, was: 'He had a drop . . . one over and nine and I'd not to stop.' The man spoke in a local accent.

Swales drove on and while the pigs were being unloaded mentioned it to Dobson and his farmhands who were working in the dark with the aid of hurricane lamps. No one could explain it; Dobson was hard of hearing and might not have heard what Swales was saying. Strangely Dobson told the court he could not remember anyone saying anything about a man lying in the field but Swales insisted, 'He was there [while pigs were being unloaded]. He could hear it.'

The one piece of evidence that turns suspicion away from Hoolhouse and strongly points to his innocence is the footprints. Yet it seemed that the evidence of Detective Sergeant Foster on this was either ignored or rejected. Detective Sergeant Foster is crucial because he was the only person to have examined the footprints found around the body. He was the scene-of-the-crime officer and arrived at around 11.15 a.m. No one else, he said, had been allowed around the body.

He found a set of footprints round the body. These matched Dobson's rubber boots and were made when he found his wife's body. Another print made by a size nine leather boot was found under one of Dobson's prints. Foster made a plaster cast of it. When the defence asked Foster, 'Has it [the plaster cast of the boot] been compared with the accused's boots?', the cautious reply was: '. . . there is not sufficient detail on the cast to show any resemblance to his foot at all.'

The defence pressed on: '. . . having thought it worthwhile to compare it with the accused's shoes, you could find no resemblance between that and the accused's shoes?' Foster replied, 'I certainly could not, sir.'

At this stage Hoolhouse's shoes Exhibit 35A and the plaster cast Exhibit 13, were produced. In fact the plaster cast was to show a large footprint interlocked by a heelmark at right angles to it. It was established that: (a) Hoolhouse's shoes had a pattern not present on the plaster so neither print could have been his; and (b) Farmer Dobson's print was the second one, the heelmark, which was made after the main footprint. The significance of this, which seems to have been wholely overlooked, is that the footprint was made *before* Dobson found his wife's body.

Foster said the footprint could have been made by 'a man standing astride with one foot on the verge, another on the soil and [who] could get back without making further marks.'

If not Dobson, police, doctor, Hoolhouse or anyone else – who could have made the print but the murderer? It was a point that seemed to defeat the defence counsel, Arthur Morley KC, who misunderstood certain points in his questioning and failed to make any reference to it at all in his summing up. As far as the judge was concerned he seemed keen to set this inconvenient piece of evidence to one side and dismiss it in his summary as 'an unresolved mystery'.

Of all the scientific evidence against Hoolhouse there is nothing that amounts to a concrete solid fact that could be held up by the prosecution. At best all that can be said for it is that it places Hoolhouse in the small category of men who may have done the crime. And that still leaves the question of why there were no semen stains on Hoolhouse's shirt when the victim was said to be matted with them.

Several aspects of scientific evidence were initially said

to lean heavily against Hoolhouse. These dealt with blood stains and hairs. In court, Dr Henry Cookston, pathologist at Sunderland Infirmary said the knife found in Hoolhouse's pocket could have inflicted the knife wounds in Mrs Dobson's neck and chest. He tested the knife and found a minute quantity of blood – not enough to prove it was human – in the thumb nail groove. He had taken the knife to pieces to look for more blood but found none. He said the blade looked as if it had been recently sharpened.

Dr Cookson was then asked if the alleged marks on Hoolhouse's face could have been caused by finger nails through the woollen gloves Mrs Dobson was wearing. 'They could do,' he said, because, 'they are a sort of knitted network and they spread out at the ends, allowing fingers to come through mesh of worsted.'

He tested the knife and he carried out an experiment with the gloves. His secretary put them on and then tried to scratch Superintendent Kirkup's face. Asked if she succeeded Cookson said, 'She would have done if she persisted. Kirkup felt the nails.' This half-baked statement was not pounced upon by the defence, and the strange matter of why Hoolhouse's scratches were not photographed by police is left unquestioned. Dealing with the bloodstains on Hoolhouse's handkerchief, Cookson said that it was not, in his opinion, like mopped blood that might come from a boil, as the young man claimed. He said he would have expected pus from a boil and had found none, but agreed in cross-examination he had examined only the three parts marked by blood.

Dr Cookson examined the bloodstains on Hoolhouse's clothes and he was emphatic that the stains could not have come from a man who cut himself shaving, but then agreed he did not think blood spurting from a knife wound would have left any blood on the assailant. The cap, he said, showed an appreciable amount of blood on the right-hand side which, given that most of Mrs Dobson's injuries were on the left side of her body would seem to be a telling fact against Hoolhouse. Home Office analyst Dr Gerald Roche Lynch said he found blood on Hoolhouse's clothes from group II and said he found nothing to support the suggestion that the blood came from a boil. Mrs Dobson's blood was group II.

Hoolhouse refused to take a blood test to establish whether the blood on his clothes was his. He was within his rights to refuse, but was he advised how this might appear in the eyes of the jury?

Next to give evidence was Professor Frederick Tryhorn, Professor of Chemistry at University College, Hull. He compared hairs taken from Hoolhouse's handkerchief, his head and from Mrs Dobson's head. He said he found differences in hair from Hoolhouse's head and handkerchief but slight similarities in hair from the hanky and Mrs Dobson. Could it have come from Mrs Dobson? 'Yes.' Further pubic hair from Mrs Dobson could have the same origin as hair found on Hoolhouse's shirt. Despite all this, Professor Tryhorn admitted under cross-examination that hair analysis is at best an inexact science. 'Would you be prepared to swear that any hair you saw came from a particular person?' 'No, I would not – it is impossible with hair.'

As the judge was to point out later the evidence regarding blood and hairs: 'really proves nothing ... it does not amount to proof', and he went on to say, 'It only proves there is nothing inconsistent found – nothing in regard to the blood or in regard to the hair, which is inconsistent with this man being the murderer. That, of course, is not the way in which guilt of a crime like this is established...'

Mr Justice Wrottensley told the jury that no motive had been established. 'The prosecution pile up suspicious circumstance upon suspicious circumstances ... it amounts to no more than this, that it is quite consistent with this man having committed the murder: but it is consistent with his not having committed it.'

At the trial the prosecution itself alluded to the thinness of what they had to go on, saying, 'Of course there is much less evidence than we usually have.'

This was putting it mildly for as the defence were to point out the prosecutor's tactic was to place suspicious circumstance upon suspicious circumstance. The jury heard both the scientific and the circumstantial evidence against Hoolhouse being attacked by the defence.

1. The blood on his clothes was not positively proven to have come from Mrs Dobson. It was a tiny amount. All that could have been said was that the blood on the woman and that on the clothes were blood group II which is shared by 40 per cent of the population.

2. The question of strange hairs found on Hoolhouse's clothing also seems to disappear on intensive examination. The scientists could not identify them as Mrs Dobson's or anyone else's.

3. Hoolhouse's clothes were carefully examined and no semen stains were found despite the fact extensive semen stains were found on the body.

4. As regards Hoolhouse's evident nervousness to the three farm workers who met him after the murder the defence counsel cited the evidence of the postman on the bus and that of his girlfriend and her aunt who said they noticed nothing wrong.

5. Swales, the pig lorry driver, and his mate Nelson failed to positively identify Hoolhouse's bike as the one they saw in the lane.

6. Swales' identification of a man seen in the field

when he passed by is inconclusive. In his evidence Swales said he saw the side of a face of a man aged about thirty (ten years older than Hoolhouse at the time) who was wearing breeches and gaiters (neither of which were worn by Hoolhouse). Swales made no mention of spectacles which Hoolhouse wore all the time. Strangely the court transcript shows that no one in court asked Swales the simple question, 'Do you see the man you saw in court today?' which might have helped answer the question.

7. The defence made the strong point that when asked to go to the police station the accused put on the very clothes that were alleged to incriminate him. At no time did he attempt to wash or disguise them in any way.

8. The crucial footprint evidence indicating that Hoolhouse was not the murderer was misunderstood by the defence counsel and not mentioned in his summing up in any way.

Summing up, the defence underlined the '... intrinsic improbability of the story; a young man of twenty-one ... going to see his girl of about the same age, from 3.30 p.m. to 4.30 p.m.; going back to his house ... changing his clothes and shaving; going back to meet his girl shortly after 7.00 p.m.: and going again the next day to do exactly the same thing ... the intrinsic probability of the suggestion that in the interval between 4.30 p.m. and 7.00 p.m. he attacked and ravished and murdered this old woman of sixty-seven is so great that, my Lord, I ventured to suggested it ought to weigh very much with your Lordship in considering the question whether this case ought to go to the jury at all.'

Mr Justice Wrottesley was new to the bench. In fact, it was his first criminal trial. He decided the case should proceed. The defence responded by calling no defence witnesses, and Hoolhouse was not called to put his story to the jury.

In his final speech to the jury, Mr Paley Scott, for the prosecution, leant heavily on forensic evidence which would have put Mrs Dobson's death at 4.30 p.m. Of the evidence that Hoolhouse was at the scene of the crime, Mr Paley Scott concluded: 'He was in a position to reach the spot where this crime was committed at the exact time – as far as we can fix it – when it was committed.'

As to why Hoolhouse might have gone to the farm, Paley Scott launched into an extensive speculation, based on the fact that Hoolhouse occasionally worked for Smith's threshing crew. Hoolhouse, he speculated, might have gone to the farm to see Smith for work, missed him and seen Mrs Dobson, who ordered him off because Mr Dobson had told the father of the accused (five years earlier) that neither he nor any of the family were allowed on the farm again.

And, having taken drink as they knew he had, Hoolhouse may have resented it, and a quarrel in which brute force was used might have followed. Hoolhouse's alleged conduct outside the newsagent's was heavily relied on by Paley Scott. Suspicion rested on him from the moment he met Smith, Collins and Fulcher outside the shop. If he were guilty he would want to conceal from the police that he was at Wolviston between 4.30 p.m. and 4.45 p.m.: 'So he gave an account to the police which said that he left Wolviston in such a time as to enable him to be back at Haverton Hill by 4.00 p.m.

'No evidence has been called by either side to say what time he got back home. The police made further inquiries into his times, and it was not until they told him that his times did not tally with those given by the people whom he had seen that he admitted that the time he had given was wrong.'

Morley, for the defence, said that Hoolhouse was a quiet man of good character who had never been in trouble with the police. He submitted that the prosecution in the case was a complete inversion of the basis of criminal law in this country. They had begun by presuming the prisoner's guilt and not that he was innocent until proved guilty.

After four hours and twenty minutes the jury – all men – trooped back into the box and announced their verdict. Guilty. They did not add a recommendation for mercy. When the foreman announced the verdict Hoolhouse appeared to be stunned. He swayed and closed his eyes tightly. When asked if he had anything to say as to why the sentence of the court should not be pronounced he remained for a time speechless. It was not until some seconds had elapsed that he was seen to mumble something to the warder on his left who told the court he had nothing to say.

After sentence Hoolhouse's parents, who had been waiting in a quiet corridor near the court, broke down. 'We are broken-hearted, it is the last thing I ever expected. We had a taxi at the door waiting to take him home,' said Mrs Hoolhouse. 'It has meant days of anguish and sleepless nights for us both. We have only seen him once since Monday.'

A newspaper report stated that: 'While Hoolhouse ... was being sentenced to death ... his parents were waiting in the precincts of the city hall in which the trial is being held so confident were they of his eventual acquittal.'

But he was fated to leave court in a black taxi. After sentence of death he was taken to the cells below the court and then escorted to the railway station whence he was conveyed to Durham Gaol.

Hoolhouse's leave for application to appeal was turned down in the Court of Appeal on Monday, 9 May 1938 despite an appeal from his solicitor, a petition signed with 14,440 names and an appeal by local Durham MPs.

The Court of Appeal heard from Mr Arthur Morley KC appearing for Hoolhouse who said, 'This is a case, if ever there was one, which ought not to have gone to the jury because there was nothing in it but suspicion. The case, having gone to the jury, ought not to be allowed to stand because the evidence admitted by the judge is only suspicion on suspicion and is consistent with innocence.'

The news of the failure of the appeal was broken to Hoolhouse's mother at her home in Haverton Hill by a newspaper reporter who wrote:

> For a few moments Hoolhouse's mother seemed to take the news quite calmly as if she did not quite understand its import.
>
> 'I am still convinced my son is innocent,' she said. 'Everybody thought that he would get off.' She then broke down and wept.

Dolly's mother Mrs Lax said that there had been a lot of gossip in the village and 'poison tongues' had been wagging. Her daughter had broken off with her boyfriend (not Hoolhouse) owing to this mischief.

Robert William Hoolhouse, twenty-one-year-old agricultural labourer of 6, Pickering Street, Haverton Hill, was executed at Durham Gaol at 8.00 a.m. on 26 May 1938.

Executioner Albert Pierrepoint entered the prison the night before, in accordance with regulation, to test the scaffold. At 7.00 a.m. a few police and press were outside the prison but by half past the number had grown to fifty. There was silence when the cathedral clock started chiming. When it had finished and began to strike the men who had gathered outside doffed their caps. A minute or two before 8.00 a.m. Pierrepoint and his assistant pinioned the prisoner and, headed by the chaplain reciting the opening sentences of the burial service, began the walk to the scaffold.

In a matter of seconds the ankle strap and noose were adjusted and the lever drawn, according to the local newspaper. Within a few minutes the customary notice was pinned to the front gate announcing the execution. A crowd pressed forward, then dispersed.

On Friday, 27 May, the *Northern Echo* reported that the Home Secretary had refused to advance a reprieve:

> 'Until then it is believed that he had been buoyed up with the hope that efforts made on his behalf would be successful. He broke down and quickly regained his composure. Throughout his incarceration in the condemned cell he conducted himself with fortitude and maintained an attitude of outward calm to the end.'

A heart-rending scene was enacted at one newspaper office as reported in the *North Eastern Gazette*. A labourer working on a nearby church site called at the newspaper office, announced he was Hoolhouse's father and asked to be told when the sentence was carried out. When the news came a reporter went to tell him. Mr Hoolhouse, visibly upset, was comforted by his fellow workmen. Then he turned away, shrugged his shoulders and said, 'It can't be helped.'

Today the account of one lady who lives in

Middlesbrough adds to worries about the scratches that Hoolhouse is supposed to have had. Mrs Freda Heath clearly recalls how her mother Mrs Margaret Barker was interrogated by detectives after meeting Hoolhouse on the night of the murder. Mrs Barker met Hoolhouse on the bus to Wolviston whilst he was on his way to take Dolly Lax to the cinema.

She had exchanged a few words with the young man – whom she knew – and during that time she had a clear view of his face and did not see any scratches.

This point was to be the subject of heated exchanges between herself and detectives who she felt were trying to trick her into saying that she could not have seen both sides of his face. Mrs Barker always insisted that she had a clear view and that there were no scratches. Sadly her voice was not to be heard by the jury.

Today Mrs Heath remembers that the detectives were 'quietly persistent' and that her mother had become annoyed at what she felt were attempts to trip her up.

Mrs Barker was a friend of the Hoolhouse family and went around the doors of the area collecting signatures for his reprieve. She was so determined in this that she got her daughter to make a packed lunch for her so she did not have to waste time travelling home.

On Hoolhouse's twenty-first birthday and again, after the appeal had been rejected, Mrs Barker travelled with Hoolhouse's mother to Durham Gaol to visit her son in prison. Mrs Heath remembers her mother describing the boy as 'very quiet'. New light is also thrown on the conviction by Mr David Simon who for many years has been a practising solicitor in the Stockton-on-Tees area. At the time of the court case he was acting as an articled clerk to Hoolhouse's defence solicitor and he remembers the crushing sense of disappointment when the verdict came through. He also remembers the deep sense of unease he felt at the conduct of the defence by Mr Arthur Morley KC. Today he prefers to keep his own counsel on how Mr Morley handled the case: 'Let's just say he was no George Carmen QC. He wasn't even a Paley Scott.'

Mr Paley Scott KC, for the prosecution, on the other hand was one of the main prosecutors on the northern circuit and was a leading star in the legal firmament of the day – a devastatingly effective prosecutor. Many years later Mr Simon met Mr Paley Scott's junior counsel at the trial, Mr Alfred Peaker, and he put it to him that there had not been enough evidence to convict. Peaker's frank reply astonished him. For Peaker said that back in 1938 as Prosecution Junior Counsel he had agreed and had suggested to his Senior Counsel Mr Paley Scott that they should offer no evidence. They discussed it at some length and eventually Paley Scott said, 'Let's leave it to the judge.'

It seems that even the prosecution were divided as to whether to proceed with the case against Robet Hoolhouse.

New regulations relaxing the rules on the release of documents allowed the Hoolhouse file to be available for public inspection for the first time in mid-1992. The yellowing documents contained in PRO HO 144/21121/80913 do nothing to dispel any of the 'lurking doubts' that surround the Robert Hoolhouse conviction. They add to them. For not only do they confirm the existence of more evidence that might have helped to clear him, they also reveal the astonishing extent of official complacency and incompetence.

They also help change the whole picture hitherto conveyed of events in Wolviston in mid-January 1938. Far from being some kind of lone cyclist it appears the roads in the area were positively abuzz with tramps, young men on bikes, tradesmen in vehicles, the unemployed, etc. And far from being 'the only man in the frame', a total of eight sighted potential suspects besides Hoolhouse were drawn up in the original police investigation. Three of them were men who were never traced.

Amongst the yellowing files is a letter from the Director of Public Prosecutions Office to the Home Office in which a civil servant admits the incredible remark: '... I think it is right to add that the evidence against Hoolhouse was never strong'.

The file also includes a doctor's report in which he says that Hoolhouse had a mental age of thirteen and a half. Included also is the statement of High Grange worker Charles Adams who claimed to have been approached for a cigarette by two drunken men on the afternoon of the murder. The statement reveals that he correctly identified one of the men from a photograph the police had of a tramp but no mention is later made of this sighting.

Crucial evidence comes in the statements of two women from whom the jury were never to hear. Mrs Doris Teale, a next-door neighbour of Hoolhouse told detectives she had seen Robert – bareheaded and without his cap – outside his house on the day and time he was supposed to be committing murder.

The encounter between Robert Hoolhouse and Mrs Margaret Barker on the bus is recorded. He is quoted as having said to her: 'Hello, missus, goodnight.' Interestingly there is no mention of Mrs Barker's claim that much of the interview consisted of her denying the detective's suggestions that he had facial scratches.

Yet another witness mentions the sighting of a possible suspect who was in the proximity to the murder at the right time, and who could not have been Hoolhouse.

At about 5.00 p.m. on Tuesday the 18th, thirty-three-year-old plater's helper Joseph Clark had finished work at a local shipyard and was cycling home via Cowpen Road towards Wolviston. At about 5.20 p.m. just outside Wolviston and near High Grant Farm he saw a youth riding a cycle 'with silvery handlebars' coming from the opposite direction. Clark emphasised that he did not see Hoolhouse but that 'if the cyclist was Hoolhouse ... I am sure I would have recognised him.'

But the single most damning piece of evidence in the file comes in the description of a meeting between the Home Secretary and Mr Justice Wrottesley, in which the good judge tries to impress on the Secretary of State his total belief in Hoolhouse's guilt. The judge had consulted the three Court of Criminal Appeal Judges and they 'all took the view that there was no doubt as to the prisoner's guilt'.

The judge himself had no doubt. And then there follows the passage that reveals the most astonishing fact about the Hoolhouse case. 'The judge pointed out that apart from the evidence revealed there was an important piece of information which the police could not use.'

Apparently a lorry driver had identified Hoolhouse cycling on the road between Cowpen Bewley and Wolviston at a time when the young agricultural labourer claimed to have been at home. The note concludes triumphantly: 'If [the driver's] evidence had been available, it would have destroyed the prisoner's statement that he got home at 5.00 p.m.'

But what this civil servant's note does not say, and what the judge did not tell the Home Secretary, was that this arbitrarily introduced evidence – not tested in court

– was fatally flawed. For when the lorry driver was confronted with an identity parade which included Hoolhouse, whom the lorry driver said he knew by sight, he failed to pick him out.

But this slightly embarrassing detail was no hindrance to the judge. He chose to believe that the same driver had correctly identified Hoolhouse as the cyclist he overtook in pitch darkness on a bend on that fatal night of Tuesday, 18 January 1938.

The secret nature of the judge's exchanges with the Home Secretary meant that the civil servant never had to reveal why he did not choose to tell the judge this point. Nor why he deigned not to tell him of all the other witnesses whose evidence was not heard in court who might have helped save Hoolhouse from the gallows.